Endogenous Innovation

Endogenous Innovation

The Economics of an Emergent System Property

Cristiano Antonelli

Professor, Department of Economics and Statistics 'Cognetti de Martiis', University of Turin and Fellow, Collegio Carlo Alberto, Italy

Edward Elgar
PUBLISHING

Cheltenham, UK • Northampton, MA, USA

Cover image: Umberto Boccioni, *Dynamism of a Soccer Player*, 1913, oil on canvas, 193.2 × 201cm. The Sidney and Harriet Janis Collection, Museum of Modern Art, New York. Source: Wikimedia Commons – public domain.

Published by
Edward Elgar Publishing Limited
The Lypiatts
15 Lansdown Road
Cheltenham
Glos GL50 2JA
UK

Edward Elgar Publishing, Inc.
William Pratt House
9 Dewey Court
Northampton
Massachusetts 01060
USA

A catalogue record for this book
is available from the British Library

Library of Congress Control Number: 2017936570

This book is available electronically in the **Elgar**online
Economics subject collection
DOI 10.4337/9781782545149

ISBN 978 1 78254 513 2 (cased)
ISBN 978 1 78254 514 9 (eBook)

Typeset by Servis Filmsetting Ltd, Stockport, Cheshire
Printed and bound in Great Britain by TJ International Ltd, Padstow

Contents

v

Figures and tables

FIGURES

TABLES

PART I

Endogenous Innovation as a Creative
Response: A Reappraisal of the
Schumpeterian Legacy

1. Standing on the shoulders of giants

Appreciation of Schumpeterian literature has been quite selective. The 1911 book *The Theory of Economic Development* and the 1942 *Capitalism Socialism and Democracy* have attracted much attention, and actually exhausted it. Other relevant Schumpeterian contributions have been gradually forgotten. The crucial essay 'The creative response in economic history' published in the *Journal of Economic History* in 1947 received little attention after its publication, and has been largely forgotten since then.[1] According to the Social Science Indicator, the essay received no citations in the time span 1985–2012. The other contributions and mainly the two books by Schumpeter received a total of 2400 citations in the same time interval.

This exclusion impedes the correct appreciation of the evolution of the Schumpeterian analysis of the role of innovation in economic growth. It also deprives economics of a framework that can accommodate in a more inclusive approach the important tools of analysis elaborated by Schumpeter in almost 40 years of activity dedicated to grasping the role of innovation in the economy and in economics. The aim of this section is twofold:

- to highlight the merits of Schumpeter's 1947 essay, articulating the view that it should be considered the result of his successful attempt to synthesize, into a single integrated and coherent framework the main results of his life work on the role of innovation in the economy and in economics;
- to show how the notion of innovation as the result of a creative reaction, conditional on the characteristics of the system, provides the foundations for new understanding of innovation as an emergent property of system dynamics.

This framework enables us to identify the limitations of the main approaches to explaining innovation and technological change, and to appreciate the contributions of the Marshallian legacy.

The new growth theory and the evolutionary approach are the two competing frameworks available in the current literature to study the economic determinants of innovation. They have provided the basic ingredients for an endogenous theory of innovation. Identification of the central relationship between the early economics of knowledge and the economics of growth is the main contribution of the new growth theory. The central role of the variety of innovations being introduced at each point in time is the main contribution of evolutionary approaches. They provide the indispensable background for any attempt to elaborate solid microfoundations of the innovation process. The limits of both approaches, however, have become more and more evident.

1.1   THE LIMITS OF THE NEW GROWTH THEORY

The new growth theory impinges upon the results of the preliminary steps of the economics of knowledge to elaborate an endogenous account of economic growth. It builds upon the results of the enquiry into the economic properties of knowledge as an economic good. Technological knowledge is characterized by limited appropriability that has the twin effect of reducing the revenue that 'inventors' can earn from its generation and – spilling through the system – reducing the costs of its generation for anybody else in the system. The non-excludable component of new technological knowledge generated at each point in time contributes directly to the increase of total factor productivity (TFP) at the system level: knowledge plays a central role as the engine of growth (Romer, 1990, 1994a, b, 2015).

The elegant and articulated frame of the new growth theory justified its success and stirred a variety of applications and empirical tests that gradually questioned its foundations. It became clearer and clearer that the new growth theory was unable to cope with the strong and shared evidence about the huge variance of total factor productivity levels and rates of increase across agents, industries, regions, countries and, most importantly, historic times (Craft, 2010).

The recent advances of new economics of knowledge, especially at the microeconomic level, questioned some of its basic assumptions. First, it became apparent that the new growth theory rested upon quite an implicit postulate about a positive sum game between the effects of the excludable and non-excludable components of technological knowledge. The new growth theory, as a matter of fact, does not provide a clear analysis of the reasons why the losses that 'inventors' suffer from the lack of appropriation of the non-excludable part of the knowledge they contributed to fund should be lower than the benefits in terms of increased total factor productivity. Actually, at the microeconomic level, it is difficult to understand why a firm should experience an increase in total factor productivity stemming from expenses that have been made without any benefit in terms of revenue. Moreover, the microeconomics of knowledge suggests that, even with a positive-sum game, the new growth theory does not provide any clue to understanding how and why opportunistic behaviour should not prevail. Even when the Romer postulate of a positive-sum game applies, in fact, each firm misses the appropriate incentives to invest resources in the generation of knowledge. The argument is stronger with a non-positive sum game, either zero or negative: firms have no incentive to invest resources in the generation of new knowledge. According to the recent advances in the microeconomics of knowledge, the new growth theory is unable to avoid the implications of Arrovian analysis of the negative effects of knowledge non-appropriability.[2]

A second bundle of problems about the limits of the assumptions of the new growth theory – that spillovers engender pure and instantaneous knowledge externalities that can be absorbed and used at no costs – became progressively clear. Recent advances in the new economics of knowledge have explored the effects of knowledge cumulability, complementarity and non-exhaustibility. They have also made clear the role of the stock of knowledge – both internal and external to each firm – in the recombinant generation of new technological knowledge. Technological knowledge is at the same time an input and an output characterized by high levels of tacitness that make access to and use of external knowledge difficult.

Agents can benefit from knowledge externalities only after appropriation lags and substantial efforts to screen, identify, absorb and recombine external knowledge as an input into the generation of new knowledge. Knowledge externalities are diachronic and pecuniary: first, knowledge appropriability is transient rather than partial. Technological knowledge can be appropriated by 'inventors' for a limited but qualified stretch of time. It becomes a public good only after some time. The flows of knowledge generated at each point in time add to the stock of public knowledge only through time. As such, knowledge externalities are diachronic as opposed to synchronic. Second, the absorption and eventual use of selected knowledge items extracted from the stock of public knowledge requires efforts and resources. External knowledge is not free. It has a cost that is lower than the cost of first generation. As such, knowledge externalities are pecuniary, as opposed to pure.

Third, the evidence confirms that innovation takes place in highly idiosyncratic conditions, with huge variance across agents, industries, regions and historic times. This evidence contradicts the assumptions of new growth theory that innovation is spontaneous, unlimited, ubiquitous and evenly distributed in time and space.

Finally, the limits of the implicit assumption that technological knowledge and technological innovation coincide seem more and more evident. The availability of knowledge externalities and, more generally, the idiosyncratic characteristics of knowledge are not sufficient to understand why firms do innovate. Knowledge externalities, in other words, are indeed a necessary condition for innovation to take place, but not a sufficient one. Firms are reluctant to introduce innovations, and they can actually innovate only when a number of complementary conditions apply. Knowledge externalities are part of the set of conditions upon which innovation is contingent, but they are not the single and most exclusive factor.

As a consequence, externalities are not only diachronic and pecuniary, but also stochastic (localized in time and space) rather than synchronic, pure or technical (ubiquitous in time and space and automatic). Structured interactions are necessary to use knowledge spillovers as inputs in the recombinant generation of new technological knowledge. Highly localized and specific circumstances make available external knowledge that can be accessed and used at costs that are below equilibrium levels. Knowledge externalities, moreover, are *a necessary but not sufficient condition* for the actual introduction of innovations and the consequent increase of total factor productivity (Antonelli and David, 2015).

1.2   THE LIMITS OF BIOLOGICAL EVOLUTIONARY APPROACHES

Different waves of evolutionary frameworks have been elaborated since the founding contribution of Thorstein Veblen (1898) focused on the role of heterogeneity of agents and institutions. After the decline of the second framework by Armen Alchian (1950), centred primarily on the role of uncertainty, evolutionary economics was revived at the end of the twentieth century by Richard Nelson and Sidney Winter with the grafting of biological metaphors. This (third) approach emphasizes the role of innovations, and made crucial contributions to understanding industrial dynamics based on the selective adoption and imitation of innovations. This evolutionary framework explores the effects of the exogenous introduction of a variety of innovations and their sequential and cumulative selection on the dynamics of market shares of firms and aggregate growth. The introduction of innovations, however, is assumed to be automatic and random. Biological evolutionary models pay very little attention to the endogenous determinants of innovation.

Evolutionary approaches that build upon the path-breaking contributions of Nelson and Winter (1982) have renewed the Schumpeterian centrality of innovation in economic theory, and shown that economic systems are characterized by perennial change both in technology and structure. To elaborate their framework, Nelson and Winter rely on Darwinistic metaphors according to which agents try to change their routines only as a reaction to adversity.[3] In the rest of their 1982 book, however, Nelson and Winter suggest that firms change their routines and introduce innovations without a specific cause. Firms learn and occasionally change their routines; but it is not clear why firms would feel the need to change. Their changes are sorted out in the selection environment: some survive and are adopted. Many fail. Occasionally firms have the chance to introduce innovations – that is, new and superior technologies: as a matter of fact innovation is random and exogenous.[4] Innovation is, in fact, the *ex post* result of the selection process.

The standard evolutionary approach misses serious microeconomic foundations of the introduction of innovations. Standard evolutionary economics has made crucial contributions to the understanding of industrial dynamics based upon the selective adoption and imitation of innovations. The standard evolutionary framework explores the effects of the exogenous introduction of a variety of innovations and their sequential and cumulative selection on the dynamics of market shares of firms and aggregate growth. The introduction of innovations, in fact, is assumed to be automatic and random.

The attempt to rely upon metaphors elaborated in biology to understand the evolution of economic systems can be regarded as the main cause of the weak microeconomic foundations of standard evolutionary thinking. As Edith Penrose (1952, 1953) had already remarked more than 30 years before the publication of *An Evolutionary Theory of Economic Change* (Nelson and Winter, 1982):

> To treat the growth of the firm as the unfolding of its genetic nature is downright obscurantism. To treat innovations as chance mutations not only obscures their significance but leaves them essentially unexplained, while to treat them directly as purposive attempts of men to do something makes them far more understandable. To draw an analogy between genetic heredity and the purposive imitation of success is to imply that in biology the characteristics acquired by one generation in adapting to its environment will be transmitted to future generations. This is precisely what does not happen in biological evolution. Even as a metaphor it is badly chosen although in principle metaphorical illustrations are legitimate and useful. But in seeking the fundamental explanations of economic and social phenomena in human affairs the economist, and the social scientist in general, would be well advised to attack his problems directly and in their own terms rather than indirectly by imposing sweeping biological models upon them. (Penrose, 1952: 819)

As a matter of fact, standard evolutionary thinking suffers all the ambiguities of the confusion between Jean-Baptiste Lamarck – revived for economics after his dismissal from biology – and Charles Darwin. According to Lamarck, the evolution of species is the result of the intentional changes made by the individual in behaviour (phenotype) to cope with adverse changes in the environment. Changes in phenotype would eventually lead to changes in genotypes. The changes in genotypes would in turn yield mutation and speciation. Mutation is fully endogenous: as such far from random and actually the outcome of an intentional action and a clear cause. Charles Darwin showed that changes in phenotype cannot yield eventual changes in genotype, and could be transmitted. Mutation and eventual speciation are the outcomes of random variations that are generated by chance. Each variation retains a change in genotype. Out of the many novelties, the selection process is able to select those that are better able to fit in the changing environment. Selection is endogenous, while mutation is exogenous.

The attempt of evolutionary economics to borrow from biological evolution has taken place with substantial ambiguity, contradiction and confusion. The grafting of the Lamarckian hypothesis requires causality: firms change behaviour (phenotypes) because of specific economic circumstances that affect their performances. The revival of the Lamarckian hypothesis leads to the failure inducement hypothesis. Innovations are introduced to cope with performances that fall below some 'satisficing' level. The grafting of the Darwinian hypothesis, on the contrary, requires that mutation is random and exogenous. Selection is endogenous, but innovation is not.

Standard evolutionary approaches suffer the contradiction between these two approaches that has never been solved. The ambiguity dates back to the founding contribution of Nelson and Winter (1982) in *An Evolutionary Theory of Economic Change*. Careful reading of their book reveals substantial ambiguity between two specifications: i) firms try to search for technological changes (innovations) randomly; ii) firms try to search for technological changes when their performance falls below a satisficing level. Nelson and Winter never acknowledge the contradiction between these suggestions and in their book never try to articulate a solution. They let the alternatives coexist. As a matter of fact Nelson and Winter swing between the grafting of the Lamarckian metaphor and the Darwinistic one without understanding their inconsistency. Let us explore them in depth.

Innovation as a Random Event

Firms are constantly searching for new and better technologies. Firms are not risk averse. They are ready to bear the risks associated with the introduction of innovations at all times and in all circumstances, irrespective of their profitability levels. They rely on automatic learning processes. Learning processes enable the accumulation of tacit knowledge. The stock of tacit knowledge keeps increasing, and firms keep searching. Nelson and Winter are very clear on this:

> In the orthodox formulation, the decision rules are assumed to be profit-maximizing over a sharply defined opportunity set that is taken as a datum, the firms in the industry and the industry as a whole are assumed to be at equilibrium size, and innovation (if treated at all) is absorbed into the traditional framework rather than mechanically. In evolutionary theory, decision rules are viewed as a legacy from firm's past and hence appropriate, at best, to the range of circumstances in which the firm customarily finds itself, and are viewed as unresponsive, or inappropriate to novel situations or situations encountered irregularly. Firms are regarded as expanding or contracting in response to disequilibria, with no presumption that the industry is 'near' equilibrium. Innovation is treated as stochastic and as variable across firms. (Nelson and Winter, 1982: 165–6)

According to them, innovation takes place as a random process. Incumbents keep changing their routines, and occasionally have the chance to introduce actual innovations – i.e. new, superior technologies. Innovation is neither determined by intentional action nor by the properties of the system. Firms that have been 'lucky' will introduce successful innovations that are adopted because they fit the changing environment. Firms do not have a strategy and a project

As a matter of fact Nelson and Winter rely on an implicit postulate according to which *homo oeconomicus* is characterized by the spontaneous propensity to innovate. Yet their postulate about the spontaneous drive to change routine and introduce, occasionally, better technologies that are *ex post* sorted out in the eventual selection process does not find the necessary support in the economics of decision-making. Agents are reluctant to make all the efforts that are necessary to innovate, for two basic reasons: first, the innovation process is characterized by radical uncertainty. Its outcome and timing cannot be predicted; second, because of limited appropriability and tradability, the economic exploitation of innovations is itself characterized by radical uncertainty. Agents need a specific motivation to try to innovate that goes beyond the need to cope with adversity and include the 'Schumpeterian' hypothesis (1942) that profits above the average feed the innovation process. Yet the large literature that builds upon the contributions by Nelson and Winter (1973, 1982) consistently does not provide a clue to understanding why firms innovate. Once again the assumptions on which Nelson and Winter elaborate their Darwinistic approach imply that innovation should take place evenly across agents through time and space.

As a matter of fact it seems difficult to distinguish the innovation process portrayed by the evolutionary approaches that impinge upon the legacy of Nelson and Winter from the 'manna' of the neoclassic theory of growth so much criticized. Neither the manna nor this evolutionary approach here is able to justify the huge variance in the distribution of actual innovation processes. Substantial evidence shows that some agents innovate more than others, some regions innovate more than others and some industries are more innovative than others: innovations cluster in time and space.

This approach impinges upon the line of analysis that pays attention to learning processes. The accumulation of competence is the outcome of learning. The introduction of innovations relies on the accumulation of tacit knowledge made possible by means of learning processes. This approach is not able to cope with the large body of evidence on the large variance among firms in terms of rates of introduction of successful innovations. It seems that some firms are better able to learn than others. This raises in turn the issue of what are the determinants of such variance. The emphasis on the role of randomness and chance seems to be the result of a clear analytical dead end.[5]

Innovation When Performance Level Falls

The alternative failure-inducement hypothesis is well articulated by Nelson and Winter (1982: 211) as follows:

> we assume that if firms are sufficiently profitable they do no 'searching' at all. They simply attempt to preserve their existing routines, and are driven to consider alternatives only under the pressure of adversity. Their R&D activity should thus be conceived as representing an *ad hoc* organizational response rather than a continuing policy commitment. This satisficing assumption is a simple and extreme representation of the incentives affecting technical change at the firm level.

In the failure-inducement hypothesis innovation is introduced only as a response to performances that fall below some satisficing level.

It seems clear that both the view that innovation is automatic and random and the failure-inducement hypothesis are at odds with the Schumpeterian literature. More specifically, the failure-inducement hypothesis contrasts sharply with both Schumpeter's (1942) analysis and the neo-Schumpeterian literature. According to Schumpeter, innovation is made possible by the accumulation of extra profits that stem from the appropriation of the rents that are engendered by the introduction of innovations. The longer the time span of appropriation, the faster the rates of introduction. The so-called Schumpeterian hypothesis has been the mother's milk of the rich neo-Schumpeterian literature that has explored the relationship between market structure, appropriability regimes, profitability and rates of introduction of innovation. The well-known conclusion has been that temporary monopolies can increase welfare because they empower the virtuous mechanism by means of which innovations breed innovations (Scherer, 1986). The microfoundations of the innovation process of the standard evolutionary approach are clearly contradictory and inconsistent with the Schumpeterian legacy.

The evolutionary literature that impinges upon the path-breaking contribution of Nelson and Winter abandons the failure inducement hypothesis. Instead, it fully retains their basic assumption that the introduction of innovations is a spontaneous and automatic process that is not characterized by intentionality and has no microeconomic foundation. The strength of this literature lies in its path-breaking analysis of the diffusion of innovations as the outcome of a selection mechanism that, out of the many innovations introduced randomly, is able to sort those that fare better. The selection mechanism is, instead, fully endogenous and allows sorting innovations, out of the many attempts, that fit better the system.[6] In the models of industrial dynamics, innovation is exogenous while diffusion is endogenous.

The history-friendly models elaborated by Malerba et al. (1999, 2001) simply assume that some firms innovate:

> At the beginning of our episode, the only available technology for computer designs is transistors. N firms engage in efforts to design a computer, using funds provided by 'venture capitalists' to finance their R&D expenditures. Some firms succeed in achieving a computer that meets a positive demand and begin to sell. This way they first break into the mainframe market. Some other firms exhaust their capital endowment and fail. Firms with positive sales use their profits to pay back their initial debt, to invest in R&D and in marketing. With R&D activity firms acquire technological competencies and become able to design better computers. Different firms gain different market shares, according to their profits and their decision rules concerning pricing, R&D and advertising expenditure. Over time firms come closer to the technological frontier defined by transistor technology, and technical advance becomes slower. (Malerba et al., 2001: 4–5)

In history-friendly models the microeconomic decision of whether or not to innovate is completely missing. Innovation is assumed as a given characteristic of the system.

The influential contributions of Iwai (1984, 2000) make this point very clearly: the analysis moves from the assumption that an innovation has been introduced. It does not explore who did try to innovate, or why, when and where. Iwai's analysis of the characteristics of the selective diffusion of many competing technologies remains one of the key contributions of the standard evolutionary literature.

The inclusive review of the evolutionary literature of Safarzyńska and van den Bergh (2010: 347) concludes that:

> Although innovations are intrinsically uncertain, and for this reason in most evolutionary-economic models treated as stochastic, it would be incorrect to consider the process of innovation as totally random. Innovations may be expected to occur in a systematic manner, namely preceded by the cumulativeness of relevant technical advances. The innovative process is often depicted as following relatively ordered technological path-ways, as is reflected by notions such as natural trajectories (Nelson and Winter 1977), technological guide points (Sahal 1985), technological paradigms (Dosi 1982), and socio-technological regimes (Geels 2002, 2005). Innovations are conceptualized in formal models in a number of ways: as a stochastic process (e.g., Poisson) that can result in structural discontinuity, variation and recombination of existing technological options, or random or myopic search on a fitness (technology) landscape. Innovations may be associated with a new vintage of capital (e.g., Iwai 1984a, b; Silverberg and Lehnert 1993; Silverberg and Verspagen 1994a, b, 1995). 'Standard evolutionary theory misses an agent based theory of innovation'.

The models of industrial dynamics that impinge upon the basic contribution of Dosi et al. (1995) assume that innovations are determined by technological opportunities; but no analysis is provided of the specific characteristics of the decision process at firm level: all firms are expected to innovate when, where and if technological opportunities are at large. The determinants of technological opportunities are missing; as such they must be regarded as exogenous.

The important contribution by Winter et al. (2000) explores an alternative route: innovation is the direct and automatic consequence of learning. Learning processes are deemed to engender the accumulation of technological knowledge and the eventual introduction of innovations. The introduction of innovations is simply the consequence of learning processes: as such they take place at all times, in all conditions and in all locations. There is no variety in these models with respect to the innovation process: all firms do learn and do innovate. The possibility that some firms innovate (more) and others do not is not taken into account.

Windrum and Birchenhall (2005) provide the basic reference for the analysis of the models of selective adoption and implementation. They highlight the role of network externalities in the selection of alternative (given) technological innovations. For a given set of potential technologies, network externalities play a critical role in sorting out those that have stronger chances of further development and implementation. Once more the analysis does not take into account the determinants of the process by which agents tried to introduce each of the many alternative innovations. The variety of possible technological innovations is assumed but not explained.

As Dawid (2006) shows in his comprehensive review of the evolutionary models of innovation and technological change that impinge upon the agent-based approach, the decision to innovate is little explored: the focus of the analytical exploration is concentrated on the characteristics of the selective diffusion process rather than on the determinants of the innovation process.

The microeconomic limits of the standard evolutionary approach are becoming more and more evident. The empirical evidence documents the large variance among firms in terms of rates of introduction of innovations as proxied by R&D expenditure and intensity, patents, total factor productivity levels and innovation counts, and calls for an effort to build consistent microfoundations of innovation.

Standard evolutionary theorizing seems to be trapped in its Darwinistic analogy where, as a matter of fact, variation is fully random and exogenous. Changes in genotype cannot be intentional, and do take place by chance. The characteristics of the new species do not reflect the purposes of their relatives. Instead, their selection is endogenous as, out of the many variations, it enables identification of those that fit better into the environment. The grafting of the Darwinistic analogy onto economics impedes understanding of the determinants of the introduction of innovations at the firm level (Antonelli, 2007a, b).

It seems more and more necessary to contribute to the evolutionary approach with an explicit analysis, at the firm level, of the determinants of innovation and the role of externalities in the decision process that leads to their (possible) introduction. To do so it is necessary to go back to the Schumpeterian dynamics, where innovation is not the outcome of a random process but the result of the creative response of firms and their intentional pursuit of new technologies made possible by the properties of the system in which the process takes place. In this context, appreciation of the Marshallian roots enables to focus attention on the role of imitation externalities not only in the selective adoption of new technologies but also, and primarily, in their introduction.

1.3　THE MARSHALLIAN FOUNDATIONS

The Marshallian legacy can be regarded as one of the basic components of the notion of creative response contingent upon the property of the systems in which firms are embedded that can be elaborated, building upon the essay published by Schumpeter in 1947.

The theoretical framework that accounts for innovation as an endogenous process that shares the basic characteristic of an emergent system property, and provides an endogenous understanding of the innovation process able to integrate the analysis at the firm level with the appreciation of the role of externalities embedded in the system, finds its origins in the Marshallian legacy. As a matter of fact the Marshallian legacy has been a constant source of inspiration for Schumpeter on which he relied systematically through all his work.

Schumpeter's (1941) essay in honour of Alfred Marshall documents how the basic ingredients of the Marshallian partial equilibrium approach enabled him to go beyond the contraposition of the 1911 book with respect to Leon Walras. In his tribute to Marshall, Schumpeter acknowledges the many contributions of Marshallian legacy to his own understanding of the role of selective competition among heterogeneous firms.

The adaptation of the Marshallian framework enabled Schumpeter to go beyond the limits of the early framework where innovation was explained by the entrepreneurship (Schumpeter, 1911/34) or just rivalry between firms and articulate a fully endogenous explanation of the innovation process (Schumpeter, 1928, 1942). Following this line of enquiry, the Schumpeterian dynamics elaborated in the 1947 essay can be considered a sequential step that builds on the selection process based on the imitation externalities of the Marshallian legacy leading to the identification of a stable equilibrium with the introduction of two critical novelties: i) the creative response of firms caught in out-of-equilibrium conditions; ii) conditional on the availability of appropriate levels of knowledge externalities so as to implement an endogenous process of technological and structural change. In the Schumpeterian approach, equilibrium takes place only when knowledge externalities are not sufficient to support the response of firms and help them become creative.

Appreciation of the Marshallian microeconomic foundations and their integration into the framework elaborated by Schumpeter is indispensable to implement the missing microfoundations of the innovation process of evolutionary economics. The Marshallian model rests on three building blocks: i) exogenous innovations; ii) no appropriability; and iii) imitation externalities. Let us consider them in turn.

Exogenous Innovations

In the Marshallian framework innovations are the starting point. Marshall acknowledges the important role of changes in the technology of the production process and the organization of firms. Innovations do play a role in the Marshallian framework. They are introduced occasionally and randomly, without any causality. Yet their introduction puts the system in motion. The influence of Marshall on *the theory of economic development* is clear. The role of entrepreneurship is a first attempt to fill the Marshallian gap in the origin of innovations. Schumpeter (1911/34) however does not really provide an endogenous account of the origin and determinants of entrepreneurship. It remains unclear whether the flows of innovations introduced by entrepreneurs and their entry are steady through time and space, or whether they exhibit relevant and systematic changes. As a matter of fact evolutionary models are intrinsically Marshallian as they rely mainly upon the Schumpeter's legacy whereby, following Marshall, innovations are exogenous as they are introduced by entrepreneurs who enter the economic system from outside without any economic causality.

No Appropriability

According to Marshall, knowledge cannot be appropriated by inventors; rather, it spills freely like information so that everybody is immediately aware of the details of best practice. Perfect access to the best knowledge at each point in time is a key aspect of the notion of 'normal' cost: 'But though everyone acts for himself, his knowledge of what others are doing is supposed to be generally sufficient to prevent him from taking a lower or paying a higher price than others are doing' (Marshall, 1920, V, 3: 199). As a matter of fact both the notions of limited appropriability and knowledge spillover, eventually elaborated by Arrow (1962) and Griliches (1979) respectively, had been introduced long before by Marshall.[7]

Imitation Externalities

The imitation of exogenous innovations introduced randomly is the focus of the analysis and the engine of the dynamics both in standard evolutionary models and in Marshall. The opportunity to imitate technological and organizational innovations introduced by third parties is the source of major externalities.

The notion of externalities is one of Marshall's most important contributions to economic theory. Externalities can be defined as the effects on efficiency and output of interactions among firms. With the notion of externalities Marshall is able to consider a wide range of interaction effects that take place in an economic system. Pure or technological externalities stem exclusively from interactions and do not require intentional actions of the recipients; pecuniary externalities stem from interactions-cum-transactions, include the purchase of inputs at prices that are lower than in equilibrium conditions and require intentional action of the recipients.

Marshall considers two types of externality: agglomeration and imitation. Agglomeration externalities have received much attention, while imitation externalities have not.

Agglomeration externalities stem from the increase in the density of firms co-localized. They are both positive and negative: the density of firms favours the reduction of production costs up to a point. Beyond that point negative externalities stemming from congestion costs are larger than positive externalities stemming from co-localization. The interplay between positive and negative agglomeration externalities identifies an optimum size of industrial districts and the equilibrium level of output.

The identification of imitation externalities, as distinct from agglomeration externalities, is a major contribution to understanding the foundations of the Marshallian selection process and its direct impact on the foundations of Schumpeterian dynamics. Moreover, it enables us to appreciate the further distinction between imitation externalities and knowledge externalities.

Imitation externalities consist in the opportunity for imitators to replicate the innovation introduced by the 'inventor'. As such it concerns the incumbent and potential competitors in the same product market. Recent contributions have clarified the role of imitation in head-to-head rivalry in the very same product market (Bloom et al., 2013; Aghion et al., 2015).

Imitation externalities differ from agglomeration externalities and, as mentioned above, have received lesser attention. More specifically, imitation externalities focus on a component of generic agglomeration externalities that stem from the opportunity of co-localized firms to access and share the competences of the most efficient firms. This chapter draws attention to Marshallian imitation externalities.

The notion of imitation externalities articulated by Marshall – and, more specifically, his analysis of their determinants and effects – reveals substantial differences and yet complementarities with Schumpeterian dynamics. They play a crucial role in both. In the former, externalities are a major propeller of the search for a stable equilibrium. In the latter, in contrast – especially in the legacy of Schumpeter (1947a) – they are a major propeller of persistent growth and evolution.

Imitation externalities are at the heart of the Marshallian dynamics that lead to equilibrium. The Marshallian model of competition, in fact, is based upon variety and selection. Marshall assumes that firms are heterogeneous: some firms perform better than others. Selective competition drives the system to generalize the competence of the best-performing firms. The selection process of heterogeneous agents characterizes the Marshallian search for a 'stable' equilibrium. In stable equilibrium the representative firm applies, while in 'temporary' equilibrium imitation externalities apply. In Marshall, equilibrium is the result of a competitive process that reduces heterogeneity to homogeneity.[8] The variety of firms is the cause of the Marshallian imitation externalities. Externalities and variety decline together, along with a competition process – intertwined with a selection process – that reduces variety, and consequently destroys the very origin of externalities. They display their effects along with the selection process and the reduction of heterogeneity to homogeneity. Marshallian imitation externalities are endogenous to the system and intrinsic to the Marshallian search for equilibrium. As such, however, they are bounded.

Marshall assumes that a variety of firms try to produce, enter and exit the marketplace. At each point in time firms are confronted with partial equilibrium that unveils their heterogeneity in terms of production costs. Less efficient firms are sorted out, while more efficient ones can enjoy the benefits of transient rents and increase their size. In the Marshallian process, new entrants and poorer-performing incumbents can imitate freely the best-performing ones. The efficiency of best performing firms spills freely through the system and can be accessed and shared by any other agent.[9] The imitative entry of new competitors and the imitation of incumbents affect the shifting position of the supply curve that engenders a sequence of lower market prices and larger quantities. The variance of profitability levels shrinks. In the long term the process leads to the eventual identification of the equilibrium price according to which only most efficient firms can survive with normal profits.

Within industrial districts, the least efficient firms, as well as newcomers, enjoy easier access to the factors that account for the superior competence of the most advanced firms: imitation is more effective and absorption costs are lower. Agglomeration increases the opportunities to benefit from the knowledge of more advanced firms: the two types of externality reinforce each other. When the number and the characteristics of firms reach the long-term equilibrium conditions, however, externalities are no longer fed by the changing levels of the output, population and density of firms. Only worst performing firms can benefit from imitation. Most advanced firms are not allowed to introduce innovations so as to further increase their efficiency. The identification of a stable equilibrium stops the endogenous generation of externalities. In equilibrium there is no growth. Growth lasts as long as the selection and imitation process that enables firms to push the allocation of inputs towards their most effective use. Marshallian externalities are endogenous, but bounded.

The Marshallian dynamics of imitation externalities provide the foundations for Schumpeter's path-breaking contribution in 1947. Marshallian and Schumpeterian externalities are much closer and more interdependent than currently assumed in the literature. As a matter of fact the limited appropriability of knowledge and its positive consequences in terms of spillover were well known by Alfred Marshall long before their Arrovian codification. In Marshall, however, only less advanced firms can benefit – by imitation – from the knowledge spilling from the most advanced firms. In the Schumpeterian tradition, instead, all firms can benefit from knowledge spillover, including the most advanced ones that can use knowledge spilling in the atmosphere as input to generate new knowledge. In the Marshallian process spillover engenders imitation that leads to the identification of a stable equilibrium, while in the Schumpeterian dynamics spillover engenders knowledge externalities that may reinforce the introduction of further innovations. The two notions of imitation externalities and knowledge externalities are highly distinct. They can be considered steps in a sequence where the Schumpeterian notion of creative reaction based on knowledge externalities implements, augments and extends the Marshallian selective search for a stable equilibrium stretching the dynamics of the typical Marshallian endogenous but bounded imitation externalities with self-reinforcing mechanisms.

Schumpeter (1947a) clearly anticipated the notion of knowledge externalities later articulated by Zvi Griliches. Knowledge externalities consist in the opportunity to use the knowledge embodied in an innovation to generate new knowledge. Knowledge externalities are not bound to an industry or a product market, as they apply to a much larger array of products and processes. While imitation externalities benefit laggards only and necessarily, knowledge externalities provide fundament inputs to all agents to innovate. Knowledge externalities are indispensable to keep innovating (Griliches, 1979, 1984).

The Marshallian analysis of the competition process assumes an exogenous variety of firms and a selection process characterized by the exit of the worst performing firms, the growth of the most efficient ones and the entry of new firms. The entry of new firms takes place because of the knowledge externalities that consist in access to the competence of the most efficient ones. At the end of the Marshallian competition, the initial heterogeneous variety disappears and is gradually reduced to homogeneity where only the most efficient firms survive. The representative agent is the result of the process. On closer analysis it is clear that the Marshallian competition process yields the selection of the best performing firms because of the externalities that enable the worst performing firms to imitate the best performing ones. When the selection process comes to an end, however, and the market has been able to reach equilibrium, imitation externalities are no longer available. In Marshall, imitation externalities are endogenous only in so far as out-of-equilibrium conditions prevail.

When the system reaches equilibrium conditions, no more knowledge externalities are being generated. The Schumpeterian analysis impinges directly upon the Marshallian legacy, but it makes a key change.[10] In the Schumpeterian approach, in fact, both variety and externalities are fully endogenous. Both are constantly reproduced within the dynamics of the creative reaction. Firms that are able to react creatively generate new variety as well as new technological knowledge. The latter in turn becomes the source of new knowledge externalities (Metcalfe, 2010).

In Schumpeter's 1947 essay variety is no longer an exogenous attribute defined at the onset of the process, as in Marshall; rather, it is an endogenous product. Schumpeterian firms, as opposed to Marshallian firms, are expected to try to change their technology as a consequence of mismatch experienced in the market place. In so doing they re-create variety that is at the same time a determinant and a consequence of the process.

In *Business Cycles* (1939) Schumpeter retains the Marshallian notion of endogenous externalities. There, externalities are the endogenous result of the concentration of innovative efforts that in turn stem from the exhaustion of investment opportunities and the decline of profitability based upon previous waves of innovation. The concentration of innovative efforts engenders knowledge spillovers that support the innovation process. Once the waves have been introduced, the density of innovation efforts declines and, together with them, the amount of knowledge externalities shrinks. In *Business Cycles* knowledge externalities are generated within the system and do not stay at given levels: they fluctuate across time and space, as they are at the same time the cause and consequence of creative reactions.

Schumpeter (1941) actually implements the Marshallian notion of endogenous externalities. In Marshall, in fact, externalities are endogenous but cannot increase beyond long-term equilibrium levels. Once the Marshallian selection process has made it possible to reduce (exogenous) variety and identify best practice, the system has reached the maximum possible output and the endogenous provision of externalities stops (Cassata and Marchionatti, 2011). The Schumpeterian process of endogenous creation of knowledge externalities is cyclical but endless, as it is associated with long-term disequilibrium.[11] The path-breaking contribution of Schumpeter (1947a) relies on both knowledge and imitation externalities. The notion of creative response he articulated can be regarded as a fully fledged evolutionary process based upon the notion of endogenous innovation as the outcome of a creative reaction that takes place in out-of-equilibrium conditions when firms' plans do not meet the actual product and factor market conditions – provided the system is able to support their reaction with the provision of knowledge externalities.

Like Marshall, Schumpeter assumes that there is a variety of firms. Each firm makes plans based upon its own expectations. It starts the production process; enters its relevant product and factor markets; and may be confronted with unexpected market conditions that engender out-of-equilibrium conditions. The entry of new competitors that rely on imitation externalities, a typical trait of the Schumpeterian dynamics – established since *Theory of Economic Development* and amplified in *Capitalism Socialism and Democracy* – is at work also in 'The creative response in economic history' (1947a). Here, however, the distinction between imitation and knowledge externalities applies and displays its powerful effects. Firms try to react: their reaction will be adaptive if no knowledge externalities are available. In this case firms can only move on the existing map of isoquants changing the techniques, but not the technology. The reaction will be creative if knowledge externalities are sufficient to support their innovation efforts. In this second case firms are actually able to introduce innovations that change the map of isoquants.

Schumpeter (1947a) makes two crucial innovations to the Marshallian frame. The first Schumpeterian graft onto the Marshallian frame consists in the notion of reaction. According to the evolutionary frame that builds upon Schumpeter (1947a, 1928), firms can try to react to unexpected mismatch between their plans and related investments, and irreversible commitments and actual conditions of product and/or factor markets. Their reaction will be either adaptive by means of sheer technical changes, consisting in movements of the existing map of isoquants, or creative by means of the introduction of innovations.

The second Schumpeterian graft concerns the appreciation of the role of endogenous knowledge externalities that are generated in the localized context of action in which each firm is embedded. Schumpeter had already made clear earlier that externalities are endogenous to the system.[12] The quality of the externalities available to each firm is the sorting device that discriminates between passive or adaptive reactions and creative ones. Adaptive reactions consist of simple movements on the existing maps of isoquants: firms are not able to innovate. Creative reactions that lead to the introduction of productivity enhancing innovations are possible only if the access to knowledge externalities and the actual conditions of use of external knowledge support the innovative attempts of firms.

The frame elaborated in Schumpeter (1947a) can be regarded as a fully fledged evolutionary process based upon the notion of innovation as a creative reaction that takes place when firms' plans do not meet the actual product and factor market conditions, provided the system is able to support their reaction with the provision of knowledge externalities. The starting point of the Schumpeterian dynamics is clearly the Marshallian representation of the working of competitive markets in the selection process that is expected to lead to the identification of the long-term equilibrium point viewed as a stable attractor (Schumpeter, 1941).

The Schumpeterian dynamics elaborated in the 1947 essay impinge upon the Marshallian dynamics and yet differ from it for four key reasons:

1. Schumpeter makes the distinction between imitation and knowledge externalities. Marshallian agents can only imitate advanced firms. Advanced firms cannot take advantage of their transient competitive advantage to introduce new innovations. Knowledge externalities, instead, make it possible for every firm to introduce productivity-enhancing innovations that keep the system in a cost-reducing process.
2. Knowledge externalities are endogenous. They may, in fact, be further reinforced by the increased level of generation of new technological knowledge that is able to reinforce the further creation of endogenous knowledge externalities.
3. In Schumpeter the creative reaction of firms supported by the self-sustained dynamics of knowledge externalities enables the introduction of innovations. Schumpeterian agents exhibit the distinctive characters of entrepreneurship that enable them to try to react to both good and bad performances. In both cases, in fact, they will try to introduce innovations either to contrast their decline and eventual exit or to take advantage of their competitive advantage and increase it with the introduction of new technologies.
4. Out-of-equilibrium conditions are not bound, like in Marshall, but may be self-reinforcing. Innovations are by definition the cause of unexpected changes in product and factor markets.

The Schumpeterian path-dependent dynamics of self-reinforcing mechanisms that may enable the continual creation of knowledge externalities that support the expansion of the generation of new technological knowledge – which in turn leads to both the introduction of productivity-enhancing innovations and the creation of new knowledge externalities – exhibits all the characteristics and the properties of complex system dynamics (Anderson et al., 1988; Arthur et al., 1997).

At the same time, appreciation of the central role played by the systemic mechanisms underlying the creation of knowledge externalities confirms that, in Schumpeterian dynamics, innovation is fully endogenous and is an emergent property of the system rather than the result of the individual entrepreneurial act (Lane, 2002; Lane et al., 2009).

NOTES

1. The outstanding work of Esben Andersen (2009) and Clemence (1989) can be considered among the few exceptions. Schumpeter's 1947 article was reprinted in Clemence (1989: 221–31), together with the companion essay, 'Theoretical problems of economic growth' (Schumpeter, 1947b).
2. See the Appendix in Chapter 4.
3. Careful reading of Nelson and Winter (1982: 211) seems to suggest that firms would change their routines and introduce innovations only as a reaction to adversity: 'we assume that if firms are sufficiently profitable they do no "searching" at all. They simply attempt to preserve their existing routines, and are driven to consider alternatives only under the pressure of adversity.' In so doing Nelson and Winter rule out the hypothesis that firms with profits above the average introduce innovations.
4. See Nelson and Winter (1982: 165–6): 'In the orthodox formulation, the decision rules are assumed to be profit-maximizing over a sharply defined opportunity set that is taken as a datum, the firms in the industry and the industry as a whole are assumed to be at equilibrium size, and innovation (if treated at all) is absorbed into the traditional framework rather than mechanically. In evolutionary theory, decision rules are viewed as a legacy from firm's past and hence appropriate, at best, to the range of circumstances in which the firm customarily finds itself, and are viewed as unresponsive, or inappropriate to novel situations or situations encountered irregularly. Firms are regarded as expanding or contracting in response to disequilibria, with no presumption that the industry is "near" equilibrium. Innovation is treated as stochastic and as variable across firms.'
5. Edith Penrose fully anticipated the problem: 'We have no reason whatsoever for thinking that the growth pattern of a biological organism is willed by the organism itself. On the other hand, we have every reason for thinking that the growth of a firm is willed by those who make the decisions of the firm and are themselves part of the firm, and the proof of this lies in the fact that no one can describe the development of any given firm or explain how it came to be the size it is except in terms of decisions taken by individual men' (1952: 808).
6. See Nelson and Winter (1973: 441–2): 'Over time, the technique used by a firm may change as a result of two kinds of search processes, either of which may be triggered when rates of return fall below target levels. One process is internal to the firm and may be identified conceptually with the firm's research and development, operations analysis, and related activities. We assume that these activities turn up possible new techniques that are more likely to be "close" to the current technique (in terms of similarity of input coefficients) than far away. In this sense we have adopted the metaphor of "local" or "incremental" search that is familiar in organization theory and also seems generally consistent with studies of technical change at the firm level. The second type of search process is an imitation mechanism: The firm is more likely to consider a given technique the greater the percentage of current industry output produced with that technique. The possibilities turned up by these search processes are then subjected to a profitability test: Is the alternative technique more profitable, at prevailing prices, than the one currently employed? If the answer is yes, the firm will switch, otherwise not.'
7. Limited knowledge appropriability and the related spillover of proprietary knowledge are at the heart of both the Marshallian and the Schumpeterian dynamics. In the former they engender imitation externalities bounded to less efficient firms. In the latter, instead, they can be used by all firms, including the most advanced ones. For this reason we shall call them, respectively, imitation externalities and knowledge externalities.
8. See Metcalfe (2007a: 10): 'In a famous passage Marshall claims that the tendency to variation is the chief source of progress . . . (Marshall, 1920, V, 4, p. 355). This telling phrase captures in a single step the deep evolutionary content of Marshall's thought but "What is meant by this?" The rest of the Principles make clear that variation and progress are connected by a variation cum selection dynamic, Marshall's principle of substitution in which more profitable firms prosper at the expense of weaker brethren.

Outcomes are tested in the market so that "society substitutes one undertaker for another who is less efficient in proportion to his charges" (Marshall, 1920, V, 3, p. 341). Indeed, in introducing a discussion of profit in relation to business ability, Marshall is quite explicit that this principle of substitution is a "special and limited application of the law of "the survival of the fittest" (Marshall, 1920, VI, 7, p. 597). Furthermore, innovation is inseparable from the competitive process. For the advantages of economic freedom "are never more strikingly manifest than when a business man endowed with genius is trying experiments, at his own risk, to see whether some new method or combination of old methods, will be more efficient than the old" (Marshall, 1920, V, 8, p. 406). The relation runs two ways and mutually reinforces the links between free competition and business experimentation.'

9. See Ravix (2012: 53, quoting Marshall, 1920, VI, VII, 1, p. 496): 'In Marshall, entry–exit appears in different contexts. For instance, economic change leads to the distinction between "those who open out new and improved methods of business, and those who follow beaten tracks".'

10. The first attempt to integrate the Marshallian externalities into the analysis of innovation as an out-of-equilibrium process dates from Schumpeter's essay 'The instability of capitalism', where the role of externalities in the innovation process is clearly identified: 'What matters for the subject of this study is merely the essentially discontinuous character of this process, which does not lend itself to description in terms of a theory of equilibrium. But we may conveniently lead up to this by insisting for the moment on the importance of the difference between this view and what I have called the received one. Innovation, unless it consists in producing, and forcing upon the public, a new commodity, means producing at smaller cost per unit, breaking off the old "supply schedule" and starting on a new one. It is quite immaterial whether this is done by making use of a new invention or not for, on the one hand, there never has been any time when the store of scientific knowledge had yielded all it could in the way of industrial improvement, and, on the other hand, it is not the knowledge that matters, but the successful solution of the task sui generis of putting an untried method into practice – there may be, and often is, no scientific novelty involved at all, and even if it be involved, this does not make any difference to the nature of the process. And we should not only, by insisting on invention, emphasize an irrelevant point irrelevant to our set of problems, although otherwise, of course, just as relevant as, say, climate-and be thereby led away from the relevant one, but we should also be forced – to consider inventions as a case of external economies. Now this hides part of the very essence of the capitalist process. *This kind of external economies – and, in fact, nearly every kind, even the trade journal must, unless the product of collective action, be somebody's business – characteristically comes about by first being taken up by one firm or a few-by acting, that is, as an internal economy. This firm begins to undersell the others, part of which are thereby definitely pushed into the background to linger there on accumulated reserves and quasi-rents, whilst another part copies the methods of the disturber of the peace.* That this is so, we can see every day by looking at industrial life; it is precisely what goes on, what is missing in the static apparatus and what accounts both for dissatisfaction with it and for the attempts to force such phenomena into its cracking frame instead of, as we think it natural to do, recognizing and explaining this as a distinct process going on along with the one handled by the static theory' (Schumpeter, 1928: 378–9; italics added).

11. See Schumpeter (1941: 242–3): 'A still more significant point comes into view if we pass from the distinction static-dynamic to the distinction stationary-evolutionary. Marshall put up, somewhat regretfully as it seems, with the static nature of his apparatus but he disliked the stationary hypothesis to the point of overlooking its usefulness for some purposes. His thought ran in terms of evolutionary change – in terms of an organic, irreversible process. And something of the flavor of it he imparted to his theorems and concepts and still more to the factual observations with which he presented them. I do not think that the theory of evolution at the back of them was satisfactory. No schema can be that does not go beyond an automatic expansion of markets – an expansion not

otherwise motivated than by increase of population and by saving – which then induces internal and external economies that in turn are to account for further expansion. But still it was a theory of evolution, an important development of Adam Smith's suggestions, and greatly superior to what Ricardo and Mill had to offer on the subject.'

12. See Schumpeter (1928: 379), as quoted in note 10.

2. Innovation as a creative response

Schumpeter in his 1947 essay proposes four crucial innovative arguments: a) the distinction between adaptive and creative responses; b) the role of the system as the source of externalities in determining whether the response will be creative or adaptive; c) analysis of the causes of mismatches; d) the historic and complex character of economic processes. Let us analyse them in turn.

2.1 ADAPTIVE VERSUS CREATIVE RESPONSES

> What has not been adequately appreciated among theorists is the distinction between different kinds of reaction to changes in 'condition.' Whenever an economy or a sector of an economy adapts itself to a change in its data in the way that traditional theory describes, whenever, that is, an economy reacts to an increase in population by simply adding the new brains and hands to the working force in the existing employments, or an industry reacts to a protective duty by expansion within its existing practice, we may speak of the development as adaptive response. And whenever the economy or an industry or some firms in an industry do something else, something that is outside of the range of existing practice, we may speak of creative response. (Schumpeter, 1947a: 149–50)

At each point in time, based on expectations, firms make plans related to organizing their production activity. When and if expectations are not fulfilled because product and factor market conditions differ from the expected ones, the firm will experience mismatch. These mismatches can be both positive and negative for performance: firms may discover they are losing money or making extra profits. Both affect the viability of existing routines. Schumpeterian firms, similar to any textbook firm, have the capability to try to react. The capability to react is a basic component of the standard theory of production. In the received tradition of standard microeconomics, however, this reaction can be only passive or adaptive. The reaction of Schumpeterian firms can be both adaptive and creative.

The textbook adaptive response consists of technical changes to the existing map of isoquants. Textbook firms adjust to new conditions in the marketplace by changing their levels of outputs and inputs and their combinations. They relocate on the existing map either to adjust factor intensity if changes affect relative factor costs and/or to adjust output levels if changes affect the desired levels of output. The outcome of an adaptive response is compatible with a standard general equilibrium. An adaptive response is nothing more than a textbook adjustment to an exogenous shock.

A creative response assumes that the firm can change its technology, and hence reshape the map of isoquants. Technological change is a consequence of an augmented and empowered reaction capability. Schumpeter extends the standard textbook argument that firms can react beyond the limits of technical change to include technological change. The outcome and viability of the creative reaction, and hence the likelihood that the reaction will lead to the introduction of innovation, does not depend only on the intrinsic characteristics of the firm. The likelihood that the reaction is actually creative is portrayed not as a deterministic attribute, but rather as the result of a stochastic process that is influenced by the specific interaction between the action of the firm and the characteristics of the system.

There is a continuum between technical and technological change. Technical change is the extreme case that emerges when responses are fully adaptive. Radical technological change emerges when responses are fully creative. Between the two extremes is a mix of technical-cum-technological change. The notion of response accommodates technical and technological change within a single framework as a possible outcome of the firm's reaction conditional on the characteristics of the system, and as such 'localized' (Antonelli, 2009).

2.2   THE SYSTEM AS THE SOURCE OF EXTERNALITIES

Rivalry, Aggregate Demand and Factor Costs Cause Mismatches

As Schumpeter notes:

> Sometimes an increase in population actually has no other effect than that predicated by classical theory – a fall in per capita real income; but, at other times, it may have an energizing effect that induces new developments with the result that per capita real income rises. Or a protective duty may have no other effect than to increase the price of the protected commodity and, in consequence its output; but it may also induce a complete reorganization of the protected industry which eventually results in an increase in output so great as to reduce the price below its initial level. (Schumpeter, 1947a: 149; internal note omitted)

Agents may face surprises and unexpected events in both factor and product markets. Unexpected changes in factor markets, seldom considered by Schumpeter in his previous works, play a major role alongside and in combination with changes in product markets. Also, changes in the level of aggregate demand are now regarded as major causes of mismatches. Here, Schumpeter considerably extends the possible causes of mismatches, and hence the inducement to introduce innovations. The traditional Schumpeterian emphasis on oligopolistic rivalry in product markets and consequent demand changes for each firm, as the single factor of change, is now relaxed. In addition to oligopolistic rivalry, Schumpeter includes unexpected changes in aggregate levels of demand and in factor markets among the possible causes of mismatches.

2.3   THE CAUSES OF MISMATCHES

The Key Role of System Characteristics

As Schumpeter notes:

> Thirdly, creative response – the frequency of its occurrence in a group, its intensity and success or failure – has obviously something, be that much or little, to do (a) with quality of the personnel available in a society, (b) with relative quality of personnel, that is, with quality available to a particular field of activity relative to quality available, at the same time, to others, and (c) with individual decisions, actions, and patterns of behavior. (Schumpeter, 1947a: 150)

Firms are able to implement a creative response if the externalities made available by the system are sufficient to support their innovative efforts. If the system is unable to support the firm, its reaction will be adaptive. The quality of the system in terms of externalities is the crucial sorting device. The characteristics of the system determine whether the adaptive or creative response will fail or succeed. The inclusion of system characteristics as a key factor in determining the outcome of individual behaviour seems to be a late discovery for Schumpeter, and the result of a final effort to bring together the different threads of his analysis in an integrated framework. The late Schumpeter is more of a system thinker than acknowledged by the received tradition according to which he highlights the central role of entrepreneurial individuals as determining the innovation process, and the chances of economic growth and system change. The intrinsic characteristics of the system dictate the ability to innovate. Innovation depends not only on the supply of entrepreneurial agents but also on the structure and architecture of interactions and transactions of the system. The very provision of knowledge externalities, however, is the endogenous product of the generalized participation of a large number of firms in the collective generation of technological innovation. The gales of innovation are the result of that collective and accelerated effort to react creatively to the generalized out-of-equilibrium conditions of the system. As such, these gales are as much the result of the conditions of the system as of the entrepreneurial efforts of firms.

2.4   THE HISTORIC AND COMPLEX CHARACTER OF ECONOMIC PROCESSES

History Matters

As Schumpeter notes:

> First, from the standpoint of the observer who is in full possession of all relevant facts, it can always be understood *ex post;* but it can practically never be understood *ex ante*; that is to say, it cannot be predicted by applying the ordinary rules of inference from the pre-existing acts. This is why the 'how' in what has been called above the 'mechanisms' must be investigated in each case. Secondly, creative response shapes the whole course of subsequent events and their 'long-run' outcome. It is not true that both types of responses dominate only what the economist loves to call 'transitions' leaving the ultimate outcome to be determined by the initial data. Creative response changes social and economic situations for good, or, to put it differently, it creates situations from which there is no bridge to those situations that might have emerged in its absence. This is why creative response is an essential element in the historical process; no deterministic credo avails against this. (Schumpeter, 1947a: 150)

Economic and historical analyses are strictly complementary and cannot be practised separately without major and mutual losses. It is only the combination of economics and historical analysis that makes it possible to investigate 'the sadly neglected area of economic change' (Schumpeter, 1947a: 149). Economic processes are definitely characterized by non-ergodic dynamics. Irreversibility is an intrinsic characteristic of economic processes. Technological change is the cause of irreversibility: the equilibrium conditions before the introduction of innovation differ from the new equilibrium conditions (Antonelli, 2015a, b).

More specifically, it is clear that for Schumpeter economic processes that necessarily consider innovation as an integral and irreducible component are path dependent, as distinct from past dependent. A process is past dependent when its non-ergodic dynamics are defined at the onset. No characteristic of the dynamics based on irreversibility can be changed along the process. Past dependence is different from path dependence. A process is indeed path dependent when it is shaped by and affected by irreversibility. However, events along the process can affect it to change its direction, speed, intensity and general characteristics. In all non-ergodic processes history matters, but it plays different roles according to the relevance of the initial conditions and the events that take place along the historic time of the process. A past-dependent process is deterministic. A path-dependent process in inherently stochastic (David, 2005, 2007).

2.5   THE GREAT SYNTHESIS

Careful reading of Schumpeter's 1947 essay suggests that it was a relevant attempt to elaborate the final synthesis of his various contributions. From this perspective, an appreciation of the 1947 work opens discussion of the asserted divides and contradictions in his earlier contributions.

Inclusive reading of Schumpeter's complete works suggests that the 1947 essay provides crucial clues to integrate his previous, different contributions as sequential steps that can be articulated in a single framework that enables us to appreciate their complementarities rather than their contrasts. The notion of innovation as creative reaction that can take place when appropriate externalities are available does not come as a surprise in the context of the large set of Schumpeterian works. The notion of creative reaction conditional upon the characteristics of the system can be regarded as the result of a major attempt to synthesize within a consistent and coherent frame the main achievements of Schumpeter's lifelong analysis of the role played by innovation in the economy and in economics.

This hypothesis contrasts with the dichotomist interpretation, made in much of the literature, of a divide between the so-called Schumpeter Mark One and Schumpeter Mark Two. According to this body of work, Schumpeter had a radical change of mind. His 1911 contribution considered the key characteristics of the European innovation system based on entrepreneurs and innovative bankers. Meanwhile, the 1942 contribution reflects the key characteristics of the American innovation system based on the corporation as a portfolio of activities that allows the systematic introduction of new activities enabled by the resources available for research and development (R&D) provided by the extra profits stemming from the introduction of previous vintages of innovations.

According to Freeman et al. (1982) the articulation between the 'first' and 'second' Schumpeter could be regarded as a form of complementarity rather than a historical sequence. The 1911 work (Schumpeter Mark One) applies to science-based industries, where scientific entrepreneurs play a central role. Schumpeter Mark Two (derived from the 1942 book) would apply to oligopolistic product markets where rivalry between large corporations is based on product innovation. This interpretation has been much implemented, with the notion of two different Schumpeterian regimes inspiring many empirical investigations (Malerba and Orsenigo, 1995, 1996).

In our view, the notion of innovation as a creative reaction makes it clear that Schumpeter had already reconciled the divide. With his 1947 contribution, Schumpeter finally elaborates a single framework in which innovation is considered the endogenous result of the efforts of entrepreneurs, including entrepreneurs at the head of incumbent corporations, and made possible and successful by the characteristics of the system. Careful reading of the 1947 work suggests that there is but a single Schumpeter who praises both the entrepreneurial action of firms able of creative reactions and the central role of the characteristics of the system in which firms are embedded as complementary and indispensable elements to provide an integrated understanding of the innovation process (Langlois, 2007).

The dynamic process established by Schumpeter in 1947 can be regarded as a major progress and a generalization of the Schumpeterian analysis elaborated in *Business Cycles*. Here Schumpeter makes clear that innovation is endogenous to the economic system:

> Those acts, the formation of companies for the exploitation of the new opportunities, the setting of the new countries, the exports into and the imports from them, are part of the economic process, as they are part of economic history, and not outside of it. Again, the invention of, say, the Montgolfier balloon was not an external factor of the business situation of its time; it was, indeed, no factor at all. The same is true of all inventions as such, witness the inventions of the antique world and the middle ages which for centuries failed to affect the current of life. As soon, however, as an invention is put into business practice, we have a process which arises from, and is an element of, the economic life of its time, and not something that acts on it from without. In no case, therefore, is invention an external factor. (Schumpeter, 1939: 15)[1]

In the following step Schumpeter makes clear that innovation is indispensable to understanding the working of economic systems: 'But what dominates the picture of capitalistic life and is more than anything else responsible for our impression of a prevalence of decreasing cost, causing disequilibria, cutthroat competition and so on, is innovation, the intrusion into the system of new production functions which incessantly shift existing cost curves' (Schumpeter, 1939: 88).

In *Business Cycles* Schumpeter updates and elaborates the foundations of his approach with respect to the Walrasian approach now enriched by a new appreciation of the Marshallian contributions:

What we are doing amounts to this: we do not attack traditional theory, Walrasian or Marshallian, on its own ground. In particular, we do not take offense at its fundamental assumptions about business behavior – at the picture of prompt recognition of the data of a situation and of rational action in response to them. We know, of course, that these assumptions are very far from reality but we hold that the logical schema of that theory is yet right 'in principle' and that deviations from it can be adequately taken care of by introducing friction, lags, and so on, and that they are, in fact, being taken care of, with increasing success, by recent work developing from the traditional bases. We also hold, however, that this model covers less ground than is commonly supposed and that the whole economic process cannot be adequately described by it or in terms of (secondary) deviations from it. This is satisfactory only if the process to be analyzed is either stationary or 'steadily growing' in the sense of our definition of the term Growth: any external disturbances may enter, of course, provided adaptation to them is passive. And this is equivalent to saying that the assumption that business behavior is ideally rational and prompt, and also that in principle it is the same with all firms, works tolerably well only within the precincts of tried experience and familiar motive. It breaks down as soon as we leave those precincts and allow the business community under study to be faced by new possibilities of business action which are as yet untried and about which the most complete command of routine teaches nothing. Those differences in the behavior of different people which within those precincts account for secondary phenomena only, become essential in the sense that they now account for the outstanding features of reality and that a picture drawn on the Walras-Marshallian lines ceases to be true—even in the qualified sense in which it is true of stationary and growing processes: it misses those features, and becomes wrong in the endeavor to account by means of its own analysis for phenomena which the assumptions of that analysis exclude. The reasonable thing for us to do, therefore, seems to be to confine the traditional analysis to the ground on which we find it useful, and to adopt other assumptions—the above three—for the purpose of describing a class of facts which lies beyond that ground. In the analysis of the process dominated by these facts traditional theory, of course, still retains its place: it will describe the responses to innovation by those firms which are not innovating themselves. (Schumpeter, 1939: 95–6)

The notion of entrepreneurship is finally clarified: it does not identify exclusively newcomers and young firms that enter the marketplace, but rather the specific function of introducing innovations:

For actions which consist in carrying out innovations we reserve the term Enterprise; the individuals who carry them out we call Entrepreneurs. This terminological decision is based on a historical fact and a theoretical proposition, namely, that earning out innovations is the only function which is fundamental in history and essential in theory to the type usually designated by that term. The distinction between the entrepreneur and the mere head or manager of a firm who runs it on established lines or, as both functions will often coincide in one and the same person, between the entrepreneurial and the managerial function, is no more difficult than the distinction between a workman and a landowner, who may also happen to form a composite economic personality called a farmer. And surely it is but common sense to recognize that the economic function of deciding how much wool to buy for one's process of production and the function of introducing a new process of production do not stand on the same footing, either in practice or logic. (Schumpeter, 1939: 100)

The foundations of the alternative Schumpeterian regimes are deprived of a solid Schumpeterian reference: entrepreneurs can be both small, young firms and larger corporations.

Finally, Schumpeter lays down the 'skeleton' of his analysis where the search for profit is assumed to be the basic incentive to innovate:

These new commodities intrude into the economic world that existed before at a rate which will, for reasons given in the preceding chapter, be too great for smooth absorption. They intrude, nevertheless, gradually: the first entrepreneur's supply will not, in general, cause visible disturbance or be sufficient to alter the complexion of the business situation as a whole, although those firms may be immediately affected with the products of which the new commodities or the commodities produced by new methods are directly competitive. *But, as the process gathers momentum, these effects steadily gain in importance, and disequilibrium, enforcing a process of adaptation, begins to show.* The nature of the effects on the 'old' firms is easy to understand. It superimposes itself on the disequilibrium caused by the setting up of the new plant and equipment and the expenditure incident thereto. But while the effects of this were, even in those cases in which they spelled net losses, softened by the flow of that expenditure, the new disequilibrium enforces much more obviously difficult adaptations. They proceed not exclusively under the stimulus of loss. For some of the 'old' firms new opportunities for expansion open up: the new methods or commodities create New Economic Space. But for others the emergence of the new methods means economic death; for still others, contraction and drifting into the background. Finally, there are firms and industries which are forced to undergo a difficult and painful process of modernization, rationalization and reconstruction . . . Profits will be eliminated, the impulse of innovation will, for the time being, have spent itself. But second, since entrepreneurial activity upsets the equilibrium of the system and since the release of the new products brings disequilibration to a head, a revision of values of all the dements of the system becomes necessary and this, for a period of time, means fluctuations and successive attempts at adaptation to changing temporary situations. This, in turn, means the impossibility of calculating costs and receipts in a satisfactory way, even if necessary margins are not altogether absent while that goes on. Hence, the difficulty of planning new things and the risk of failure are greatly increased. In order to carry out; additional innovations, it is necessary to wait until things settle down as it was in the beginning to wait for an equilibrium to be established before embarking upon the innovations the effects of which we are now discussing. (Schumpeter, 1939: 139; italics added)

In *Business Cycles* Schumpeter argues that innovation takes place only in the proximity of equilibrium where there are no profits and the risks are too high. According to Schumpeter (1939: 169), it is clear:

not only that the entrepreneurial impulse impinges upon an imperfectly competitive world but also that entrepreneurs and their satellites almost always find themselves in imperfectly competitive short-time situations even in an otherwise perfectly competitive world. In fact, evolution in our sense is the most powerful influence in creating such imperfections all around. Hence we now drop the assumption of perfect competition altogether, as well as the assumption, made at the threshold of this chapter, that there is perfect equilibrium at the start. We can assume, instead, that both competition and equilibrium are, independently of the effects of our process, imperfect from the start, or even that the system is inactive in the sense defined in the second chapter.

The notion of gales of innovations, introduced in *Capitalism, Socialism and Democracy*, is clearly based upon the analysis elaborated in *Business Cycles*. According to Schumpeter (1942, 83):

> The opening up of new markets and the organizational development from the craft shop and factory to such concerns as U.S. Steel illustrate the process of industrial mutation that incessantly revolutionizes the economic structure from within, incessantly destroying the old one, incessantly creating a new one . . . [The process] must be seen in its role in the perennial gale of creative destruction; it cannot be understood on the hypothesis that there is a perennial lull.

Business Cycles had laid down the foundations of the gales of innovations highlighting the complementarity of the efforts of myriad firms that try to react to a generalized downturn of profitability. Specifically, Schumpeter gathers historical evidence to support the hypothesis that the gales of radical innovations are introduced in downturns of long-term business cycles when investment opportunities, due to previous gales, decline. The new gales of radical innovations are the result of the collective reaction of multiple firms to the lack of profits.

In this context, the 1947 approach seems to solve the apparent contradiction of the *Theory of Economic Development* (1911/34), whose first part is devoted to praising Walras and the general equilibrium approach, while the second part stresses the crucial role of the entrepreneur as an exogenous factor in the introduction of innovations and wreaking of creative destruction. According to the 1947 contribution, equilibrium is possible. However, it is one of the possible outcomes that take place when the reaction of firms is adaptive as opposed to creative. Consistently, with the 1947 contribution, Schumpeter, relying on his 1941 appraisal of Marshall, substitutes the Walrasian framework with the Marshallian framework, where production and variety precede exchange to confirm but delimit the relevance of equilibrium.

The mismatch between expectations and consequent plans and actual market conditions is very much rooted in the Marshallian analysis of the temporary partial equilibrium that emerges after production, and is far removed from the Walrasian world where production takes place after equilibrium has been identified. Marshall provides the platform for the introduction of innovation as part of the competitive and selective process that sorts out the original variety identifying the most efficient firms and technologies. A quote from his essay on Marshall seems useful here:

> Marshall was one of the first economists to realize that economics is an evolutionary science (although his critics not only overlooked this element of his thought but in some instances actually indicted his economics on the very ground that it neglected the evolutionary aspect), and in particular that the human nature he professed to deal with is malleable and changing in function of changing environments. (Schumpeter, 1941: 237)

The Schumpeterian dynamics excludes all possibilities of a stable attractor. It is clear, in fact, that in Schumpeter there is a spiralling loop at work where innovations are at the same time a cause and a consequence of the dynamics. Innovations are at the origin of mismatches that induce the creative reaction of firms towards the generation of new technological knowledge. This not only leads to the introduction of new destabilizing innovations – now a consequence; it also leads to the creation of new knowledge externalities that in turn – now a cause – make the generation of technological knowledge by means of the additional knowledge externalities even easier, with increasing chances that the reaction of firms become creative (as opposed to adaptive) and hence feed further loops of innovation and creative destruction. Innovation exhibits all the typical characteristics of a system-emergent property based upon the interaction between the entrepreneurial reaction of firms and the actual availability, defined at the system level, of knowledge externalities (Martin and Sunley, 2012).

In the Schumpeterian dynamics that builds upon Schumpeter (1947a) only the decline of the mechanisms that generate knowledge externalities can stop the process. If effective knowledge governance mechanisms remain at work, no stable attractor exists. Periods of self-sustained introduction of innovations that build upon the endogenous and self-reinforcing generation of knowledge externalities can alternate and can stop only if and when the creation of new knowledge externalities is inhibited by the decline of knowledge governance mechanisms engendered by institutional problems and congestion.

When and if knowledge governance fails and knowledge externalities are no longer available, the reaction of firms will become adaptive instead of creative. Firms will not be able to introduce technological or organizational innovations. Their reaction will consist simply of technical adjustments on the existing map of isoquants. When and if no knowledge externalities are available and the system is not able to create them from inside – or economic policy is not able to foster their creation – the Marshallian attractor comes back into play. The Marshallian equilibrium that takes place when the selection among existing techniques has produced all its positive effects in terms of increased efficiency at the system level lies at the other extreme of the Schumpeterian dynamics. The Marshallian equilibrium occurs when the Schumpeterian dynamics are exhausted.

The Schumpeterian dynamics of self-reinforcing mechanisms that enable the continual creation of knowledge externalities that support the expansion of the generation of new technological knowledge – which in turn supports both the introduction of productivity-enhancing innovations and the creation of new knowledge externalities – exhibit all the characteristics and properties of complex system dynamics (Anderson et al., 1988; Arthur et al., 1997). At the same time, the appreciation of the central role played by the systemic mechanisms underlying the creation of knowledge externalities confirms that, in the Schumpeterian dynamics, innovation is an emergent property of the system rather than the result of the individual entrepreneurial act (Lane, 2005; Lane et al., 2009).

The reaction of individual agents – both at the knowledge frontier and behind it – is indeed crucial. Its positive outcome in terms of generation of new technological knowledge and eventual introduction of productivity-enhancing innovations depends strictly upon the system conditions that enable the generation of knowledge externalities, and hence the generation of new technological knowledge at costs that are below equilibrium level. In a system where technological knowledge can be generated in equilibrium conditions there is no possibility to introduce productivity-enhancing innovations. The system is doomed to adaptive reactions, and hence to an equilibrium in which a stable Marshallian attractor freezes the system for ever with no chance of further growth and change.

The evolutionary complexity implemented by Schumpeter (1947a, 1928) articulates knowledge, variety, innovation and growth as emergent properties of an economic system that stems from the self-sustained interactions between individual actions and the changing structure of the system (Antonelli, 2008a, b, 2001). The Marshallian and Schumpeterian frameworks can be regarded as two outcomes of the same basic process (Caldari, 2015). The Schumpeterian framework applies to all the agents in the system, and takes place if and only if the properties of the system make possible the creative reaction. According to the levels of knowledge externalities, all incumbents can innovate and increase their efficiency levels. This in turn engenders new variance and new opportunities for imitation and the generation of further externalities. Innovation takes place with all the characteristics of an emergent system property. If, instead, the quality

Table 2.1   From Marshallian to Schumpeterian dynamics

	Externalities	Variety	Process	Outcome
Marshallian dynamics	Imitation externalities available only to poorer performing firms	Exogenous	Selection-cum-imitation leads to homogeneity	Equilibrium takes place when all firms use the best available technology
Schumpeterian dynamics	Knowledge externalities available to all firms	Endogenous	Selection-cum-endogenous innovation leads to reproduction of variety	Evolutionary complexity that keeps evolving provided knowledge externalities are reproduced

of knowledge externalities is low, the Marshallian framework applies. The reaction is adaptive rather than creative. The Marshallian equilibrium prevails. Table 2.1 synthesizes the key points of the analysis.

Economics of innovation has made considerable progress in the last decades. It is now recognized as specialized field of research and is taught in most universities. The discovery of the residual and its crucial role in the increase of total factor productivity, and hence in economic growth, has given it a central place in economics (Solow, 1957). The understanding of the determinants of innovation, i.e. the cause of more than 50 per cent of US economic growth in the years 1909–49, became indispensable for economics to survive as a science able to explain economic activity. Moving from the study of the consequences of technological change on the working of the economic system, economics of innovation has made it possible to better understand the processes by means of which innovation is being introduced in the economy.

We know much better how and where innovation takes place. Yet, we know very little about why innovation is introduced and even less when. The understanding of the determinants of innovation is still unclear. The ambition to understand innovation as an endogenous product of the working of economic activity has not yet been fulfilled. The promise of evolutionary economics and new growth theory to go beyond the limits of standard economics, where technological change falls like manna from heaven, did not yield the expected results (Antonelli, 2008a, 2009).

The retrieval and the implementation of the notion of creative response introduced by Schumpeter in his 1947 essay provide crucial clues to understanding innovation as the endogenous result of reactions – as opposed to a planned conducts of firms caught in out-of-equilibrium conditions by the mismatch between the expectations that are necessary for the rolling activities of firms and the actual conditions of the ever-changing factor and product markets, conditional upon the endogenous availability of knowledge externalities. The notion of creative response provides crucial clues to provide economics of innovation with a new analytical platform that integrates many different analytical traditions, including the tools of the economics of complexity, and enables us to understand innovation as an endogenous process (Antonelli 2008a, 2009, 2011, 2015a).

Retrieval of Schumpeter's (1947a) legacy enables us to express a satisfactory explanation of the endogenous determinants of innovation introduction elaborating a comprehensive framework based on the notion of evolutionary complexity in understanding why and when innovations are being introduced. This enables us to go beyond the ambiguities and dead-ends of both approaches building upon biological metaphors and the so-called new growth theory. Within the framework of economic complexity, innovation can be usefully viewed as an emergent property that is shaped and explained by the interactions between heterogeneous agents, embedded in the organized complexity of the economic system (Anderson et al., 1988; Arthur et al., 1997; Lane et al., 2009; Antonelli, 2009; Arthur, 2009, 2010, 2015; Fransman, 2010).

The empirical evidence on the strong, diachronic and synchronic variance of innovative activity, measured with any possible indicator – from innovation counts to patents, including total factor productivity rates of increase, across agents, industries, regions, countries and historic time – questions not only the new growth theory but also (and primarily) the evolutionary accounts as it raises the key question: why such a variance if all agents are equally eager to innovate (Craft, 2010)?

The innovation process in evolutionary approaches that use biological analogies is not endogenous as it stems from random events. In the Darwinistic approach, in fact, the generation of variety takes place randomly without any specific causality about the rate and the direction of the introduction of innovations.[2] Only the Darwinistic selection among the many innovative attempts can be grounded on solid economic foundations. Only innovations that actually fit into the specific economic conditions will be sorted and diffused. The others will fail.[3]

The search for an endogenous causation of innovation does not end with standard evolutionary approaches. It is still necessary to understand why firms try to innovate. Along the same lines, it remains unclear why the rates of innovation introduction differ across economic space and, most importantly, historic times.

2.6   THE SCHUMPETERIAN PLATFORM

Schumpeter's 1947 essay provides the opportunity to expand on an analytical platform able to integrate different and yet complementary approaches elaborated in the literature so as to grasp innovation as the endogenous product of economic activity. Antonelli (2008a, 2011, 2015a) analyses in detail Schumpeter's 1947 essay, highlighting its key contributions:

- Schumpeter makes clear that firms are reluctant to engage in innovation activities: when there is no mismatch between expected and actual product and factor market conditions, firms are not considering the possibility to innovate. They are well aware of the radical uncertainty that characterizes the knowledge generation process and the actual outcome of the full range of innovation activities. They try to innovate only when the actual conditions of product and factor markets do not meet their expectations. This takes place both when profits and performance at large are below and above the average.
- The distinction between creative and adaptive response made by Schumpeter stresses the role of the co-occurrence of (knowledge) externalities in determining whether the reaction of firms can be actually creative or simply adaptive.[4] The mismatches without knowledge externalities – as much as knowledge externalities without mismatches – are not sufficient to engender the creative reaction that leads to the introduction of innovations.
- The creative reaction engenders new mismatches and new knowledge externalities. Firms' creative reaction and the consequent introduction of innovations cause out-of-equilibrium conditions for other firms which may be able to react creatively and engender new out-of-equilibrium conditions for yet other firms. These latter, in turn, may be able to react creatively, provided that the structural characteristics of the system – now fully endogenous – are able to continue to provide a flow of knowledge externalities that enable creative reaction (Antonelli, 2008a, 2011; Antonelli and Scellato, 2013).

The 1947 contribution can be regarded as the synthesis of the different contributions elaborated by Schumpeter that enables us to build a comprehensive platform that allows the integration in a single framework of the following analytical blocks: a) reactive decision-making; b) the neo-Schumpeterian approach; c) classical legacies; d) the new economics knowledge; e) the selective diffusion of innovations. Let us consider them in turn.

Reactive Decision-Making

The Schumpeterian focus on response rather than on planned conduct of firms and agents enables us to take advantage of the behavioural analysis of decision-making. In an evolutionary complexity that builds on the notion of innovation as a creative response, the attributes of economic agents in terms of rationality acquire substantial relevance. The analysis of the limits to Olympian rationality and notions of bounded and procedural rationality matter to understanding and implementing Schumpeterian dynamics based on decision-making procedures and the reaction and inter-actions among agents in the system (Simon, 1947).[5]

Herbert Simon notes that procedural rationality is the result of sequential reactions that take place when expectations and related decisions do not match the actual conditions of product and factor markets. At each point in time, agents try to articulate expectations upon which to base their choices. When these expectations do not match actual market conditions, agents are forced to react. Bounded rationality and the burden of sunk costs enable them to rely on procedural rationality that is contingent on their specific conditions and on past decisions.

The prospect theory of Kahneman and Tversky (1979) and the regret theory elaborated by Loomes and Sugden (1982) apply very well to make clear how difficult it is to change the current way of doing business. Firms can overcome their reluctance to abandon current routines only when unexpected circumstances expose them to either major opportunities or major problems. The decision to try to innovate is taken only when the reluctance to change is overcome by unforeseen prospects for high profits or major losses that are engendered by emerging mismatches between expected and actual product and factor market conditions. This approach contrasts with the theorizing of Darwinistic ascent according to which the innovative behaviour of firms is spontaneous and automatic: firms would try to innovate without any specific inducement mechanisms. Here, instead, it is clear that the attempt to innovate is considered a possible strategy only when firms are exposed to unexpected events.

Unexpected events affect the performance of firms. Reaction takes place when unexpected events expose firms to performances that are far from equilibrium, both below and above average. When firms experience equilibrium performances there are no reasons to try to react. Firms try to react when performance is negative and exposes them to failure. In this case the reaction is necessary in order to survive. The failure mechanism is put in place. Firms also try to react, however, when performance is well above equilibrium levels. Fast rates of growth in demand and high levels of profitability make it possible to fund innovative activities (Bandura and Cervone, 1986; Rizzello and Turvani, 2002).[6]

The context in which firms react has a strong bearing on the characteristics and effects of their reactions. The outcome of their reactions is contingent on external conditions. At each point in time, agents try to do their best within the strict limits of their bounded rationality; since they do not have access to all the relevant information and are not able to process all the information they are able to access, they cannot foresee the future. Each contingent decision at time t affects the range of possible choices at time t + 1 and constrains the kinds of reactions they are able to articulate. The external context, in turn, exerts strong effects on the actual outcome of the specific and constrained reaction (Simon, 1969, 1979, 1982). Decision-making is intrinsically context dependent.[7]

Social interactions affect not only the behaviour of agents in the formation of their preferences as consumers and their strategies as players in product and factor markets; they also shape their capability to generate new technological knowledge by providing access to external knowledge. The framework within which such interactions take place plays a central role (Antonelli and Scellato, 2013).

The integration of behavioural analyses of decision making makes it possible to regard the creative response as an entrepreneurial action that characterizes and applies both to incumbent firms and agents. The contradiction between the exclusive role of the entrepreneur as an outsider who innovates and enters the marketplace elaborated by Schumpeter (1934) and the corporation praised by Schumpeter (1942) as the engine for innovation can be reconciled with the appreciation of the entrepreneurial function that can be performed both by incumbents and outsiders when the appropriate conditions are given (Audretsch, 2007).

The distinction introduced by Milton Friedman (1953) between subjective and objective rationality – and his claim that only the latter is relevant in economics since the market will always be able to select out firms that make the wrong choices so as to restore equilibrium conditions – no longer holds. The equilibrium conditions after the introduction of innovation are no longer the same as before. The distribution of agents unable to foresee the future and to make valid long-term plans has important consequences for economics, at least when agents are put in the position of being able to implement successful creative reactions. Friedman's argument that markets are able to sort out agents that fail to make rational choices with no consequences for general equilibrium conditions is no longer valid. The introduction of innovation changes the fundamentals of the system; sub-optimal choices have long-lasting consequences.

Market Rivalry in the Neo-Schumpeterian Approach

The core of Schumpeter's 1947 contribution identifies the causes of mismatches – which, combined with entrepreneurial resources and crucial knowledge externalities, qualify the systemic conditions as determinants of the stochastic and contingent possibility of creative responses and introduction of innovations – in the unexpected changes that occur in both factor and product markets. The neo-Schumpeterian literature, which blossomed in the US and was influenced primarily by Schumpeter (1942), concentrated much attention on product markets. It emphasized the role of the corporation engaged in oligopolistic rivalry in product markets as the main, actually exclusive, factor in mismatches (Scherer, 1982). This literature elaborated the so-called 'Schumpeterian hypotheses'[8] according to which:

- Large firms are more likely to engage in R&D and introduce innovations than small firms, because of greater opportunity to appropriate the benefits of innovations and economies of scale in conducting R&D activities (Fisher and Temin, 1973).
- Firms engaged in oligopolistic markets are more likely to introduce innovations than firms active in markets characterized by either perfect competition or monopoly (Dasgupta and Stiglitz, 1980).

A large amount of empirical evidence tested the Schumpeterian hypotheses, with mixed results. Audretsch (1995, 2006) provides strong evidence of the central role of small firms and entrepreneurship in the introduction of radical innovations, showing that corporations failed in the key technologies – biotechnology and informatics – that characterized technological change in the late decades of the twentieth century.[9] Aghion et al. (2005) confirmed the inverted-U relationship between market form, number of firms and innovative effort. The importance of oligopolistic rivalry in stirring innovative effort is not questioned; only its assumed exclusivity seems a limit.[10]

The Inclusion of the Classical Legacies

Schumpeter's 1947 contribution enables us to go beyond the neo-Schumpeterian framework and broaden the analytical context, accommodating among the causes of mismatches not only the oligopolistic rivalry in product markets or in the exogenous supply of entrepreneurs, but also the changes that take place in factor markets and product markets. This allows grafting the classical contributions onto the economics of technological change. Marx and Smith shared the same strong assumption that technological change is endogenous, but regarded it as taking place in response to changes in factor demand and aggregate demand, respectively. A large body of literature has been built on this legacy elaborating the induced technological change approach and the demand pull hypothesis. Both can be integrated successfully into the creative response framework and considerably enrich the scope of analysis.

Along these lines, analysis of the direction of technological change within the induced technological change approaches elaborated by John Hicks (1932) and Vernon Ruttan (1997), based on early Marxian intuition, can contribute to evolutionary complexity. Inclusion of the induced technological change approach helps integrate analysis of the effects of changes in the factor markets not only on the rate of introduction of innovations but also on its direction.

The notion of technological congruence is useful in this context. Technological congruence is an emergent system property defined by the match between the relative size of outputs' elasticity with the relative abundance and cost of inputs in local factor markets. With given total costs, output is greater the larger the output elasticity of the cheapest input. It is consequently clear that all changes in factor markets are likely to induce creative responses that: i) consist of the introduction of new technologies; ii) are biased – that is, characterized by changes in the composition of the output elasticity of inputs that reflect the new conditions in factor markets; and iii) help increase or restore the levels of technological congruence with positive effects on total factor productivity (Antonelli, 2016). The hypothesis that both the rate and the direction of technological change are induced by changes in factor markets that push firms to introduce directed technological change is perfectly consistent with the Schumpeterian platform, where firms innovate while trying to react to unexpected changes in the economic conditions on which their tentative equilibrium solutions had been built (Antonelli, 2008a).[11]

Similarly, contributions to the demand pull approach – based on the intuition of Adam Smith and later elaborated by Allyn Young (1928) and Nicholas Kaldor (1981) – on the central relationship between the extent of the market, the degree of division of labour and hence of specialization, can be successfully accommodated as major sources of mismatch. This dynamics is especially effective when user–producer knowledge interactions enhanced by increased levels of competent demand provide opportunities for learning and eventually generating new technological knowledge and introducing innovations (Schmookler, 1966). In the Schumpeterian synthesis, changes in the aggregate levels of demand matter as much as changes to the individual demand curve of oligopolistic corporations for altering the expected equilibrium conditions.[12] Recent attempts in evolutionary economics to better consider the active role of demand in shaping both structural and technological change contribute to this line of analysis (Saviotti and Pyka, 2013).

The New Economics of Knowledge

The new growth theory has shown the central role of technological knowledge in understanding technological change and growth. The Schumpeterian platform enables the integration of recent advances in the economics of knowledge. The new economics of knowledge, in fact, has greatly enriched analysis of the economic properties of knowledge, and investigated not only knowledge appropriability but also knowledge cumulability, non-exhaustibility and complementarity.

After much emphasis on the aggregate technology production function, where knowledge enters as an input into the generation of any other good, the attention concentrated on the generation process of knowledge, viewed as an intentional and dedicated activity characterized by the recombination of existing knowledge items. Once more the Schumpeterian legacy provides basic guidance: the generation of new knowledge, and consequently the introduction of innovations, is the result of the recombination of existing knowledge items. As Schumpeter puts it: 'To produce means to combine materials and forces within our reach . . . differently' (1911/34: 65). According to Brian Arthur, who elaborates the Schumpeterian legacy: 'new technologies were not "inventions" that came from nowhere. All the examples I was looking at were created – constructed, put together, assembled – from previously existing technologies. Technologies in other words consisted of other technologies, they arose as combinations of other technologies' (Arthur, 2009: 2).

The stock of public knowledge enters as an indispensable input into the generation of new knowledge. At each point in time the new knowledge generated adds to the stock of knowledge, which keeps increasing. The generation of additional knowledge may benefit from the increasing size of the stock of quasi-public knowledge, provided that the costs of external knowledge keep declining.[13] The generation of knowledge acquires the typical traits of a non-ergodic process where the present is influenced, at each point in time, by the past. This approach has important implications: i) the characteristics of the stock of existing knowledge shape the direction and rate of the generation of new knowledge; ii) the larger the stock of knowledge – and the better its composition in terms of coherence, complementarity and rarity of its components – the lower is the cost of knowledge as an input into the recombinant knowledge generation, the lower is the cost of knowledge as an input and hence, for a given budget, the lower is the cost of knowledge as an output[14] and the larger is the knowledge output and the likelihood that the creative reaction takes place with the eventual introduction of innovations and the increase of total factor productivity.[15]

The stock of public knowledge is an essential input into the generation of new knowledge: no new knowledge can be generated by an individual agent without access to and use of knowledge generated by third parties. Its accumulation and access conditions are determined by the organization and the composition of learning activities that take place within each system, and by the quality of the market transactions and availability of qualified and fertile knowledge interactions.

It is not only the size of the stock of public knowledge that matters; its composition also matters. Understanding of the heterogeneity of knowledge enables important progress in the exploration of a new dimension: the role of the composition, next to the size, of the stock of external knowledge. The coherence, relatedness and rarity of the components of the knowledge stock play important positive roles in the generation of innovation.[16] The stock of knowledge of different economic systems exhibits high levels of longitudinal and cross-sectional variance in terms of organized complexity.[17] Analysis of the co-occurrences of patents in the different technological classes enables us to appreciate the composition of the stock of knowledge in terms of coherence and complementarity (Nesta and Saviotti, 2005, 2006).[18]

In the new economics of knowledge the generation of new knowledge is viewed more and more as the collective and systemic result of the recombinant integration of different kinds of knowledge as inputs.[19] External knowledge can no longer be regarded as a supplementary factor that can augment output; rather it is complementary, indispensable inputs that are strictly necessary to generate new technological knowledge and introduce technological innovations.[20] The generation of knowledge is the result of both the efforts and actions of individual agents and of the intrinsic characteristics of the system, in terms of organized complexity and knowledge connectivity, in which agents are embedded (Antonelli and Link, 2015; Antonelli and David, 2015).[21]

The joint appreciation of the effects of knowledge cumulability, complementarity and non-exhaustibility – together with the new appreciation of the transient character of knowledge appropriability – enables us to grasp the dynamics and the role of diachronic knowledge externalities. At each point in time the flows of knowledge generated add to the stock of public knowledge, but only with a time lag. Knowledge producers, in fact, can retain control of their 'inventions', albeit for a limited stretch of time. At the firm level knowledge non-appropriability limits its exclusive, internal cumulability: proprietary knowledge gradually, but inevitably, spills and becomes a public good (Griliches, 1986, 1992). Knowledge cumulability displays its powerful effects mainly at the system level as it allows all firms to use knowledge components again and again for a wide variety of purposes often quite different from the original ones. Nevertheless, accumulation of knowledge and competence also exerts important effects at the firm level, at least in the short term.

The long-term laws of accumulation of the stock of public knowledge play an important role in this context. Integration of the flows of new knowledge into the stock of public knowledge may be more or less effective both with respect to size and composition. Knowledge flows can remain dispersed and fragmented in the system, or be added in a systematic, coherent and effective way. Accumulation is more effective the higher the levels of knowledge connectivity. Consequently, the higher the knowledge connectivity and the better the size and composition of the stock of knowledge, the higher the levels of diachronic and pecuniary knowledge externalities. The knowledge connectivity of the system plays a second important role as it engenders different levels of absorption costs of the stock of public knowledge. Once more, the higher the levels of knowledge connectivity, the lower will be the costs of accessing and using the stock of public knowledge and the larger the pecuniary knowledge externalities.

The recombinant generation of technological knowledge benefits from the access and use of the stock of public knowledge as an input. External knowledge however is not free. Knowledge interactions are strictly necessary because of the strong and irreducible tacit and sticky content of all kinds of existing knowledge. Knowledge differs from information exactly because of its tacit content. In turn, the tacit content of knowledge makes knowledge interactions strictly necessary to access existing knowledge external to each agent. As a consequence, access to and acquisition of external knowledge are not free, and may take place only in specific circumstances. Relevant activities are necessary in order to screen, identify, access and finally use external knowledge that is spilling into the system because of transient appropriability. Because of the strong tacit content of technological knowledge, both transactions and interactions are necessary in order to absorb external knowledge.[22] Knowledge externalities are pecuniary rather than technical (Antonelli, 2008b; Aghion and Jaravel, 2015).

Appreciation of the key role of the size and composition of the stock of knowledge and the consequent levels of knowledge externalities as endogenous elements of the system dynamics enables us to acknowledge, within the Schumpeterian platform, the amount of knowledge available within the system – and the structure of the interactions of components in which each knowledge item is stored – as the result of past creative reactions.[23] The quality of the knowledge governance systems in place plays a crucial role in shaping their distribution in time and space. As a consequence, the distribution in space and time of knowledge externalities is far from ubiquitous and homogeneous. Knowledge externalities are highly localized in their specific context of transactions and interactions, and are exposed to the interaction of various factors. Levels of knowledge externalities are strongly affected by the access, absorption and use cost of external knowledge. The quality of the knowledge governance mechanisms in place in each system and at each point in time is crucial to assess actual levels of access and absorption cost. The stock of quasi-public knowledge may increase over time, but its composition and the quality of knowledge governance mechanisms may decline. Its decay may be engendered by the very same increase in the stock of quasi-public knowledge: congestion may reduce the actual knowledge connectivity of the system. Consequently, knowledge externalities are stochastic rather than deterministic: they are, in fact, an emergent property of the system that may take place with varying levels of strength, including both increase and decline (Antonelli and David, 2015).

The Schumpeterian platform based upon the 1947 essay makes it possible to implement a dynamic understanding of the origin of and changes in innovation systems as the endogenous result of the interaction of the creative response of agents and the (changing) system characteristics that define the endogenous availability of knowledge externalities, and ultimately the cost of external knowledge. Systems of innovation keep changing size, density, borders, specialization and, ultimately, connectivity levels (Nelson, 1993; Malerba, 2005; Martin and Boschma, 2010).

Their punctuated distribution affects the Schumpeterian dynamics. At one extreme we can identify situations where the poor quality of knowledge governance mechanisms weakens the accumulation of the stock of knowledge and the access conditions so as to impede creative reactions: the system copes with mismatches simply by means of technical change, with the eventual reproduction of Marshallian equilibrium. At the other extreme we find the possibility of persistent innovation in economic systems, qualified by high-quality knowledge governance mechanisms that support the accumulation of large stocks of coherent knowledge. Thus the flows of pecuniary knowledge externalities in turn favour the regeneration of strong knowledge externalities that support, over an extended period of time, a self-sustained innovative process based on the continual introduction of innovations that increase the generation of new knowledge externalities and the widespread occurrence of creative reactions in the system. Between the two extremes are systems that may be able to support creative reactions for a limited time: following a first round of innovations the system can no longer feed a sustained process and the Marshallian equilibrium takes over again.

The Selective Diffusion of Innovations

The Schumpeterian platform can integrate the substantial advances made by standard evolutionary economics in the analysis of selective diffusion processes. This literature has provided a strong and sophisticated analytical framework to understand the selective diffusion of some innovations with respect to others (Foster and Metcalfe, 2012).

The Schumpeterian platform can benefit from biological analyses of the selection of the species that have been – randomly – generated. In fact it provides useful hints to understanding the characteristics of the processes and the underlying factors that allow some of the many innovations that have been randomly and accidentally introduced to eventually diffuse through the economic system, while others are not adopted. The intuition that at each point in time many alternative innovations compete – and that only a few succeed and will be eventually adopted and diffused – is an important contribution of standard evolutionary approaches that can be successfully retained in the broad Schumpeterian platform (Nelson and Winter, 1973, 1982).

By the same token, the Schumpeterian platform can integrate the replicator analysis that provides important insights into the effects on economic growth of the variety of technologies 'exogenous' at each point in time (Metcalfe, 2007b; Metcalfe and Boden, 1992). In so doing, it provides a new analytical framework to study the consequences of innovation within the limits of the assumption that qualified circumstances impede the agents belonging to a failing species in any creative reaction that would increase variety endogenously. Like other approaches based upon biological metaphors, the replicator analysis is not able to incorporate the endogenous emergence of innovations.

In this context, the notion of dominant design can be regarded as a major analytical tool that helps substantiate the notion of emergence. At each point in time firms try to introduce many different innovations. Only a fraction of them fit the (new) product and factor market conditions. Their selection is partly influenced by their potential complementarities that are reinforced and valorized by the introduction of incremental innovations. This process of selection and convergence leads to the eventual identification of a dominant design (Utterback, 1994; Anderson and Tushman, 1990).

In sum, it seems that Schumpeter's (1947a) insight enables us to elaborate a comprehensive and integrated Schumpeterian platform that goes beyond both the evolutionary approaches of biological ascent and the new growth theory, which, as a matter of fact (although with different assumptions), share the basic assumption that the diversity of agents and alternative technologies, including innovations, are spontaneously reproduced by the system as the result of automatic processes.

The Schumpeterian platform provides the basic tools to account for endogenous innovation, implementing the notions of rugged landscapes introduced by Paul Krugman (1994, 1995) and of ecosystem framed by Martin Fransman (2010).

NOTES

1. All extracts/quotations from Schumpeter (1939) are drawn from the abridged version with introduction by Rendigs Fels, available at http://classiques.uqac.ca/classiques/ Schumpeter_joseph/business_cycles/business_cycles.html (last accessed April 2017).
2. It seems quite surprising that little effort has been made to graft the Lamarckian hypothesis that the phenotype can change the genotype to the economics of innovation. The Lamarckian approach provides an evolutionary framework in which the causality and intentionality of the introduction of innovations might be better elaborated.
3. As a matter of fact the approach elaborated by Nelson and Winter (1982) is not able to go beyond the results of Alchian (1950: 214), who writes: 'Plants "grow" to the sunny side of buildings not because they 'want to' in awareness of the fact that optimum or better conditions prevail there but rather because the leaves that happen to have more sunlight grow faster and their feeding system became stronger. Similarly, animals with configurations and habits more appropriate for survival under prevailing conditions have an enhanced viability and will with higher probability be typical survivors.'
4. Note that we follow the Schumpeterian use of the notion of adaptive reaction as a form of passive attitude when no changes to the existing technology are possible. In fact the adaptive response is not defined as passive, but simply included in established practice. The possibility of technological change is not considered. In complexity theory, adaptive responses are an active choice that includes possible introduction of changes to the system by agents who try to adapt to its new characteristics. Following the Schumpeterian lexicon this would be a creative reaction (Miller and Page, 2007).
5. It seems appropriate to note that Schumpeter's 'Creative response in economic history' and Simon's *Administrative Behavior* were both published in 1947.
6. Antonelli and Scellato (2011) tested the hypothesis of a U-shaped relationship between profitability and innovation that has its minimum in the proximity of average levels of profitability.
7. Albin (1998: 71) provides a clear definition of the notion of context-dependent decision making: 'A robust alternative to the rational choice program must also be more explicitly context dependent . . . But one promising path to discovering a knowable orderliness in human behavior that is context dependent and computationally bounded is to ask whether and when the social environment favors some behaviors over others and why. Evolutionary models in which the distribution of strategies in a population change in response to their success and in which mutation and innovation lead to new behaviors are a logical way to attach these issues.'

8. See Kamien and Schwartz (1982: 22): 'We attribute these hypotheses to Schumpeter because that is how they are commonly referred to in the literature on the subject.'

9. The empirical evidence of Antonelli and Colombelli (2015b) shows that the relationship between size and innovation holds only with respect to the size of the stock of knowledge. Firms with a large stock of internal knowledge are more likely to introduce innovations than firms with a small stock of knowledge. This relationship is not confirmed when size is measured with other indicators such as sales and employment. The Schumpeterian hypothesis holds because of the recombinant character of the knowledge-generation process.

10. Aghion et al. (2015), following the neo-Schumpeterian literature that impinges upon the legacy of Schumpeter (1942), does not take into account the hypothesis that firms may be induced to innovate by their negative performances. In the failure-induced approach, instead, firms introduce innovation not only to gain monopoly rents but also as a creative reaction to their falling profitability (Antonelli, 1989). The evidence provided by Antonelli and Scellato (2011) shows that there is a U relationship between profitability and innovation. Firms introduce innovations both when their profitability is negative and when their profitability is very high. Both stem from out-of-equilibrium conditions. In the former case the failure-inducement mechanism takes place. The introduction of innovations is determined by efforts to cope with adverse market conditions. In the latter case the large profitability reduces the liquidity constraints and provides firms with the opportunity to cope with the high levels of uncertainty of the innovation process.

11. Antonelli and Quatraro (2010) provide strong empirical evidence of the causal relationship between changes in factor prices, the introduction of directed technological changes and the increase in total factor productivity. Antonelli (2015b) articulates a model of Schumpeterian growth based on the endogenous accumulation of capital and the related reduction of its relative user cost that induces the search for higher levels of technological congruence based on the introduction of capital-intensive technological change.

12. Antonelli and Gehringer (2015b, c) test the competent demand pull hypothesis, according to which demand actually pulls technological change and total factor productivity growth only when it is associated with effective knowledge interactions that parallel market transactions along vertical value chains between competent users and producers.

13. The increase in the stock of quasi-external knowledge and the introduction of innovations may undermine the quality of the knowledge-governance mechanisms engendering congestion effects and, more generally, changing the structure of interactions and transactions that enable access to the stock of knowledge.

14. The empirical evidence of Antonelli and Colombelli (2015b) shows that the amount and structure of external knowledge and the internal stocks of knowledge that firms can access and use in the generation of new technological knowledge help firms reduce the costs of knowledge. The empirical section is based upon a panel of European public companies for 1995–2006 for which information on patents was gathered. Econometric analysis of the costs of knowledge explores the role of R&D expenditure and the stock of knowledge internal and external to each firm on the unit costs of patents. In order to articulate the different facets of the external knowledge that is made accessible by proximity with firms co-localized in the same region (NUTS2), they take into account other variables as proxies for regional variety, complementarity and similarity. The results confirm the hypothesis that the size and composition of the stock of external knowledge play key roles in reducing actual costs of the generation of new technological knowledge at the firm level.

15. Antonelli and Gehringer (2016) articulate the hypothesis that the use of external knowledge is necessary to complement the recombinant generation of new knowledge. The empirical evidence of 20 OECD countries in 1975–2010 confirms that, when access to the external knowledge occurs at costs below the social value of knowledge, firms benefit from pecuniary knowledge externalities, and are actually able to introduce productivity-enhancing innovations so that the growth of total factor productivity

is negatively associated with the costs of knowledge. Total factor productivity thus increases faster where and when the costs of knowledge are lower.

16. See Antonelli et al. (2016) for an empirical analysis of the role of Jacobs externalities in the knowledge-generation function.

17. The composition of the stock of knowledge in terms of variety, rarity and relatedness changes across systems and, most importantly, over time. Composition quality can rise as well as fall, as the application of the methodology first elaborated by Hidalgo and Hausmann (2009) to study the composition of the stock of knowledge enables us to measure.

18. Antonelli et al. (2010) show how analysis of the co-occurrence of technological classes within two or more patent applications allows identification and measurement of the levels of coherence and complementary of the stock of knowledge. Their empirical investigation confirms that the recombination process has been more effective in countries characterized by higher levels of coherence and specialization of knowledge stock. Countries better able to master the recombinant generation of new technological knowledge have experienced higher rates of increase in national multifactor productivity growth.

19. Antonelli et al. (2016) introduce the notion of Jacobs knowledge externalities to study the effects of the composition of the stock of knowledge of European regions and test their relevance in knowledge generation.

20. Antonelli and Colombelli (2015a) test the hypothesis that external and internal knowledge are strictly complementary inputs in the recombinant knowledge-generation process. Neither input can fall below minimum levels without putting at risk the production of new technological knowledge.

21. As a matter of fact the notion of non-appropriability was first introduced by Schumpeter. Innovators can command the benefits of their innovations only for a limited time. Eventually, and inevitably, competitors react. Knowledge has the same property of profit that is intrinsically transient: it 'has the most lamentable similarity with the drying up of a spring' (Schumpeter, 1934: 209). In Schumpeter innovators enjoy the appropriation of the rents stemming from the introduction of innovations, albeit for a limited time. Eventually, in fact, the exclusive command of the new technology leaks out; imitation takes place together with entry. Market prices fall together with profits. In Schumpeter there are no appropriable and non appropriable components of innovations. All innovations are first appropriable and later become public goods. The sequence between the first appropriation and the eventual leakage is intrinsically Schumpeterian.

22. To explore the endogeneity of knowledge externalities Lane and Maxfield (2005: 48) introduced two key notions. The first is generative relations, for example: 'the generative potential of their relationships with other agents. We then show how semantic uncertainty may emerge in the context of generative relationships – and how this uncertainty may give rise to new attributions of identity that may then be instantiated in new artifacts or new kinds of agent roles and relationships' The second is scaffolding structures: 'to show how market systems emerge through the construction of scaffolding structures in agent space. Through these structures, the agents who operate within the market system jointly confront their ontological uncertainty. Scaffolding structures provide a framework for controlling the kinds of new entities – both agents and artifacts – that enter the market system, and for aligning the attributions of agents in the market system about one another and the artifacts they make, exchange, install, maintain and use. Through scaffolding structures, agents can consolidate a zone of agent-artifact space, making it sufficiently stable to support both markets and the generation of new artifacts to be traded within those markets.'

23. See Appendix in Chapter 4.

3. Towards an evolutionary complexity of endogenous innovation

The Schumpeterian platform provides the foundations of an evolutionary complexity approach that enables us to understand:

- the systemic determinants of innovation as an endogenous process that is based on reactive decision-making highly sensitive to the institutional characteristics of the system in terms of the structured organization of the micro-level interactions of heterogeneous agents that make possible the generation and use of knowledge at costs that are below equilibrium levels;
- the consequences of the sequential bifurcations that are determined by the aggregate consequences of the micro-level interactions of heterogeneous agents credited with the ability to introduce technological and structural changes that alter the organized complexity of the system;
- the role of thresholds and non-linearity in the relations between the key components of the system dynamics stressing the effects of 'small events' that are able to change the levels of organized complexity of the system, the consequent availability of pecuniary knowledge externalities and the non-ergodic dynamics of the system (Lane and Maxfield, 1997; Lane et al., 2009; Bonifati, 2010; Arthur et al., 1997; Miller and Page, 2007).[1]

The Schumpeterian legacy accommodates the basic tools of complexity economics: feedback, emergence, organized complexity and knowledge connectivity, endogenous variety and path dependence. Let us consider them in turn.

3.1 FEEDBACK

According to the Merriam-Webster dictionary, feedback is 'the return to the input of a part of the output of a machine, system, or process'. In economics the notion of externalities accommodates effectively the basic feedback mechanism. Externalities, in fact, account for the changes of individual action and performance engendered by the effects at the system level of prior action. The introduction of innovations as the result of a creative response to a mismatch between expected and actual market conditions, conditional on the availability of effective knowledge externalities, provides the case of augmented and multiple feedback. While standard feedback usually consists in one-sided effects, the innovation process is a vector of multiple feedbacks that can be both positive and negative. The innovation process is likely to stir a three-pronged system of feedback: i) economic feedback concerning product and factor markets; ii) knowledge feedback concerning the composition of the stock of quasi-public knowledge; iii) knowledge-governance feedback concerning the mechanisms that rule the conditions of access and use of the stock of quasi-public knowledge. The direction and intensity of each may differ from the others. The successful introduction of innovations may have positive effects both in terms of increased levels of total factor productivity and increased quality of the knowledge stock and knowledge governance. It may also have positive economic effects coupled with negative ones if and when it undermines the quality of the stock of knowledge in terms of composition and/or of the knowledge governance mechanisms, engendering an increase – rather than a decrease – in the costs of accessing and using the stock of quasi-public knowledge (North, 2010).

3.2 EMERGENCE

The application of the notion of emergent system property to the economics of innovation provides a fertile context into which the Schumpeterian notion of innovation as a creative reaction – contingent upon the system characteristics that arise in special circumstances when a variety of specific conditions apply and the interactions between the agents and the characteristics of the system engender multiple feedbacks – can be generalized and implemented. Innovation is the endogenous result of the combination of mismatches with the micro-level interactions of heterogeneous agents that, for given characteristics of the organized complexity of the system, may yield the creation of positive pecuniary knowledge externalities (Antonelli, 2008a, 2009, 2011).

The notion of emergent system property elaborated by complexity theory is most useful to accommodate and yet implement the Schumpeterian notion of innovation as a creative reaction. As stated by Arthur (2014): 'An emergent system property takes place when the elements in a system react to the outcome those agents together create.' Consequently, emergence is both a product and process; it has both static and dynamic aspects that may be both positive and negative.

Analysis of the crucial role of the interplay between individual decision-making based on the notion of reaction and the sorting role of the characteristics of the context of action of each individual agent makes clear that innovation is an emergent property of the system rather than the result of individual action. The role of the economic environment in assessing the real possibility that the reaction of individual agents may be creative as opposed to adaptive stresses the systemic character of the innovation process. The characteristics of the system are central to assessing the rate and direction of the innovative process. From this viewpoint, the notion of innovation as an emergent property of the economic system in which the agents are embedded reduces the weight of the individual entrepreneur, stresses the collective role of the innovation process and highlights the weight of the system.

Mismatches can lead to creative reactions, and hence to actual introduction of innovations only if the system is endowed with appropriate levels of organized complexity that make knowledge externalities available, and hence make the generation of new technological knowledge not only possible but also cheaper than in equilibrium conditions. Without appropriate levels of organized complexity, knowledge externalities are not sufficient to enable the generation of new technological knowledge at costs that are below equilibrium, and agents are bound to adaptive reactions. See region A in Figure 3.2, which shows how the bifurcation takes place.

Emergent properties can be contrasted with so-called resultant properties, understood as the properties of wholes that are possessed by the individual elements comprising those wholes. Whereas the existence of emergent properties requires that certain elements stand in specific relations to each other, thereby forming a particular structure or whole, resultant properties are possessed by the individual elements irrespective of how they are related to one another. These resultant properties obtain even when those elements are taken in isolation or when the elements occur as an unstructured aggregation or 'heap' (Harper and Lewis, 2012).

The distinction between system and resultant properties is most important for the economics of innovation. As long as innovation is the ultimate cause of the increase in total factor productivity levels it is, in fact, quite difficult (if not impossible) to regard it as the outcome of the resultant property of individual action. Understanding of total factor productivity relies upon the answer to the key question of why the individual agent would have not been able to maximize the use of inputs that cause innovation so that their marginal productivity would match their costs; but this remains unexplained. Taking advantage of the notion of emergent system property, it is impossible to accept the hypothesis that innovation is the result of individual action irrespective of its localized context. The identification of innovation as an emergent system property allows us to regard the structure of the system in terms of interactions and connections, quality and size of the stock of quasi-public knowledge and the consequent access costs as the necessary complementary factors that – together with individual action – explain the endogenous causation of innovation, and hence of total factor productivity increase.

At each point in time the introduction of innovations and the consequent creative destruction engenders new mismatches between plans and actual market conditions. The introduction of innovations is the primary source of the unexpected changes in product and factor markets that stir the reaction of firms. Firms try to cope with unexpected product and factor market conditions. The reaction of each individual firm will be creative and consist in the introduction of further technological changes if and when the system is – *again* – able to support individual entrepreneurial action with the accumulation of the stock of knowledge and the consequent provision of appropriate amounts of knowledge externalities.

At each point in time the *changing* levels of the stock of knowledge (both in terms of size and composition) and of the quality of knowledge-governance mechanisms – and consequently of the actual levels of pecuniary knowledge externalities – are crucial and far from deterministic. Their levels in fact are not given, as they depend upon the changing levels of organized complexity of the system. The generation of additional knowledge and the introduction of innovations at time t + 1 may undermine the quality of both the knowledge-governance mechanisms and the stock of knowledge in terms of composition at time t2, and hence lead to an increase in – rather than the reduction of – the costs of accessing, absorbing and using the stock of quasi-public knowledge as an input in the generation of additional knowledge.

The characteristics of the system in which firms are localized, and specifically its levels of organized complexity and knowledge connectivity, are not given as they keep changing and are not exogenous – as it is assumed in NK models – but intrinsically endogenous.[2] The dynamics of the system feeds continuously on the interplay between out-of-equilibrium conditions, firms' reactions, accumulation of large and coherent stock of knowledge, and effective external knowledge search; low-cost generation of new technological knowledge; the (eventual) introduction of productivity-enhancing technological innovations; price reductions; and eventual new out-of-equilibrium conditions. This dynamics is characterized by structural and technological changes that – at each point in time – reshape the levels of knowledge connectivity as well as the size and composition of the knowledge stock that firms can access and the amount of knowledge externalities actually available to firms. Such changes can have both positive and negative effects on the cost of access to the stock of quasi-public knowledge. Endogenous knowledge externalities are as much at the heart of the innovation system as endogenous innovation.[3]

3.3 ORGANIZED COMPLEXITY AND KNOWLEDGE CONNECTIVITY

The composition of the system in which reaction can be either adaptive or creative is crucial and endogenous. The organized complexity of a system differs according to its composition in terms of the characteristics of its components and their relations. A wide range of mesoeconomic characteristics play a role in assessing the changing size and composition of the stock of knowledge. These include:

- the distribution of clusters;
- the architecture of interactions and transactions within districts and networks;
- the levels of skilled worker mobility;
- the types of institutional set-up;
- the openness to international trade;
- the architecture of value chains; and
- the role of the key sectors and technologies from which knowledge flows, as synthesized by the sectoral architecture.

The new understanding of knowledge heterogeneity adds a new layer to the composition of the system: beside firms, regions and industries, the types of knowledge that characterize the stocks of both internal and external knowledge play an important role. Because of the intrinsic heterogeneity of knowledge, stocks of knowledge differ in terms of specialization, diversification, complementarity, coherence, interrelatedness and rarity, interoperability and interdependence. The mix of knowledge items that characterizes the stock of knowledge can be more or less effective in supporting the availability of knowledge externalities, and hence the likelihood of creative reactions. Moreover, the changing composition of the stock of quasi-public knowledge may have both positive and negative effects on the generation of new knowledge. Figure 3.1 details the working of the organized complexity.

Not all systems enjoy the advantages of organized complexity and knowledge connectivity at all times and forever. Systems endowed with

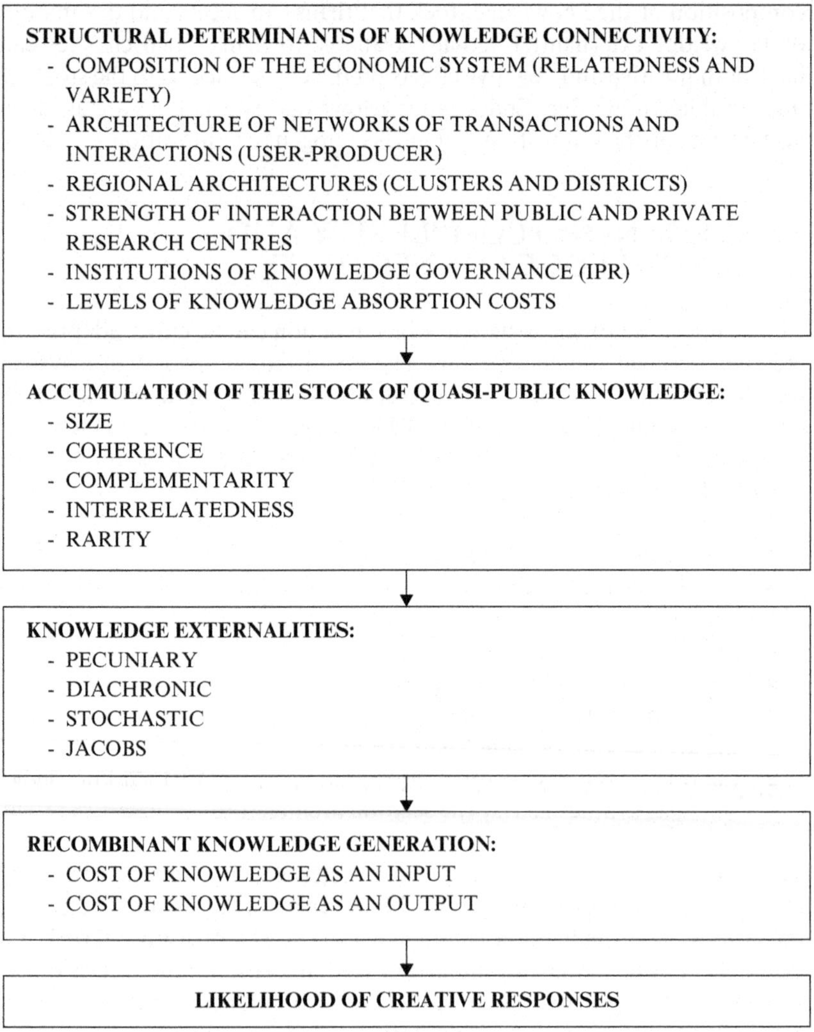

STRUCTURAL DETERMINANTS OF KNOWLEDGE CONNECTIVITY:
- COMPOSITION OF THE ECONOMIC SYSTEM (RELATEDNESS AND VARIETY)
- ARCHITECTURE OF NETWORKS OF TRANSACTIONS AND INTERACTIONS (USER-PRODUCER)
- REGIONAL ARCHITECTURES (CLUSTERS AND DISTRICTS)
- STRENGTH OF INTERACTION BETWEEN PUBLIC AND PRIVATE RESEARCH CENTRES
- INSTITUTIONS OF KNOWLEDGE GOVERNANCE (IPR)
- LEVELS OF KNOWLEDGE ABSORPTION COSTS

↓

ACCUMULATION OF THE STOCK OF QUASI-PUBLIC KNOWLEDGE:
- SIZE
- COHERENCE
- COMPLEMENTARITY
- INTERRELATEDNESS
- RARITY

↓

KNOWLEDGE EXTERNALITIES:
- PECUNIARY
- DIACHRONIC
- STOCHASTIC
- JACOBS

↓

RECOMBINANT KNOWLEDGE GENERATION:
- COST OF KNOWLEDGE AS AN INPUT
- COST OF KNOWLEDGE AS AN OUTPUT

↓

LIKELIHOOD OF CREATIVE RESPONSES

Figure 3.1   The working of organized complexity

high levels of organized complexity (and hence knowledge connectivity) are better able than others to sustain the accumulation of a large and coherent stock of knowledge, and hence support the generation of new knowledge externalities and the introduction of innovations. This capability is not given once and for ever, as it keeps changing in both directions: progress and decline (Page, 2011).

Thomas Jefferson's famous candlelight metaphor is most useful to grasp how the institutional and structural organization of a system plays the key role of dissemination mechanism of the knowledge flows that enable the creative reaction, and hence the introduction of innovations.[4] The system's organized complexity plays the same role as the Jeffersonian architectural design of the distribution of mirrors, which is able to maximize the amount of light produced by each candle.

The architecture of the interactions and transactions among learning agents in terms of networks and percolation structures has a central role in explaining the accumulation of the stock of knowledge in terms of size and composition, generation of knowledge externalities, the consequent generation of technological knowledge and the eventual introduction of innovations. The rates of introduction of innovations, and consequently the rates of increase in total factor productivity, are likely to be larger the better is the organized complexity and the consequent knowledge connectivity of the system.

The quality of organized complexity plays a key role as the sorting device of the dynamics of the system. When the quality of organized complexity is high – and the knowledge connectivity is strong enough to favour the accumulation of the stock of knowledge – the system enters a loop of self-sustained creative reactions, technological and structural changes, and generation of both new knowledge externalities and new mismatches that feed further changes. The dynamics of the system can stop when the generation of new knowledge, the introduction of technological and structural changes have negative – rather than positive – effects on the quality of both the composition of the stock of quasi-public knowledge and the organized complexity of the system.

At the other extreme, there is equilibrium: one of the many possible outcomes of Schumpeterian dynamics. It takes place when the levels of organized complexity are not appropriate to favour the accumulation of a large and well-structured stock of knowledge that generates sufficient amounts and quality of knowledge externalities that are necessary to make the reaction of firms creative. With low levels of organized complexity and poor knowledge connectivity, the reaction of firms is adaptive and leads to equilibrium conditions. Innovations are not introduced; no new mismatches and no new knowledge externalities are being generated; no forces are any longer at play to modify the decisions of agents. The Marshallian selection of variety takes place, and the dynamics of the system expires. Equilibrium is a possibility, and it is actually a frequent outcome that takes place when no innovative feedbacks are at work and externalities are no longer available.

The levels of organized complexity of a system are endogenous to the system itself, as they depend upon the structure and architecture of knowledge interactions and transactions that take place within the system.

They are far from automatic, as they are the result of processes that are dynamic, endogenous, non-ergodic and far from deterministic. The introduction of innovations has multiple effects:

- to create mismatches between expectation and the actual conditions of product and factor markets;
- to reshape the organized complexity of the system changing the levels of knowledge connectivity determined by the structure of knowledge interactions and transactions;
- to change the size and composition of the stock of public knowledge upon which the provision of knowledge externalities depend; and
- to shape the generation of additional technological knowledge.

The creative reaction affects the levels of knowledge connectivity – with effects that may be both positive and negative – and hence the amount of knowledge externalities without which the introduction of innovations is impossible.

At each point in time each firm discovers that, because of the creative destruction following the introduction of innovations, the actual conditions of: i) product and factor markets; ii) the organized complexity of the system and the levels of knowledge connectivity; iii) the size and composition of the stock of knowledge; and iv) the actual levels of knowledge externalities are no longer the expected ones. Again, each firm considers the possibility of coping with unexpected mismatches either by adaptive responses that consist in movements within the existing technology and the existing structure of the economy or creative responses that consist in technological and structural changes. Here the structural consequences of the introduction of innovations on the organized complexity of the system become crucial. Because of the introduction of innovations at time t, the structural conditions of the system at time t + 1 may now be different. Previous creative responses may have affected the conditions that are necessary for the generation of new additional technological knowledge. The introduction of innovations may have changed the structure of interactions and transactions, and hence the levels of knowledge connectivity and consequently the size and composition of the stock of knowledge and the actual amount of knowledge externalities available in the system, either increasing or decreasing their levels.

The dynamics of creative reactions can be self-feeding and persistent, so that the introduction of innovations at time t is the cause of the introduction of further innovations at time t + 1 only when two conditions are fulfilled. This result, in fact, takes place only in specific circumstances, if and when the introduction of innovations – besides the effect of engendering mismatches in product and factor markets – has the complementary effect of increasing the levels of knowledge connectivity, and consequently the stock of knowledge and the amount of knowledge externalities without reducing them to below the threshold levels that are necessary to support the reaction and make it creative. In these special conditions creative reactions cause creative destructions that support the further introduction of innovations. In this case the consequences of the introduction of innovations are the causes of the introduction of further innovations.

When, instead, the introduction of innovations not only engenders mismatches in product and factor markets but also has negative effects on the organized complexity of the system that are at the origin of the deterioration and reduction of the levels of knowledge connectivity and the size and composition of the stock of knowledge – hence of the availability and levels of knowledge externalities – the chances that the creative reaction may take place again are reduced.

The generation of additional technological knowledge and the introduction of innovations may have negative consequences on the quality of the stock of quasi-public knowledge and on the levels of organized complexity of the system, and hence on the amount of knowledge externalities increasing the levels of search, absorption, decodification costs and, in general, of the entire range of activities that are necessary to access and use external knowledge as an input into the recombinant generation of new knowledge. The generation of additional technological knowledge and the introduction of innovations may have structural consequences that affect the levels of knowledge connectivity of the system, and hence the size and composition of the stock of knowledge affecting the viability and sustainability of the mechanisms of knowledge governance and the institutional set that had been effective until then. The generation of additional technological knowledge and the introduction of innovations may have reduced the levels of knowledge connectivity, the coherence, variety and rarity of the stock of knowledge and the scope of activity of the key sectors, created diseconomies of agglomeration and excess density. The basic mechanisms of knowledge governance may no longer be appropriate to coordinate the division of creative labour and the dissemination of knowledge.[5]

With lower levels of knowledge connectivity and a reduction in the rates of accumulation of the stock of quasi-public knowledge, the decline of knowledge externalities, the reaction of each firm may become adaptive. The system is no longer able to support the continual introduction of innovations, and the dynamics converge to equilibrium levels. Firms adjust quantities to prices and prices to quantities without any further changes in product and factor markets.

Region B of Figure 3.2 shows the working of the second bifurcation. If the changes in technological knowledge and in the organized complexity

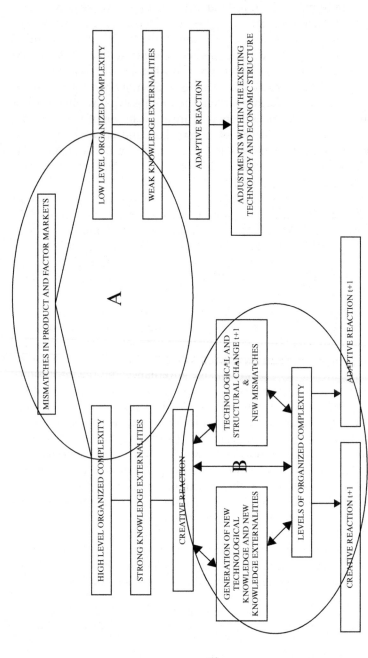

Figure 3.2   Endogenous innovation and organized complexity as emerging system properties

of the system increase its knowledge connectivity so as to favour the generation of new knowledge externalities, the innovation process maintains momentum. If, instead, the technological and structural changes reduce the levels of knowledge connectivity of the system and undermine the size and composition of the stock of knowledge – and hence the knowledge externalities available within the system – the chances of a creative reaction taking place decline and the innovation process stops.

In Schumpeterian dynamics the levels of organized complexity, however, are themselves endogenous and can improve or deteriorate according to the structural and technological changes that are introduced along the process. The levels of organized complexity and knowledge connectivity are themselves a system-emergent property.

Understanding of the fortuitous, punctuated and stochastic character of the organized complexity that engenders endogenous knowledge externalities enables us to account for the great diachronic and synchronic variance of the rates of introduction of innovations and the rates of increase in total factor productivity (Mokyr, 1990; Craft, 2010).

3.4   ENDOGENOUS VARIETY

In the Schumpeterian dynamics of endogenous innovation the variety of agents plays a central role and is itself endogenous. Agents are heterogeneous because of their location in the different spaces that constitute the system, and the consequent participation in the differentiated activities that take place within it. Agents react in different ways to mismatches between planned and actual market conditions, according to the number of knowledge externalities that are available in their proximity. The variety of agents and the heterogeneity of the system are the endogenous products of the reactive dynamics, built into Schumpeterian dynamics. Appreciation of the endogeneity of variety has the immediate consequence of drawing attention to the characteristics of the dynamics of the heterogeneity within the system and its endogenous organization.

3.5   PATH DEPENDENCE

The grafting of tools of complexity analysis and the retrieval of a correct appreciation of the Schumpeterian legacy makes it possible to understand the historical and endogenous character of economic change achieving a much stronger foundation and broader scope of application for the economics of innovation. The process of economic change – including the

generation of technological change, the introduction of innovations and
the transformation of the structure of economic systems – can be better
understood as a path-dependent, non-ergodic endogenous dynamics where
history matters, and yet the changing conditions in which the dynamics
displays its process affect its changing speed, direction and very survival
(Blume and Durlauf, 2006).

The generation of technological knowledge is itself a non-ergodic
process characterized by diachronic knowledge externalities. The generation of new knowledge in fact consists in the recombination of existing
knowledge items. The stock of existing knowledge is an indispensable
input into the generation of knowledge as an output. The flows of new
proprietary knowledge generated at each point in time – with due lags
engendered by the limited duration of appropriation of inventors – add
to the public stock of knowledge. The changing composition and size of
the stock of public knowledge yields changes in the flows of diachronic
knowledge externalities that enable reduction in the costs of knowledge as
an input, and hence of knowledge as an output.

The loop of endogenous accumulation of the stock of knowledge, generation of technological knowledge and innovations is a possible dynamic
process that is far from deterministic. The process is indeed non-ergodic,
as events that take place in the past effect firms' choices and the types of
reaction that they can practise, but it is heavily affected by events that
occur during the process.[6] A system can support and assist in the creative
reaction of agents for a given length of time until the continuous introduction of additional innovations engenders the increasing size, composition
and accessibility of the stock of knowledge, and hence the generation of
positive externalities. The characteristics of the system are not defined for
ever at the outset of non-ergodic dynamics; rather, they are exposed to
contingent events during the process, including the endogenous introduction of innovations (David, 2005).

Path dependence is intrinsic to evolutionary complexity because the
interplay between the innovative efforts of the agents surprised by out-
of-equilibrium conditions, the characteristics and the effects in terms of
limited reversibility of their decisions taken at time $t - 1$, and the characteristics of the system does not only affect the type of reaction – adaptive
or creative – and the outcome of the innovative efforts; it also affects the
structure of the system and its ability to provide access to knowledge externalities. Structural and technological changes are intertwined in a dynamic
process that is intrinsically historical and, as such, affected by the effects
of contingent events that are determined by the stochastic evolution of
events.[7]

The context in which firms try to react to mismatches between expectations and the actual conditions of product and factor markets is shaped at each point in time by decisions taken in the past. In other words, reactions are contingent on the conditions determined by the choices made in the past. As such, their effects are non-ergodic and *path* dependent as opposed to *past* dependent because the new choices may correct the old ones and direct the process towards unexpected outcomes.

The creative response and the consequent introduction of innovation are not only consequences of system characteristics, but also cause a second type of feedback and endogenous process. The introduction of innovations is likely to affect the very conditions that make further creative response possible. In other words, it is clear that knowledge externalities are indeed external to each firm but absolutely endogenous to the system. The introduction of a specific innovation, in a specific context and at a specific time can reinforce the provision of knowledge externalities as much as it may weaken it. Once again, the process dynamics is typically historical – that is, non-ergodic but path dependent as opposed to past dependent.

In this context, longitudinal correlation of the sequence of events that take place along time can exhibit non-transitive properties such that, while the correlation between event A at time t_1 and event B at time t_2 and the correlation between event B at time t_2 and event C at time t_3 happen to be strong, the correlation between event A and C may be very weak (David, 2005, 2007).

Appreciation of the path-dependent character of these dynamic processes questions the use of standard Markov chains. Standard Markov chains are dynamic stochastic processes characterized by the presence of discrete values of the states and, more importantly, by the fact that the conditional probability of a state at time t depends exclusively on the state at time $t - 1$. This implies that the process has no memory and only the last state influences the subsequent state. If the process is path dependent, instead, Multiple Probability Transition Matrices (MPTMs) apply. MPTMs rely on the computation of different probability transition matrices in relevant sub-periods that are identified by significant contingent events that are expected to affect the transition probabilities between the innovative and non-innovative status of the agents. Comparison of the MTPM parameters in different sub-periods allows better identification of the path-dependent character of the innovation process. In particular, observation of significantly different MTPM parameters in different sub-periods might be an indication that the extent of the hysteresis is affected by contingent events and, hence, the innovation process can be qualified as path dependent (Antonelli et al., 2015).

The Schumpeterian platform shares the intrinsic characteristics of a high order emergence. The notion of third order emergence nicely accommodates this dynamics. According to Martin and Sunley (2012: 341), third order emergence comprises:

> emergent phenomena and systems characterized by 'memory' where an amplification of high-order influences on parts is combined with a selective sampling of these influences which reintroduces the parts into different realizations of the system over time, imparting both continuity with and divergence from prior states of the system.

The dynamics of diachronic knowledge externalities that stem from the accumulation of the stocks of public knowledge is at the centre of the non-ergodic characters that shape endogenous innovation.

In fact, we see that at each point in time key characteristics of the system – determined by the past and yet exposed to contingent changes – qualify the reaction of agents caught in out-of-equilibrium conditions, whether creative, allowing them to introduce innovations through access to knowledge externalities at time t, or adaptive because they have no access to knowledge externalities. The occurrence of the systemic characteristics that qualify the levels of knowledge connectivity and make knowledge externalities available – combined with the entrepreneurial attributes of the managers of incumbent corporations and the entry of new firms – make the mismatch between expected and actual conditions in both product and factor markets endogenous. The accumulation of the stock of knowledge and the consequent flows of knowledge externalities are at the same time the result of individual action and its cause.

NOTES

1. Agent-based simulation (ABS) is a powerful methodology that is able to mimic the dynamics of complex systems characterized by thresholds and non-linearity that determine the outcome of the micro-level interactions among heterogeneous agents framed into scaffolding structures. Antonelli and Ferraris (2011) apply an ABS model to explore the characteristics of the organized complexity of an economic system as the determinant of endogenous technological and structural change.
2. NK models assume the characteristics of the knowledge landscape to be exogenous (Levinthal, 1997; Sorenson et al., 2006).
3. Antonelli and Ferraris (2017) elaborate an agent-based model to analyse the dynamics of endogenous knowledge externalities.
4. Jefferson's wrote: 'He who receives an idea from me, receives instruction himself without lessening mine; as he who lights his taper [candle] at mine, receives light without darkening me. That ideas should freely spread from one to another over the globe, for the moral and mutual instruction of man, and improvement of his condition, seems to have been peculiarly and benevolently designed by nature, when she made them, like fire, expansible over all space, without lessening their density in any point, and like the air in which

we breathe, move, and have our physical being, incapable of confinement or exclusive appropriation.' Note that the distinction between non-rivalry in user value and non-rivalry in exchange value is most relevant in this context.

5. Antonelli et al. (2011) test the hypothesis of a non-linear (inverted-U) relationship between density and knowledge externalities and show that – beyond a threshold – excess agglomeration of innovative activity has negative effects on knowledge governance mechanisms, with the consequent reduction in the quality and availability of pecuniary knowledge externalities.

6. Audretsch et al. (2015) elaborate the interesting notion of 'spillover entrepreneurship' to stress the crucial role of entrepreneurship as an intentional activity that is necessary to accessing and using knowledge spillovers. Knowledge spillovers are far from spontaneous and automatic, and cannot be accessed by passive users.

7. For empirical evidence on the role of contingent events on the persistence of innovative activity, see Antonelli et al. (2012, 2013, 2015).

4. Innovation as an emergent system property

The Schumpeterian essay of 1947 has provided the basic inspiration to elaborate a theoretical platform able to move away from the limitations and ambiguities of the evolutionary approaches that impinge upon biological metaphors, and to accommodate the new developments of evolutionary complexity that enable us to account for innovation as an emergent system property. The new approach builds upon a few critical assumptions: let us consider them in turn.

First, firms are characterized by bounded rationality that impedes the perfect forecast on the future conditions of product and factor market conditions. Firms rely on procedural rationality that makes it possible to try to react to the evolving conditions of product and factor markets, assuming the actual consequences of the choices that have been made until that time. Procedural rationality implies, as a consequence, that weak irreversibility qualifies the decision making of firms. They can change their assets and their market conduct only within a limited range of alternatives.

Second, the reaction can be creative only if and when appropriate knowledge externalities are accessible. Innovation requires two strictly complementary conditions: the entrepreneurial vision of firms exposed to unexpected mismatches, as much as the appropriate characteristics of the system in which the reaction takes place. From this viewpoint innovation is a participated activity that can succeed only when the tacit competences of a variety of agents are able to complement each other in a collective effort, integrating the economics of innovation. The new understanding of the unique features of the activities that enable the generation and use of technological knowledge for the introduction of innovations contributes to an appreciation of the crucial role of the system in which agents are embedded in their efforts to try to react to unexpected events by innovating. The characteristics of the system can support or contrast their efforts (Antonelli and David, 2015).

Third, and consequently, it is clear that the characteristics of the system are endogenous and dynamic. This in turn makes it clear that history matters for explaining the intertwining relations between the outcome of innovative efforts and the characteristics of the system, but not in a deterministic way. The dynamics is non-ergodic and path dependent as opposed to past dependent. Here the analysis of the self-reinforcing mechanisms that take place in the phases of introduction of radical innovations laid down by Schumpeter in *Business Cycles* (1939) are generalized beyond the cycle so as to characterize the general innovation process. As his 'Instability of capitalism' (1928) had already made clear, externalities are both crucial and endogenous.

Fourth, technological and structural changes are intertwined and inseparable within a historical process where the past – stochastically as opposed to deterministically – affects the future path of the dynamics. The gale of innovations, introduced by Schumpeter in *Capitalism, Socialism and Democracy* (1942), becomes a general attribute of the system dynamics.

The appreciation of these 'tacit' assumptions embedded in the notion of creative reaction contingent on endogenous externalities paves the way to a new understanding of innovation as an endogenous and systemic process that can be usefully analysed with the notion of emergent system property. The correct appreciation of the Schumpeterian legacy, and specifically the correct understanding of the evolution of his analysis, provides a major contribution to the economics of innovation as an emergent system property articulating in an integrated frame the following key notions: i) procedural rationality based on the notion of reaction; ii) feedback based on knowledge interactions; iii) endogenous externalities; iv) innovation as the product of an emergent, systemic process rather than individual action; and v) non-ergodic path-dependent dynamics (Lane and Maxfield, 2005; Lane et al., 2009; Louçã, 2010; Fontana, 2010).

The prospects for important progress in the economics of innovation along these lines of enquiry are most promising: the Schumpeterian notion of creative reaction paves the way to implementing a complex evolutionary approach that can overcome the limits of both biological evolutionary approaches and new growth theory (Anderson et al., 1988; Arthur et al., 1997; Arthur, 2010; Foster and Metcalfe, 2012). Let us analyse them in turn.

Evolutionary approaches built upon biological metaphors are in fact unable to explain the origin and the endogenous determinants of the introduction of innovations. The implicit assumption that variety is continuously regenerated within the system by random recombination limits the scope of the economics of innovation – it is no longer able to explain why innovation is introduced, but only how and possibly where (Nelson and Winter, 1973, 1982). In standard evolutionary approaches innovation, in fact, is ultimately regarded as the product of spontaneous and automatic recombinations that have no economic intentionality. In this approach technological change does not fall like manna from heaven, but shares the intrinsic economic exogeneity of standard economics. Animal spirits substitute for the manna.

Standard evolutionary approaches fail to elaborate this theory of endogenous innovation, but succeed in providing an endogenous theory of the selective diffusion of innovations. Here the notion of dominant design, eventually elaborated by James Utterback, can be regarded as showing how the selection environment is able to identify and sort the innovations that fit better, out of the array of tentative innovations generated by random recombination (Utterback and Abernathy, 1975; Utterback, 1994).

The new growth theory suffers quite the same limitations. The generation of technological change and the introduction of innovations that make the increase of total factor productivity possible take place because of the automatic and spontaneous spillover of technological knowledge that is characterized by non-exhaustibility and non-appropriability. Technological knowledge spills from knowledge producers to knowledge users who can access and use it with no effort and at no cost. Technological knowledge does not fall from heaven like manna, but shares the characteristics of the atmosphere (Romer, 1994).

The notion of innovation as an emergent system property stemming from the implementation of the Schumpeterian creative reaction contingent on endogenous knowledge externalities can be much enriched, including in an integrated framework the theories of endogenous innovations elaborated in the history of economic analysis and, specifically, the notion of induced technological change and the notion of demand pull. Building upon the reappraisal of the Schumpeterian legacy, innovation can be viewed as the result of the creative reaction to unexpected mismatches between the plans elaborated by firms and the actual conditions of product and factor market evolving conditions, that is contingent on the quality and availability of endogenous knowledge externalities. Innovation can no longer be regarded as a resultant property (that is, a property valid both at individual and system level), but only as an emergent system property (a property of the system into which the action of innovators takes place). The quality of the system in terms of structure of interactions and transactions among firms and between the business sector and the public scientific infrastructure including the supply of human capital is not set forever by external conditions. It is determined within the system and keeps changing. The direction of such change can be both positive and negative. The generation and exploitation of technological knowledge that is necessary for the introduction of innovations may increase the amount of knowledge externalities as much as reduce it. The introduction of innovations changes the architecture, composition and organization of the system. The effects can be positive as well as negative with respect to a system's actual ability to support or contract the innovative efforts of agents (Antonelli, 2008, 2011, 2015).

The contribution by Schumpeter (1947a) can be regarded as the synthesis of a long exploration into the economics of innovation in which the most important results are brought together in a consistent and highly innovative frame that deserves to be fully appreciated and implemented. The 1947 work in fact provides a simple yet powerful platform able to integrate within a systemic and dynamic framework a variety of partial explanations, and to provide a systematic understanding of the endogenous origin of innovation that impinges upon the identification of the notion of creative reaction as the product of two strictly complementary processes: individual – entrepreneurial – action and appropriate levels of endogenous knowledge externalities at the system level.

This achievement is quite remarkable since in the neoclassical world there is no way to explain why firms would not continuously increase their innovation activity to the point where its marginal product matches their costs. Standard evolutionary approaches have the same limits as neoclassical analysis: firms innovate by chance, without any economic rationale. Evolutionary economics based on biological metaphors explains the causes and consequences of selective adoption and diffusion of innovations rather than the causes of their introduction. New growth theory assumes that knowledge externalities are not endogenous and do not require the dedicated action of prospective users. New growth theory, like standard evolutionary economics, is not able to go beyond the basic assumption that the generation of technological knowledge and the introduction of innovations are the spontaneous and automatic products of economic activity. The new knowledge economics fails to appreciate that the availability of knowledge externalities is *a necessary but not sufficient condition* for the actual introduction of innovations' increase in total factor productivity. Innovations are introduced when two complementary conditions apply: i) the possibility to generate new technological knowledge at costs below equilibrium levels; and ii) the effort of firms to generate and use it to introduce technological innovations. Analysis of the working of these to joint conditions can be implemented successfully with the notion of system-emergent property.

Schumpeter (1947a) provides an integrated framework in which a new economics of innovation is able to recognize the crucial role of the collective and systemic processes that make it possible. The notion of creative reaction, contingent on the characteristics of the system into which it may take place, stresses the crucial role of the evolving structure and architecture of knowledge interactions and transactions that qualify the system in which the reaction may be creative.

The Schumpeterian notion of innovation as the result of a creative reaction contingent on the endogenous and evolving characteristics of the system makes it possible to use economics of complexity tools to overcome the limits of standard evolutionary and new growth theory implementing the notion of innovation as an emergent system property.

The claim that evolutionary economics drawing upon biological metaphors can explain why innovation is endogenous and does not fall like manna from heaven has yet to be justified. Variety and innovation are automatically reproduced within the system, without any intentionality and any causality. Biological evolutionary economics is exposed to the same basic criticism of new growth theory, where innovation is determined by exogenous forces: respectively, unlimited and automatic knowledge spillover, and a spontaneous and automatic drive to introduce innovations.

Understanding innovation as an endogenous and economic process can no longer rely on the assumption that the variety within a system be perennially renewed by random recombinations of its agents' basic traits. At the same time, assumptions of spontaneous and unlimited generation of knowledge spillovers, upon which the new growth theory impinges, appear less and less reliable. The new analysis of the generation of technological knowledge confirms that knowledge externalities are far from being automatic and ubiquitous. Quite the opposite: knowledge externalities are available only in the specific circumstances, highly localized in space and time, of organized complexity that make external knowledge not only available but also accessible at costs that are below the equilibrium levels of reproduction.

Schumpeter's 1947 essay is a quasi-forgotten landmark that makes it possible to implement a robust analytical platform for a broader and more inclusive economics of endogenous innovation that accommodates five new radical elements:

1. Innovation is the result of an unplanned response to unexpected occurrences.
2. Changes in factor markets, together with all changes in product markets as much as in the levels of aggregate demand, play a role in causing the mismatches that push firms to try to innovate.
3. The chances for creative responses to mismatches to take place are strictly contingent on the characteristics of the system and the availability of knowledge externalities.
4. The introduction of new technologies alters the fundamental characteristics of the organized complexity of the system with respect to levels of knowledge connectivity, and hence the number of knowledge externalities that are available at each point in time.

5. The generation of both technological and structural change is endogenous as they are emergent and path-dependent system properties.

Innovation takes place and total factor productivity actually increases only when two conditions jointly apply:

1. The endogenous structure of the system attains levels of organized complexity and knowledge connectivity that support the accumulation of a stock of accessible quasi-public knowledge, and hence enables firms to generate new technological knowledge at costs that are below equilibrium levels.
2. Firms caught in out-of-equilibrium conditions are actually able and ready to take advantage of knowledge externalities and actually introduce innovations.

The first key bifurcation takes place when the levels of organized complexity and the consequent levels of knowledge externalities are sufficient to support the reaction of firms and enable them to be creative instead of adaptive (Antonelli, 2008, 2011, 2013).

At each point in time a second basic bifurcation takes place in the process. This is because the introduction of innovations does not only affect product and factor markets; it also affects the organized complexity of the system and the working of knowledge connectivity in terms of accumulation of stocks of knowledge and the consequent generation of knowledge externalities, with both positive and negative effects. The structural effects of innovations shape the alternative between a dynamics of self-sustained introduction of innovations and the convergence of the system to equilibrium. If and when the effects are not negative, a new wave of creative reactions can take place so as to allow the introduction of further innovations that reproduce variety within the system and to push forward the technological frontier that supports the continual expansion of the economic system and the rates of economic growth.

If and when, because of congestion, the levels of knowledge connectivity decline together with the rate of knowledge accumulation, and the effects on availability, the levels of knowledge externalities are negative and the quality of the systems of innovations declines, firms will no longer be able to elaborate creative reactions. They will try to cope with mismatches between expected and actual conditions of product and factor markets by means of adaptive reactions. Equilibrium is one of the many possible outcomes.

The Schumpeterian platform enables us to appreciate the systemic and yet punctuated determinants of innovation as an endogenous process based on individual reactions that are highly sensitive to the institutional characteristics of the system in terms of the structural organization of the micro-level interactions that make possible the accumulation, generation and use of knowledge in society. In this context, agents' procedural rationality plays a central role. Agents try to innovate only as a reaction to unexpected changes. Schumpeterian firms make relevant mistakes, are caught in out-of-equilibrium by unforeseeable events, and only then consider as a possible solution the introduction of an innovation. Reaction is a typical form of procedural rationality: firms consider opportunities and perspectives only after the occurrence of a sequence of unexpected events. Their success is contingent on the system characteristics that become apparent *ex post*.

The Schumpeterian creative response empowers and specifies the notion of stratified and multiple feedback. The grafting into the Schumpeterian platform of the tools of complexity economics – and specifically notions of emergence, path dependence, endogenous variety and organized complexity and knowledge connectivity – provides a comprehensive and robust evolutionary complexity framework in which to study innovation as a system property (as opposed to a resultant property) that is an endogenous, dynamic, non-ergodic and stochastic process with intrinsic systemic characteristics. Its path-dependent dynamics is shaped by the changing levels of system complexity in terms of composition, organization, architecture and institutional context within which agents interact and participate in the collective endeavour of accumulation, generation and use of technological knowledge. Economics of innovation can finally rely on an analytical framework based on evolutionary complexity that is able to account for its endogenous determinants.

APPENDIX TO PART I

As is well known, the new growth theory builds upon the intuition of Zvi Griliches about the affect of knowledge externalities on levels of total factor productivity (Griliches, 1979, 1984, 1992). Griliches introduced the 'technology production function' where internal knowledge (IK) – the stock of knowledge that each firm can appropriate – enters with its output elasticity (c), next to the standard inputs of capital (C) with its output elasticity (a), labour (L) with its output elasticity (b). The output of each firm is influenced by the stock of quasi-public knowledge that spills into the atmosphere (EK) and accounts for total factor productivity (A):

$$Y = A \, (C^a \, L^b \, IK^c) \tag{4.1}$$

$$A = (EK) \tag{4.2}$$

Griliches did not pretend to elaborate a theory of growth: he provided the methodology to assess the role of knowledge externalities. As Griliches (1995: 63) notes: 'This formulation was applied to R&D expenditures by Griliches (1979) and rediscovered by Romer (1990).'

Romer did attempt to extract a theory of economic growth from the notion of spillovers. With respect to Griliches' specification, Romer takes into account total knowledge (K = IK + EK) and splits its output elasticity (γ) into two components: the appropriable (g1) and the non-appropriable ($\gamma2$). Total factor productivity is accounted for by the non-appropriable component ($K^{\gamma2}$). Increasing returns do take place at the system level but not at the firm level. Firms fund research and development activities according to the marginal productivity of the appropriable component ($\gamma1$).

The crucial hypothesis specified by Romer reads as follows:

$$Y_i = A \, (C^a \, L^b \, K^\gamma) \tag{4.3}$$

where $(a + b + (\gamma1 + \gamma2)) > 1$.

At the system level there are increasing returns that stem from the characteristics of knowledge. At the firm level, however, because of the limited appropriability of knowledge, firms have no access to increasing returns, but enjoy the positive effects of access to knowledge spillover on total factor productivity:

$$Y_i = A \, (C^a \, L^b \, K^{\gamma1}) \tag{4.4}$$

where $a + b + \gamma 1 = 1$.

$$A_i = f(K^{\gamma 2}) \tag{4.5}$$

Romer's specification is problematic from two viewpoints: i) it is not clear what the idiosyncratic characteristics are that discriminate between the appropriable and the non-appropriable components of knowledge; as a consequence ii) it is not clear what the ratio is between the first and the second. This ambiguity has major effects with respect to the coherence between the firm level of action and the aggregate behaviour. Analysis of the derived demand of knowledge (Antonelli, forthcoming) is most useful:

$$dY/dK = (\gamma \ Y/K \ p_Y) \tag{4.6}$$

Firms have no incentive to invest more than the value of the marginal product of the knowledge that they can appropriate ($\gamma 1 \ Y/K \ p_Y$), and no incentive to generate the equilibrium amount of knowledge defined by the value of its total marginal product ($\gamma \ Y/K \ p_Y$). Arrovian market failure takes place together with the undersupply of knowledge.

In our approach, the distinction between appropriable and non-appropriable components does not take place instantaneously and synchronically. The distinction takes place through time, diachronically. Actually there is no static distinction that would stem from intrinsic properties of knowledge. The distinction is dynamic: all knowledge is proprietary and can be appropriated for a short period of time, just as all knowledge eventually spills and adds to the stock of public knowledge, with a time lag.

The notion of diachronic knowledge externalities enables us to overcome the limits of the standard specification of the new growth theory. In this approach firms can fully appropriate the economic benefits stemming from the generation of new technological knowledge and the eventual introduction of innovations, but only for a limited stretch of time. After the closure of the time window of appropriation, flows of new technological knowledge add to the stock of quasi-public knowledge. Hence the total knowledge generated by each firm (K) splits into two components:

$$K = IK + EK \tag{4.7}$$

The flow of knowledge produced each year by each firm (K) splits and adds either to the stock of internal knowledge (IK) that can be appropriated or to the stock of quasi-public knowledge (EK). The stock of quasi-public knowledge is the summation, after a short time window (n), in the time interval (N − n) of the flow of knowledge generated at each point in time (K). The stock of proprietary knowledge (IK) is the summation – just for a short time window of appropriation (n) – of the knowledge (K) generated by each firm.

$$EK = g\left(\sum_{i=1}^{N-n} K_i\right) \tag{4.8}$$

$$IK = \sum_{i=N-n+1}^{N} K_i \tag{4.9}$$

The generation of technological knowledge is, in fact, itself the result of a dedicated economic activity that can be analysed by means of the knowledge generation function. The generation of technological knowledge, however, is characterized by high levels of risk. Only firms in out-of-equilibrium conditions are able to take such risks. The knowledge generation function is activated primarily if not exclusively by firms that experience mismatch between expected and actual conditions of product and factor markets with performances that are either below or above equilibrium. Firms facing exit and bankruptcy are forced to try to generate new technological knowledge in order to survive. Firms that enjoy extra profits can afford the risks associated with the generation of new knowledge because of low levels of opportunity costs stemming from the relative abundance of liquidity and resources. Firms that are in the proximity of equilibrium conditions with performances close to the average are reluctant to engage in the generation of new technological knowledge and in the eventual introduction of innovations.

The notion of diachronic knowledge externalities enables us to integrate the knowledge generation function, next to the technology production function, as an indispensable component of the following system of equations:

$$K = (EK^a \ IK^b \ R\&D^c) \tag{4.10}$$

$$C_K = z \ EK + v \ IK + rR\&D \tag{4.11}$$

$$z = h \ (EK, KCON) \tag{4.12}$$

$$Y = A \ (C^a \ L^b \ IK^c) \tag{4.13}$$

$$C_Y = wL + rC + uIK \tag{4.14}$$

K is produced by means of the recombination of the knowledge items that are available in the stock of quasi-public knowledge (EK) and in the stock of proprietary knowledge (IK) that each firm can command for a limited period of time, and of R&D activities. The use of both IK and EK takes place at a cost: respectively, v measures the unit cost of the resources that are necessary to retrieve and use the stock of internal knowledge; z measures the unit cost of the resources that are necessary to select, draw, access and use the relevant and complementary units of knowledge that are available in the stock of quasi-public knowledge; R&D activities have a unit cost r.

As equation (4.12) makes clear, the cost of external knowledge (z) changes with the size and quality of the stock of quasi-public knowledge (EK) and the levels of knowledge connectivity of the system (KCON). The laws of accumulation of the stock of quasi-public knowledge and of the changing quality of the knowledge connectivity of the system play a central role in the dynamics of the system. The actual accumulation of the stock of quasi-public knowledge is far from deterministic. The new knowledge items can remain dispersed and fragmented in the system, or contribute to the accumulation of a well-structured, coherent and inclusive stock of quasi-public knowledge that can be used and accessed effectively. The new flows of quasi-public knowledge may have both positive and negative effects on the actual cost of accessing and using the stock. The organized complexity of the system and its levels of knowledge connectivity can improve as well as decline over time.

The laws of accumulation of the stock of quasi-public knowledge (EK) and the costs of accessing and using it as an input into the generation of new knowledge define the levels of the costs of external knowledge (z) have powerful effects directly on the knowledge generation function (4.10) and indirectly on the technology production function (4.13). The levels of costs of accessing and using the stock of quasi-public knowledge (z) in fact have two effects:

1. In the knowledge generation function (4.10) where the stock of public knowledge (EK) enters as an indispensable input, next to internal knowledge (IK), it is clear that the lower the costs of external knowledge (z), the lower the unit costs of knowledge as an output (u).
2. In the technology production function (4.13) knowledge produced (K) upstream enters as an input, next to capital (C) and labour (L). Hence with a given budget, the lower the cost of external knowledge (u), the larger the amount of knowledge (K) that contributes as an indispensable complementary input to the production of the output Y, and the lower the unit costs of output Y.

The difference between the actual, historic levels of the cost of external knowledge, respectively as an input (z) in the knowledge generation function and the cost of knowledge as an input (u) in the technology production function and the equilibrium levels – based on the assumption that knowledge is a standard good so that its cost equals its marginal productivity – accounts for the levels of total factor productivity as measured by the ratio of the actual, historic levels of Y to the expected levels of output when the price of inputs is in equilibrium (Antonelli, 2013).

The stock of quasi-public knowledge affects the working of the system with two distinct mechanisms: i) a direct role exerted by the effects of knowledge externalities in the generation of new knowledge; and, consequently, ii) an indirect role in the downstream technology production.

Firms are able to try to take advantage of the low cost of knowledge made possible by the high quality and size of the stock of quasi-public knowledge only when exposed to mismatches between expected and actual factor and product market conditions. The mere availability of knowledge externalities is not sufficient for firms to try to innovate as much, as mismatches without appropriate levels of knowledge externalities are not sufficient to account for the successful introduction of innovations.

PART II

New Frontiers in the Economics of
Knowledge: The Appropriability Trade-Off
Reconsidered

5. A bird's-eye view of the economics of knowledge

The economics of knowledge consists in the analysis of the economic properties of knowledge as an economic good, a central input into the production of all goods – including new knowledge – and the result, itself, of an intentional and dedicated production process. The path-breaking contribution by Arrow (1962) has opened this fertile field of investigation comparing knowledge to standard goods.[1] With respect to standard economic goods, knowledge is characterized by highly idiosyncratic features such as limited appropriability, non-rivalry in use, limited divisibility, non-exhaustibility, cumulability and complementarity, and low reproduction costs.

So far attention has concentrated on the effects of the Arrovian properties of knowledge on its supply, and has largely disregarded their bearing on knowledge demand. Joint analysis of the effects of the limited appropriability of knowledge on both the demand and the supply of knowledge leads to uncovering the appropriability trade-off. Understanding of the knowledge appropriability trade-off is the result of a long-standing process started with the identification of the peculiar characteristics of knowledge as an economic good.

Since Richard Nelson's pioneering article of 1959 – 'The simple economics of basic scientific research' – the issue of the undersupply of knowledge has been central in the economics of knowledge. Nelson opens up the enquiry into the economic properties of knowledge as an economic good and their economic consequences. He elaborates upon the well-known Schumpeterian analysis of the limits of perfect competition:

> The introduction of new methods of production and new commodities is hardly conceivable with perfect – and perfectly prompt – competition from the start. And this means that the bulk of what we call economic progress is incompatible with it. As a matter of fact, perfect competition is and always has been temporarily suspended whenever anything new is being introduced – automatically or by measures devised for the purpose – even in otherwise perfectly competitive conditions. (Schumpeter, 1942: 105)

The 'Arrovian postulate' about the failure of the market place as the institutional mechanism for the correct allocation of resources to the generation of knowledge is set. Since then, analysis of the supply of knowledge has attracted most attention, with strong economic policy implications (Antonelli and David, 2016). The literature elaborated the basic argument that policy interventions should remedy the lack of incentives to the generation of knowledge, pushing it closer to the benchmark conditions that would apply for standard economic goods. An array of tools has been consequently put in place to increase incentives to generate new knowledge. Such tools include intellectual property (IP) rights aimed at increasing levels of appropriability; public subsidies for research and development (R&D) aimed at compensating private investors for lost revenue; and a public research infrastructure including universities and other institutions aimed at generating upstream scientific knowledge that could support the downstream generation of knowledge by the business sector.

The extended production function introduced by Zvi Griliches (1979) elaborates on the Cobb–Douglas production function with the formal inclusion of knowledge, measured as R&D capital stock (or patent or innovation indicators) regarded as an additional input that contributes explicitly to the production of output alongside 'physical' capital and labour. The extended production function becomes a pillar of the applied economics of knowledge. It provides the basic framework to investigate empirically the role of knowledge in the economy (Griliches, 1984; Link and Siegel, 2007).

The inclusive and quite exhaustive review of the large body of econometric research by Hall et al. (2010) confirms that knowledge is a key input in the long-run production process. It also shows that social returns tend to be much higher than private returns, due to positive knowledge externalities and, in particular, from the public research system to the business sector. Recent empirical research provides additional evidence confirming that social returns to R&D are estimated to be at least twice as high as private returns (Wolff, 2012; Bloom et al., 2013).

Analysis of knowledge as the output of a dedicated activity can be dated back to Schmookler (1966), who identified the knowledge generation process as the result of investment in capital goods and the consequent implementation of formal research activities. The specification of a fully fledged knowledge generation function was formalized by Griliches (1979) and eventually implemented by Pakes and Griliches (1984) and Jaffe (1986).

The parallel introduction of the knowledge generation function paved the way to a rich and still increasing empirical literature in which knowledge – usually measured by patents or innovation counts – is the output of an activity that uses a variety of inputs. These range from R&D expenditure by each firm, their stock, as well as the level and the range of

R&D activities – and/or their output in terms of patents and innovation counts – carried out by other firms in regional, industrial, technological or cultural proximity.

Following Griliches's discovery of the positive aspects of limited appropriability in terms of knowledge spillover in assessing total productivity growth (Hall et al., 2010), much attention has been paid to exploring the characteristics of spillovers and the mechanisms by which they display their positive effects on productivity. Three significant distinctions have been made: i) imitation externalities vs knowledge externalities; ii) pure vs pecuniary externalities; iii) synchronic vs diachronic externalities. Let us consider them in turn.

Imitation externalities take place when the first Arrovian property of knowledge, its well-known limited appropriability, and the consequent uncontrolled leakage of proprietary knowledge enable imitators to 'steal' innovations from 'inventors', enter the very same product market, reduce the price of products and shrink innovators' profits. Imitation externalities take place in the same product markets where 'inventors' introduced the innovation (Bloom et al., 2013; Aghion et al., 2015). Imitation externalities are mainly, if not exclusively, negative. *Knowledge externalities*, on the other hand, take place when the knowledge inputs that have made the innovation possible are accessed and reused as intermediary inputs for the generation of new technological knowledge and the eventual introduction of innovations in other industries. Knowledge externalities apply in a wide range of industries and are not bound to the sector and product market of introduction (Scherer, 1982). The effects of knowledge externalities are mainly, if not exclusively, positive. Knowledge externalities enable full advantage to be taken of the positive effects that stem from the dynamic increasing returns engendered by the other Arrovian properties of knowledge – that is, limited divisibility and exhaustibility of knowledge are taken into account (Griliches, 1979, 1984, 1992).

Pure (technical) externalities take place when spillovers can be accessed and used at no cost and do not require transactions and interactions among the parties involved. *Pecuniary externalities* apply when, on the other hand, the use of and access to spillovers requires both interactions and transactions, dedicated resources and specific absorption costs. Technological knowledge spills freely into the atmosphere, but the acquisition and use of knowledge spillovers are far from free: their access and use require dedicated activities to absorb the necessary external knowledge (Cohen and Levinthal, 1989, 1990). Antonelli (2008) suggests that knowledge externalities are pecuniary rather than pure. The higher the absorption costs and the lower the pecuniary knowledge externalities, the lower the positive effects of the amount of knowledge available. This in turn implies that low absorption costs of external knowledge enable a reduction in knowledge cost as an input in the technology production function of all the other goods and, most importantly, in the knowledge generation function of new technological knowledge.

The initial understanding of knowledge externalities as pure and synchronic has been eventually substituted by seeing them as pecuniary and diachronic. The distinction between synchronic and diachronic knowledge externalities is relevant in this context. According to Griliches's first specifications – further elaborated by Romer (1990, 1994a, b) – knowledge externalities stem from the spillover of the non-appropriable component of the knowledge generated by each firm. As such, knowledge externalities are implicitly synchronic. As a matter of fact, the distinction between the appropriable and the non-appropriable components of knowledge remains unclear. Griliches (1979, 1992) provided the methodology to measure their effects, but did not venture into any *ex ante* distinction. Romer did, but with unclear results.

The notion of diachronic knowledge externalities enables this ambiguity to be overcome. All newly generated knowledge can be appropriated, but only for a limited stretch of time. Eventually, in fact, all knowledge becomes public. The distinction between appropriable and non-appropriable components disappears. The two effects do take place, but in sequence. Mansfield (1985), using survey data, finds that knowledge of a research project is in the hands of competitors within roughly 18 months. Adams and Clemmons (2013) calibrate diffusion lags among fields and sectors for science, finding that the mean lag is about six years in standard data.

According to Antonelli (2017, forthcoming), knowledge externalities should be regarded as diachronic, and the appropriability of knowledge transient rather than partial. All knowledge generated at each point in time can be appropriated by 'inventors'. The windows of appropriation, however, are narrow. Eventually all knowledge becomes public. Knowledge externalities stem from the summation of all the flows of knowledge, generated at each point in time but with a lag determined by the windows of appropriation. The notion of diachronic knowledge externalities enables the problematic distinction between appropriable and non-appropriable components of knowledge and the related problems regarding the incentives to actually fund R&D activities to be overcome.

At each point in time there is a large stock of public knowledge and a 'small' stock of private knowledge. The former is the result of the spillover of proprietary knowledge, and the latter is the result of the short-term appropriation of proprietary knowledge by its producers. The laws of accumulation of the stock of public knowledge play a central role. The higher the level of knowledge connectivity of a system is, the more effective the actual accumulation of the stock of public knowledge. In other words, the flows of proprietary knowledge eventually but inevitably become public and add to the stock. Inventors can retain the benefits of their proprietary knowledge only for a limited stretch of time.

Equation (5.1) specifies the laws of accumulation of the stock of public knowledge (*SPT*) as a function of the summation of the yearly flows of new knowledge (T_t) in the long term (*N*), after accounting for the narrow time window of appropriation [*n, N*]:

$$SPT = f\left(\sum_{t=n}^{N} T_t \right) \qquad (5.1)$$

The quality of the accumulation process matters. The effective accumulation of a well-structured and organized stock of public knowledge is not obvious. It depends on the level of knowledge connectivity of the system in which each firm is embedded. If connectivity is higher and accumulation is faster and more effective, then access to the stock of external knowledge will be less expensive. Consequently, the better the knowledge governance mechanisms implementing the knowledge connectivity of the system and the larger the stock of public knowledge, the lower the costs to access and use it.

The effects of pecuniary and diachronic knowledge externalities can be explored by means of the knowledge generation process where external knowledge spilling from third parties favours the generation of new knowledge. The new economics of knowledge has in fact progressively shifted analysis away from the properties of knowledge as an economic good towards the characteristics of the knowledge generation process as a dedicated economic activity aimed at its generation. Study of the knowledge generation process has shown that, together with current R&D expenditure, the stock of knowledge (both internal and external to each agent) plays a strong role as an indispensable and complementary input. According to the latest advances in the economics of knowledge, new technological knowledge is generated by means of a recombination of the existing technological knowledge (Weitzman, 1996). It becomes increasingly clear that the lower the costs of accessing and using the existing stock of knowledge, then the greater the amount of external knowledge that each agent can access at low absorption costs and the more cost-effective the knowledge generation process.

The growing empirical evidence provided by the economics of knowledge confirms that the generation of new technological knowledge consists in the recombination of existing modules of knowledge, and is characterized by complementarity between internal research activities and external knowledge. Jaffe (1986) first estimated a knowledge generation function that takes knowledge externalities into account. Arora and Gambardella (1990, 1994) show that technological knowledge, external to each firm, is an indispensable input for the generation of new technological knowledge. Cassiman and Veugerlers (2006) confirm the role of external knowledge and the related sourcing activities required to identify, access and use it in the generation of new technological knowledge. Lööf and Johansson (2014) articulate the complementarity between internal and external knowledge, showing that internal research activities are essential to accessing and using external knowledge in the same way that access to external knowledge is indispensable when performing effective R&D activities intramuros. Antonelli and Colombelli (2015a) show that the knowledge generation function displays the typical traits of an O-ring technology in which no input or stock of internal knowledge or stock of external knowledge can fall to zero levels. Antonelli et al. (2010) show the relevance not only of the size but also of the composition of the knowledge stock available in a context – in terms of coherence and complementarity – in supporting the generation of new technological knowledge.

The properties of the system in which firms are embedded play a crucial role in assessing the actual access and use conditions of the stock of public knowledge. The quality of knowledge governance of an economic system improves actual access to the stock of knowledge and reduces its absorption costs without endangering the incentives to generate it. High absorption costs of existing knowledge, in fact, are likely to reduce the positive effects of the dynamics of the stock of knowledge. The higher the connectivity of the system, the lower the knowledge absorption costs. Knowledge connectivity, in turn, is determined by knowledge governance: the set of rules, procedures, modes and protocols that organize the generation, dissemination and use of knowledge in an economic system as a collective process. This includes the conditions that make possible the actual use of the scientific knowledge supplied by the State for economic purposes through its direct support to the academic system and the intellectual property rights regime (Antonelli and Link, 2015).

When and where the quality of knowledge governance and system connectivity is rich and access to existing technological knowledge can take place at low cost, new technological knowledge can be generated at costs that are below equilibrium levels. The supply curve of technological knowledge shifts downwards and identifies an equilibrium supply of technological knowledge that can be even larger than in the case of technological knowledge with quasi-perfect appropriability conditions. In such an extreme case, the Arrovian postulate needs to be reconsidered: there is no need for public intervention to support the supply of additional technological knowledge in order to compensate for market failure in terms of quantity. Instead, there is a strong need to remedy the qualitative market failure stemming from the selective exclusion of high-quality research projects.

When, on the other hand, the quality of knowledge governance and system connectivity is poor, the cost of access to the stock of existing knowledge is high – and not even the positive quantitative effects of the increasing size of the stock of public knowledge take place. Intellectual property rights regimes characterized by strong exclusivity and long duration may actually impede access to the existing stock of knowledge. When the quality of the knowledge governance is poor and the institutional set-up of the system is weak, access to external knowledge is too expensive to compensate for its transient appropriability.

These advances in the economics of knowledge need to be integrated in a single framework so as to better appreciate the full range of their economic effects. To this end, the constructionist design methodology (CDM) approach marks a major step as it provides a systemic framework in which it is possible to analyse the simultaneous interaction of the technology production function and the knowledge generation function (Crépon et al., 1998).

The CDM framework can be further enriched so as to take into account knowledge externalities explicitly. This is not straightforward since it should in principle be done at the level of each of its three layers of equations. Knowledge spillovers enter the upstream knowledge generation function as an input into the recombinant generation of new knowledge, and exert their positive effects in terms of reduced costs of knowledge. Knowledge spillovers however also enter the downstream technology production function as they provide knowledge ready to be used again. Knowledge spillovers enter directly, providing knowledge externalities in the knowledge generation function. The very same knowledge spillovers exert their indirect effects on the downstream technology production function as they provide knowledge at a cost that is below equilibrium levels. Finally, knowledge spillovers enter directly in the downstream technology production function, in terms of imitation externalities, as they enable firms to access knowledge ready to be used again as such (Antonelli and Colombelli, forthcoming).

The CDM approach prompts new reflection on the role of the demand for knowledge as an intermediary input. The demand for knowledge as an intermediary input is clearly the necessary interface between the knowledge generation function and the augmented production function. The CDM systemic approach induces us to reconsider the early analyses of Ken Arrow and Dick Nelson so as to raise the question: did both founders of the economics of knowledge assume that the undersupply of knowledge was the consequence of the reduction of supply of knowledge-intensive products only? To what extent did they consider also the changes in the derived demand (and supply) of knowledge?

Building on the tools implemented by the CDM approach – with integration of the knowledge generation function and the extended production function in a single system of equations – it seems possible to articulate the view that the limited appropriability of knowledge affects not only the downstream production of knowledge-intensive products but also the demand of knowledge together with the upstream generation of knowledge, and hence its supply.

NOTE

1. Following Arrow and the literature that impinges on his contribution, knowledge is used here to identify a broad array of overlapping activities including research and learning, competence, experience and know-how, as well as information about scientific technological, organizational and scientific procedures that can be embodied both in tangible and intangible products ranging from capital goods to services. As such, knowledge exhibits varying levels of tacit and codified contents embedded not only in protocols and routines but also, and primarily, in skills.

6. The derived demand for knowledge

An effort seems necessary to extend the CDM framework by appreciating the role of knowledge as an – indispensable – intermediary input, and hence including the specification and estimation of the derived demand for knowledge equation (Antonelli, 2007). This seems appropriate not only from a theoretical but also from an empirical viewpoint. From a theoretical viewpoint it enables us to understand the effects of the Arrovian properties of knowledge in the downstream markets of the final goods – that have been produced by means of knowledge – on the upstream demand of knowledge both within and between firms. Analysis of the derived demand for knowledge within firms enables us to grasp the effects of the price of the final goods on the internal shadow prices of knowledge within the boundaries of the corporation. It is clear that there is a strong positive relationship between the price of the final goods and the position of the derived demand of knowledge: the higher the latter, the further on the right the former.

Analysis of the demand for knowledge is relevant also when it takes place between firms and knowledge-intensive business services (KIBS) in the markets for knowledge. From an empirical viewpoint in fact the study of the demand for knowledge is becoming more and more relevant because of the increasing specialization of advanced countries in knowledge-intensive activities. These are emerging as fully fledged industries composed of firms that produce and sell knowledge embodied in patents and knowledge-intensive services to other firms which use them to produce other goods, both services and other tangible goods – including new knowledge.

From a historical viewpoint, the twenty-first century is witnessing the progressive vertical disintegration of the generation of knowledge from the augmented production function. What used to be vertically integrated within firms (groups or corporations) is becoming the object of specialized activities (KIBS) that sell knowledge embodied in products and services in the new emerging markets for knowledge (Abramovitz and David, 1996; Arora et al., 2001; Tassey, 2005; Shearmur and Doloreux, 2013). The R&D management literature has elaborated the open innovation approach that stresses the reduction in the in-house generation of knowledge and the increasing role of knowledge outsourcing (Chesbrough, 2003; Chesbrough et al., 2006).

One cannot proclaim that the notion of demand for knowledge was ignored in the early economics of knowledge, which is associated here with the groundbreaking contributions of Arrow, Griliches and Nelson. But it remained largely implicit and its importance was not stressed. A major exception is Schmookler (1966), as recognized in the illuminating analysis by Nathan Rosenberg (1974) that identifies the analytical core of the former's argument on the causal relationship between the demand for a good (typically capital goods) and the consequent – derived – demand for scientific work. The increase in demand causes increased profitability in the generation of the related knowledge that attracts an increase in the demand for scientists working in that field, and ultimately an increase in the amount of knowledge generated.

The following section provides a simple framework to assess the chain of effects of the Arrovian properties of knowledge on the price of innovated goods in downstream markets, and consequently on the upstream demand of knowledge as an intermediary input, both in terms of quantity and price.

This chapter applies the Arrovian methodology to compare the work of the marketplace for standard goods to the market for knowledge when it is characterized by Arrovian properties. Because of the limited appropriability of knowledge, the price of knowledge-intensive products will be lower than it should have been had knowledge been a standard economic good (Dasgupta and David, 1994).

The producers of knowledge-intensive goods risk not only missing the full stream of benefits that stem from the introduction of an innovation made possible by the use of knowledge; they may also fail to recover the expenses incurred to produce the goods themselves or to purchase the knowledge needed to implement process and/or product innovations. Because of limited appropriability, competitors can imitate and produce innovated goods without bearing the costs of knowledge. Their entry and growth will shift the supply schedule of the innovated products downward. Innovators are exposed not only to missing profits but also to emerging losses. The price in the final markets, in fact, will be determined by the costs of imitators who do not bear the costs of research activities. It seems clear that the price of the innovated goods that use knowledge characterized by Arrovian properties as an input is lower than it would be in benchmark product markets where all firms bear the costs of R&D.

Figure 6.1 provides a simple graphical analysis of the consequences of the limited appropriability of knowledge in the downstream markets for goods produced with knowledge as an input. Let us start with the equilibrium condition E_1 in the industry before the introduction of innovation (BeforeINnovation). In the equilibrium condition firms produce

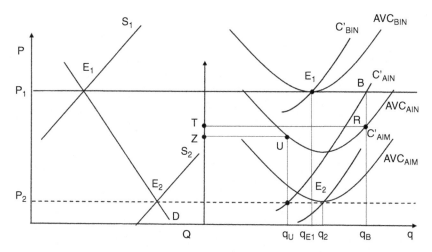

Figure 6.1 *Appropriability and imitation:* lucrum cessans *and* damnum emergens

q_{E1}, the quantity where marginal costs C'_{BIN} equal AVC_{BIN}. Let us now assume that a firm is able to use knowledge as an input to introduce an innovation. Its marginal cost C'_{AIN} and average cost AVC_{AIN} after innovation (AfterINnovation) fall. The firm that can appropriate the benefits of the innovation would fix prices in B, sell the quantity q_B and earn extra profits, identified by the surface of the rectangle P_1BTR. If and when appropriability is not possible, however, other firms can benefit from the knowledge costs incurred by the innovator. They can imitate the innovation. Their average and marginal costs, after imitation, C'_{AIM} and AVC_{AIM}, are actually lower than the innovator's costs (AfterIMitation). For them the cost of knowledge is 0. If everybody can imitate the innovation, the supply schedule of the industry S_1 shifts to the right towards S_2, where the new equilibrium price P_2 equals the marginal and average costs of imitators. The innovator's cost is now above the new equilibrium level. The innovator will sell the quantity q_U at a cost that is actually higher than the new equilibrium price P_2, incurring losses defined by the rectangle ZP_2Uq_U. The innovator is not able to earn any profit (*lucrum cessans*) but incurs actual losses (*damnum emergens*).

As a consequence, the derived demand for knowledge (that is, the marginal product of knowledge as an input in the extended production function in value) expressed by downstream activities to specialized upstream knowledge producers – both within vertically integrated firms that carry out intramural R&D and in the markets for knowledge,

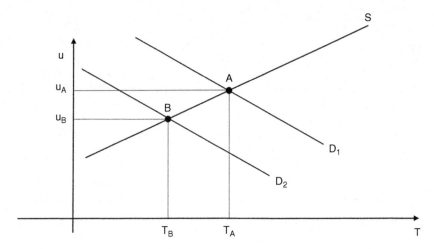

Figure 6.2   The shift of the derived demand of Arrovian knowledge with respect to the benchmark demand of a standard good

between downstream knowledge users and upstream knowledge producers (KIBS) – will be lower than it would have been had knowledge been a standard economic good.

The position of the derived demand of knowledge depends upon the actual levels of knowledge appropriability: it will be lowest when appropriability in the downstream markets is zero. With higher levels of appropriability in the downstream markets, the position of the derived demand schedule of knowledge will shift upward. When there is full appropriability in the downstream markets the position of the derived demand of knowledge will overlap with the benchmark – namely, that of knowledge as a perfect economic good.

As Figure 6.2 shows, the derived demand curve of knowledge as an input in the augmented production function – with its actual "Arrovian" economic properties, D_2 – lies below D_1, the benchmark demand curve for knowledge as a standard input, next to S the benchmark supply curve for knowledge.

With a given knowledge supply schedule (S), the derived demand of knowledge – characterized by its Arrovian properties – leads to the reduction of both the quantity (T) and the price of knowledge (u).

The Arrovian postulate about market failure is confirmed and actually enriched. The standard Arrovian market failure consists in the undersupply of knowledge ($T_A > T_B$). The analysis implemented so far enables us to appreciate a second aspect of market failure: the depreciation of knowledge ($u_A > u_B$).

The depreciation of knowledge stemming from the downward shift of the demand curve, determined by its limited appropriability and the consequent fall in the price of goods produced using it as an input, is itself a cause of a specific and new type of market failure. It engenders, in fact, the exclusion of high productivity and large-scale projects that can no longer be afforded. The fall in the price of knowledge is the cause of an additional market failure: the excess and adverse selection of research projects. The system is able to implement minor research projects that are likely to yield incremental innovations. Large-scale and high-quality projects that are likely to favour the introduction of radical innovations are sorted out. The downward shift in the demand for knowledge is the cause of selective undersupply: the undersupply of high-quality large-scale research projects.

These effects may be mitigated by the possibility that the limited appropriability of knowledge not only the affects derived demand of knowledge but also has – positive – effects on the supply of knowledge. External knowledge, in fact, spills and enters the knowledge generation function as an input. The cost of knowledge – now regarded as an output – is lower because of the effects of spillover on the knowledge production function (Adams, 2006).[1]

Analysis of the economic properties of knowledge and identification of its limits and idiosyncratic characters has been most successful. For quite a long time, the literature has focused on the effects of the economic properties of knowledge on the supply of knowledge-intensive products. Advances in the economics of knowledge – and specifically identification of the augmented production function and the knowledge generation function and their systemic combination into the CDM approach – provide a fertile framework. In fact, they enable us to single out and investigate the effects of the economic properties of knowledge not only on the supply of knowledge-intensive products, but also on the demand and supply of knowledge. Indeed, in this context appreciation of the role of knowledge as an intermediary input and an output yields important insights. The demand for knowledge is very much influenced by the outcomes of competition in the downstream markets, where the goods that have been produced using knowledge as an input are sold.

The derived demand for knowledge is affected, as much as its supply, by its limited appropriability, asymmetric information, non-rivalry in use, radical uncertainty in its generation and exploitation. Agents are not only reluctant to generate knowledge. They are also reluctant to purchase and use it as an input in the production of other goods. As a consequence, the derived demand for knowledge lies far on the left of the benchmark-derived demand for knowledge were it a standard good, and its price risks being lower than for standard goods. By the same token, limited appropriability, however, exerts positive effects on the production of knowledge. Analysis of the effects of the leftward shift of the derived demand for knowledge, combined with appreciation of the effects on the supply of knowledge, questions the economic rationale of public policies centred on supply. Supply-side policy interventions can enhance the supply of knowledge and favour the decline of the price of knowledge below benchmark levels, but cannot contrast the excess selection of large-scale and high-quality research projects.

NOTE

1. In the recombinant knowledge production function, external knowledge is an indispensable input strictly complementary to internal R&D activities and other inputs. According to the knowledge appropriability levels, the costs of external knowledge fall below the benchmark levels that would take place were all inputs standard goods. The effects of spillovers on the cost of external knowledge depend on the actual conditions of absorption and use of knowledge as an input on the production of new knowledge. The lower the level of knowledge costs as an input, the lower the cost of knowledge as an output (Griliches, 1979, 1986, 1992; Pakes and Griliches, 1984; Cohen and Levinthal, 1989; Weitzman, 1996).

7. The knowledge appropriability trade-off

7.1 KNOWLEDGE APPROPRIABILITY AS A PROBLEM

Analysis of the negative implications of the limited appropriability of knowledge, laid down by Richard Nelson, opened this line of analysis with identification and exploration of the consequences of limited appropriability of knowledge and articulated the distinction between the social and private profit of knowledge:

> The quantity of resources that a society should allocate to basic research is that quantity which maximizes social profit. Under which conditions will private-profit opportunities draw into basic research a quantity of resources that is socially desirable? If all sectors of the economy are perfectly competitive, if every business firm can collect from society through the market mechanism the full value of benefits it produces, and if social costs of each business are exclusively attached to the inputs it purchases, then the allocation of resources among alternatives uses generated by profit maximizing will be a socially optimal allocation of resources. But when the marginal value of a 'good' to society exceeds the marginal value of the good to the individual who pays for it, the allocation of resources that maximizes private profits will not be optimal. (Nelson, 1959: 298)

The comparative analysis of knowledge and standard economic good enabled Kenneth Arrow (1962) to generalize Nelson's intuition and to identify a broader and more inclusive set of peculiar and idiosyncratic knowledge characteristics, such as limited appropriability, poor excludability and negligible reproduction costs. Because of the limited appropriability of knowledge 'inventors' can retain only a fraction of the economic benefits of the knowledge they generate.

Limited appropriability of knowledge exerts negative effects on the price of goods that include knowledge as an input in the production process. As a consequence, its derived demand is lower than the derived demand of a standard production input. In the Arrovian framework – because of the lower price of output – the equilibrium price of knowledge is below the competitive level. Because of the limited appropriability of knowledge and the divergence between its generation and reproduction costs, the market price of the product that it embodies can actually be so low that it does not allow recovery of the costs incurred to purchase – and use – knowledge.

In extreme Arrovian conditions, the use of knowledge with very low levels of appropriability, high generation costs and very low reproduction cost, in other words, can be at the origin not only of *lucrum cessans* (missing profitability) but also of *damnum emergens* (emerging losses). In competitive markets, where both incumbents and entrants can imitate and use the knowledge generated by inventors, the market price would rapidly fall to levels below the marginal cost incurred by the inventor. These levels, in fact, would take into account all other costs incurred by every other firm, except the costs of knowledge paid to inventors. Knowing their inability to appropriate knowledge, the inventor lacks incentive to innovate, and the classic Arrovian market failure occurs.

The Arrovian analysis focused on the effects of the properties of knowledge on the levels of knowledge produced and used by firms. Because of the reduction in the private rates of return measured by the marginal productivity and profitability of knowledge – caused by its limited appropriability – firms generate and use (at the same time) less knowledge than would have been the case had knowledge been a standard good (Arrow, 1962, 1969). This effect results in negative incentive that leads to generating less knowledge than socially desirable.

This represents the Arrovian hypothesis of "failure of the market" as the appropriate institutional setting for the allocation of resources to the generation of knowledge. Markets are unable to allocate and produce the correct amount of knowledge. Because of the idiosyncrasies of knowledge as an economic good the market place is doomed to undersupply knowledge. The Arrovian framework has so far provided the foundations of an economic policy aimed at remedying knowledge market failure (Antonelli and David, 2015).

Arrow's (1962) analysis is not only a foundation stone for its normative implications; it is also an important methodological contribution as it relies on the comparative analysis of 'knowledge as a standard good' with respect to 'knowledge as a special good'. The comparative approach remains at the core of the economics of knowledge, and enables us to identify the full range of implications and consequences of the properties of knowledge both for economics and economic policy.

Recent contributions have further elaborated on and developed the Arrovian analysis, qualifying the context: limited appropriability of knowledge exerts strong negative effects on the price of innovated goods mainly (if not especially) through the dynamics of imitation by competent rivals in the same product markets. Rivals active in the same markets can easily take advantage of the novelties contained in each innovation and reproduce the knowledge on which they rely, at low cost (Akcigit et al., 2015). The price of innovated goods falls and affects directly the position of the derived demand of knowledge. The negative effects of the limited appropriability of knowledge are much lower when knowledge spillover concerns unrelated agents active in other product markets for two reasons:

- The risks of imitative entry, and hence the risks of missing revenue stemming from the spillover, are much lower.
- The ability of agents to actually reuse the spillover as input in their own knowledge generation processes is hindered by absorption costs that are higher the larger the distance in cognitive and product spaces.

7.2 KNOWLEDGE APPROPRIABILITY AS AN OPPORTUNITY

The Arrovian framework was questioned by the intuition of Zvi Griliches (1979, 1992) that the limited appropriability of knowledge may have some beneficial consequences due to the occurrence of positive externalities that favour the recipients of spillovers, rather than just negative ones due to missing incentives and the consequent underproduction of knowledge. The knowledge that inventors cannot appropriate *spills* into the atmosphere and, because of its non-exhaustibility, contributes to the stock of quasi-public knowledge that can be used by third parties at low costs.

Griliches provides the first definition of knowledge spillover:

> The last major issue is that of 'spillovers', the effect of 'outside' knowledge capital – outside the firm or industry in question – on the within-industry productivity. The level of productivity achieved by one firm or industry depends not only on its own research efforts but also on the level of the pool of general knowledge accessible to it. Looking at a cross section of firms within a particular industry, one will not be able to distinguish such effects. If the pools of knowledge differ for different industries or areas, some of it could be deduced from inter-industry comparisons over time and space. Moreover, the productivity of own research may be affected by the size of the pool or pools it can draw upon. This would lead to the formulation of models allowing for an interaction between the size of individual and aggregate research and development effort. (1979: 102)

With respect to standard goods, in fact, knowledge is characterized by a second set of characteristics such as indivisibility (and hence complementarity) and non-exhaustibility (and hence cumulability). As a consequence the portion of its marginal productivity that could not be appropriated by its producer adds to the stock of quasi-public knowledge and can be used – again – by third parties. This has positive consequences on the system as a whole. Because of knowledge non-exhaustibility, in fact, the same knowledge spillover can be used again and again at almost no cost. Knowledge non-exhaustibility augments the positive effects of knowledge spillover on the costs of new knowledge and on the scope for further generation of innovation. Specifically, the cost of knowledge stemming from the use of external knowledge, coming from third parties as an input in a further innovative process, is lower the weaker the appropriability provided by excludability based on secrecy or intellectual property and the greater its cumulability. This approach has been implemented by the notion of absorption costs introduced by Cohen and Levinthal (1989, 1990) that has stressed the role of the tacit content of knowledge as a barrier to its secondary uses. External knowledge spills freely into the system because of its limited appropriability; but its identification, selection, retrieval and actual use is not free. Firms need to implement dedicated and resourceful activities to actually access the stock of knowledge available in the system to use as input in the generation of new knowledge (Aghion and Jaravel, 2015).

7.3   THE TRADE-OFF

The introduction by Griliches of the notion of knowledge spillovers revealed the positive role of the stock of knowledge that becomes available for further use in the generation of new knowledge, more and more viewed as a process of recombination of existing knowledge items. Because of knowledge indivisibility, the stock of existing knowledge is an indispensable input for the generation of new knowledge that stems from its limited appropriability. This approach reveals the other side of the well-known problems raised by analysis of the limited appropriability of knowledge in terms of missing incentives, undersupply and, more generally, market failure framed by Nelson (1959) and Arrow (1962). The knowledge appropriability trade-off is set. With respect to standard goods, knowledge has peculiar characteristics that exert both positive and negative externalities.

The former consist in the fall of the price of innovated goods stemming from the ease of imitation in head-to-head competition with the consequent downward shift of the derived demand of knowledge and reduction in incentives to the generation of knowledge. The latter stem from the availability of a large stock of knowledge as a quasi-public good that (may) lead to a reduction in the cost of external knowledge, and hence compensate for the reduction in demand for knowledge. The quality of the knowledge connectivity of the system here plays a crucial role: the better the knowledge connectivity, the lower knowledge absorption costs and hence the larger the actual positive externalities.

The new methodological advances of the economics of knowledge with the introduction of the technology production function and the knowledge generation function (Griliches, 1979; Pakes and Griliches, 1984) eventually framed by the CDM approach (Crépon et al., 1998), and analysis of the derived demand of knowledge (Antonelli, 2017) and of the knowledge cost function (Antonelli and Colombelli, 2015b) enable us to appreciate in an integrated and comprehensive framework the dual role of knowledge externalities (Antonelli and Colombelli, 2017).

The analysis carried out so far can be synthesized by a model that can be used to explore the consequences of a new understanding of knowledge properties and externalities for analysis of their effects on the economic system. The model consists of a simple Schumpeterian quality ladder framework with two groups of firms: final goods producers and monopoly producers of intermediate goods (Aghion and Howitt, 1997). Technological knowledge (T) is regarded as an intermediary good, innovation occurs in the final goods sector and producers of competitive final goods (Y) employ a range of intermediates across different lines. As the quality of these goods rises, overall productivity in the final goods sector improves. Hence, the generation of technological knowledge is external to the final goods sector and appears as productivity gains in that sector, rather than in the intermediate goods sector where innovation takes place. Each producer of an intermediate good is a monopolist as long as the level of quality is not leapfrogged by an even higher quality. This framework provides equilibrium conditions for firms in each sector, including the generation of technological knowledge in the intermediate goods sector. The set-up of the model is as follows:

$$Y_t = \left(\frac{L}{M}\right)^{1-\alpha} \int A_{it}^{1-\alpha} X_{it}^{\alpha} \, di \tag{7.1}$$

This is the final goods production function; the term before the integral is labour input per intermediate (to remove scale effects: L/M is a constant); in equilibrium the integral, which is taken over the continuum of intermediates, generates aggregate productivity; X_{it} is the amount of intermediate of type i; and A_{it} is its quality. Final goods are the numeraire and the price of Y_t is unity.

Intermediate goods producers set the price P_{it} of each intermediate (which is treated as perishable and lasting one period) equal to its value marginal product in the final goods sector. Therefore,

$$P_{it} = \frac{\partial Y_t}{\partial X_{it}} = \alpha \left(\frac{L}{M}\right)^{1-\alpha} A_{it}^{1-\alpha} X_{it}^{\alpha-1} \tag{7.2}$$

Since each unit of the intermediate is produced one-for-one from the final good, the monopoly producer's profit is the price of the intermediate times its quantity, minus a price of unity (the numeraire price) times quantity. Hence,

$$\Pi_{it} = \alpha \left(\frac{L}{M}\right)^{1-\alpha} A_i^{1-\alpha} X_{it}^{\alpha} - X_{it} \tag{7.3}$$

The maximum value of profits from an intermediate is

$$\Pi_{it}^* = \pi \left(\frac{L}{M}\right) A_{it}, \ \pi \equiv (1-\alpha)\alpha^{\frac{1+\alpha}{1-\alpha}} \tag{7.4}$$

Plugging (7.4) into (7.1) yields (7.5), which defines the maximum value of the final goods production function with an aggregate productivity of

$$A_t = \int_0^N A_{it} \tag{7.5}$$

This is an index of quality that can be interpreted as the level of technology (N is the measure of time).

To determine the value of investment in R&D that is necessary to generate technological knowledge (T) and eventually introduce technological innovations, assume for simplicity's sake that leapfrogging takes place after ρ periods (a more general approach lets the period of the intermediate follow an exponential distribution) and that the intermediate is at that time replaced by a higher quality intermediate. Here, n is an inverse indicator of the speed of replacement or obsolescence. The value of an innovation, assuming a one period lag between invention and implementation, is

$$V_{it} = \sum_{\tau=t+1}^{\rho} \frac{1}{(1+r)^{\tau-t}} \pi \left(\frac{L}{M}\right) A_{it} = \frac{1}{r}\left(1 - \frac{1}{(1+r)^{\rho-t}}\right)\pi \left(\frac{L}{M}\right) A_{it} \tag{7.6}$$

In this equation r is the interest rate. As r falls, V_{it} also falls. Let the probability of discovery be

$$\phi = \eta \left(\frac{T_{it}}{A_{it}}\right)^{\theta} S_t^{\sigma} \tag{7.7}$$

where η reflects the extent of the knowledge externalities generated by firms; θ is the fraction of output that can be appropriated by a private innovator; S_t is the, for now, exogenous stock of public knowledge; T_{it}/A_{it} is R&D effort (internal knowledge) normalized by quality, indicating that more advanced goods have higher R&D costs; and s is the elasticity of substitution. The expected net benefit from R&D is then

$$\phi V_{it} = T_{it} \tag{7.8}$$

Now take the derivative of (7.8) with regard to T using (7.6) and (7.7), and set this equal to zero. The result is:

$$T_{it}^* = A_{it}S_t^{\sigma/(1-\theta)}\left[\theta\eta\frac{1}{r}\left(1 - \frac{1}{(1+r)^{n-t}}\right)\pi\left(\frac{L}{M}\right)\right]^{1/(1-\theta)} \tag{7.9}$$

It is clear that the equilibrium amount of R&D activities (T^*), a measure of the demand for knowledge, increases with the stock of public knowledge but decreases as n decreases. The stock of public knowledge increases research, but a decline in the period of appropriation of the returns decreases research.

Let us now explore the consequences of the framework with a simple graphic exposition of the market for knowledge. In Figure 7.1 the demand curve of knowledge (D) is analysed as a derived demand so that its position is determined by the marginal product in value of technological knowledge as an intermediate product in a technology production function, and its supply curve (S) is analysed as the standard horizontal summation of the marginal costs of knowledge as defined by a knowledge generation function. In standard market conditions that would apply if knowledge were a 'standard' good, supply and demand find an equilibrium that identifies the equilibrium quantity and price of knowledge. This benchmark is confronted by the market conditions that take place when the Arrovian properties of knowledge are considered.

Figure 7.1 with the price of knowledge (u) on the vertical axis and the quantity of knowledge (T) on the horizontal axis, explores the full range of effects of knowledge properties:

- Because of the well-known negative effects of the transient appropriability of knowledge on the price of goods produced using knowledge as an input, the derived demand of knowledge as a standard good shifts to the derived demand of knowledge as a good characterized by transient appropriability. Due to well-known transient knowledge appropriability and the consequent negative effects of imitation externalities, in fact, the price of the final goods produced using knowledge as an input – after a short time window – falls below the levels of the benchmark case of a standard economic good because of the entry of imitators that do not bear the costs of knowledge. Consequently, the demand for technological knowledge shifts downwards, below the benchmark levels of a standard good. The intercept of the actual derived demand for technological knowledge – characterized by the Arrovian properties – is consequently lower than the benchmark derived demand of technological knowledge if it were a standard good.

- Because of the positive effects of knowledge indivisibility and non-exhaustibility, the supply of knowledge as a standard good shifts to the right. We assume in fact that the stock of all the existing knowledge generated until that time is a complementary, indispensable input for the generation of new technological knowledge. Its use is not free: it can take place at a specific cost that accounts for a wide range of activities that are needed to absorb and use it. Due to the positive effects of knowledge externalities, the larger the stock of public knowledge, the better the knowledge governance mechanisms are and the lower the cost of knowledge as an intermediary input – itself an output of the knowledge generation activities. Consequently, the larger the stock of quasi-public knowledge, the lower the knowledge supply schedule in the markets for knowledge.

The literature has very much emphasized the first case, that is the shift in the derived demand of knowledge, but it has paid little attention to the second case – the shift of the supply curve. The latter takes place when the cost of accessing external knowledge and using it as an input for the generation of new knowledge is low, and does not take place when, on the contrary, the cost is high.

Let us analyse these in turn. When the system is not able to support the generation of agents' knowledge with appropriate levels of pecuniary knowledge externalities, and the stock of knowledge available in the system is small, the supply curve of knowledge as a standard good and the supply curve of knowledge as an Arrovian good in equilibrium define a large u: the standard knowledge market failure applies. External knowledge is indispensable, but its use cannot exert any positive effect on u. Transient knowledge appropriability displays all the negative effects of imitation externalities on the knowledge demand curve, with no positive effects on the long-term knowledge supply curve in terms of knowledge externalities. Figure 7.1 shows the typical situation of undersupply that is determined by the backward shift of the knowledge demand curve with a given supply curve, and the consequent shift of the equilibrium quantity of knowledge produced. There are actually two negative effects: i) the equilibrium quantity is lower; and ii) high-quality research projects can no longer be considered in the market place. There is a twin market failure.

The first effect is the basic reference for much work on the notion of knowledge market failure and the consequent knowledge undersupply that has provided the rationale for a public policy aimed at supporting an increase in the generation of additional knowledge through direct supply by the State with the funding of public research centres and universities, the provision of public subsidies to firms funding R&D activities and public procurement.

The second source of market failure has been little appreciated so far. Traditional market failure analysis, in fact, has not paid sufficient attention to the second negative effect: the selective exclusion of high-quality projects. The downward shift in the derived demand of knowledge engenders a reduction in the consumer surplus: the demand for knowledge as a standard good lies above the demand for knowledge as an Arrovian good. Even when and if the equilibrium demand for knowledge is larger than the equilibrium demand for the standard good, the downward shift entails the loss of the upper portion of the derived demand. Since the position and slope of the derived demand are defined by the marginal productivity in value of research activities, it seems clear that the downward shift in the derived demand implies that the high-quality research projects represented by the upper slice of the demand curve are no longer viable. A portion of the high-quality research projects is cut off. A reduction in the cost of research stemming from access to the stock of quasi-public knowledge favours the implementation of lower-quality research projects, but does not solve the problem of exclusion of high-quality projects.

When the stock of knowledge available in the system is large and knowledge governance mechanisms are effective, diachronic pecuniary knowledge externalities are relevant. Transient appropriability displays both positive and negative effects, where the former can compensate for the latter. The cost of knowledge as an output is below equilibrium levels. In this case, the notion of market failure needs substantial reconsideration.

With large spillovers complemented by good knowledge governance protocols and a large stock of public knowledge available within the system, the generation of technological knowledge can rely on access to external knowledge at low absorption costs. In the recombinant knowledge generation process, firms can take advantage of the low price of knowledge so as to substitute R&D activities with the use of 'cheap' existing external knowledge. The general costs of knowledge decline with the downward

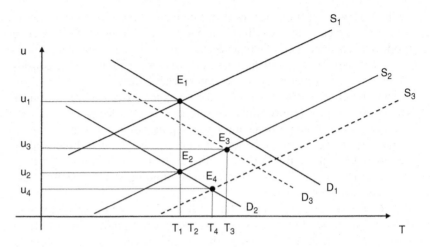

Figure 7.1   Shifts in actual demand and supply of Arrovian knowledge with respect to the benchmark demand and supply of a standard good

shift of the long-term knowledge supply curve from S_1 to S_2. Now, in the system, the amount of knowledge generated can match the equilibrium conditions so that $T_E = T_B$. The standard hypothesis about undersupply no longer applies. Moreover, the cost of technological knowledge is lower than in equilibrium. As Figure 7.1 clearly shows, $u_1 > u_2$.

In the extreme case, shown by Figure 7.1, the recombinant generation of technological knowledge that takes place in a system – endowed with a large stock of public knowledge and able to support it with high-quality knowledge governance – where it can take advantage of major pecuniary knowledge externalities, even after taking into account the downward shift in the demand of knowledge engendered by transient appropriability, leads to an equilibrium supply of technological knowledge that is actually as high as expected in equilibrium, and yet cheaper. A significant portion of the high-quality demand of knowledge, however, has been sorted out.

These effects may be mitigated by the possibility that the limited appropriability of knowledge affects not only the derived demand of knowledge but has – positive – effects on the supply of knowledge as well. External knowledge, in fact, spills and enters the knowledge generation function as an input. The cost of knowledge – now regarded as an output – is lower because of the effects of spillover on the knowledge production function (Adams, 2006).

In the recombinant knowledge production function, external knowledge is an indispensable input strictly complementary to internal R&D activities and other inputs. According to the knowledge appropriability levels, the costs of external knowledge fall below the benchmark levels that would take place were all inputs standard goods. The effects of spillover on the cost of external knowledge depend on the actual conditions of absorption and use of knowledge as an input on the production of new knowledge. The lower the cost of knowledge as an input, the lower is the cost of knowledge as an output (Griliches, 1979, 1984, 1986, 1992; Cohen and Levinthal, 1989; Weitzman, 1996).

Let us explore in detail the full range of effects of the limited appropriability of knowledge. Figure 7.1 presents:

- the shift in derived demand from the benchmark D_1 to D_2 – as determined by the effects of knowledge limited appropriability on the output and the downstream price of the goods produced using knowledge as an input, and consequently on the derived demand; and
- the shift in the supply curve from the benchmark S_1 to S_2 – as determined by the positive effects of knowledge spillover and externalities on knowledge marginal costs. (The dotted lines D_3 and S_3 show the effects of policy interventions on the demand and supply of knowledge respectively.)

Let us consider, for the sake of armchair theorizing, the interesting case that takes place when the shifts of S_2 and D_2 are symmetric. The new equilibrium is found in E_2, where the amount of knowledge as a standard good and as an Arrovian one is exactly the same ($T_1 = T_2$) while its price, u, is much lower ($u_1 > u_2$).

Analysis of the sheer quantities reveals that, when the positive effects of knowledge spillovers on the supply of knowledge are taken into account, together with the negative effects on its derived demand, there is no expected undersupply of knowledge. The positive effects of spillover on the supply side compensate for the negative effects on the demand side. This is an important result. Besides the effects on quantity, however, there are also effects on the price of knowledge. Joint analysis of the supply and the derived demand of knowledge – characterized by its Arrovian properties – enable us to grasp the problem of the depreciation of knowledge.

The derived demand of knowledge, in fact, can be regarded as an ordered structure of investment projects: those with higher levels of marginal productivity are placed in the upper part of the curve. As Figure 7.1 shows, the depreciation of knowledge that stems from the downward shift of the derived demand curve has negative effects in terms of adverse selection with the exclusion of the high-quality and high-yield projects. High-quality research projects can no longer be afforded because of the reduction in the price of goods produced using knowledge as an input.

Identification of the causes and consequences of knowledge depreciation is important. The depreciation that stems from the downward shift of the supply curve, instead, yields the typical positive effects of increased consumer surplus. The latter compensates for the shift in demand, but only with respect to low-quality projects.

The simultaneous solution of the CDM system of equations enriched by the knowledge derived demand equation that underlies this study enables us to take into account the feedback from the decrease in the price of knowledge as an input and the consequent 'additional' downward shift in the derived demand of knowledge.

When the effects of interventions through the provision of public subsidies and scientific knowledge generated by public research systems are taken into account, we see that the dotted line S_3 shifts further to the right of S_2. The amount of knowledge increases; the price of knowledge declines further, away from the benchmark situation that would take place if knowledge were a standard good; and the consumer surplus increases. The adverse selection however is not reduced. Only interventions on the demand side (the dotted line D_3) are able to increase the price of knowledge and avoid the negative effects of the adverse selection of high-quality research projects.

The Arrovian remedy, fully concentrated on the supply side, favours the increase in the supply of low-quality projects, but does not take into account the negative effects of the shift in the derived demand on the price of knowledge in terms of adverse selection. The discovery of knowledge depreciation seems to be an important contribution to the economics of knowledge as well as to the identification of its causes, whether determined by shifts in the supply or the demand curves. The effects of knowledge depreciation depend upon the cause: they are positive if they stem from a shift in the supply curve and negative if they depend on a shift in derived demand.

Let us now summarize the analysis. When only the effects of the transient appropriability of knowledge on the derived demand of knowledge are accounted for and the effects on the supply curve are not considered or are not empirically relevant, as in the standard knowledge market failure approach, the demand schedule for knowledge exhibits a downward shift from D_1 to D_2. The new equilibrium is found in A, where the amount of knowledge $T_A < T_E$.

When and if, however, the 'positive' effects of transient knowledge appropriability on both the supply and the demand curve are taken into account but the institutional set-up of the system endowed with a large stock of knowledge is able to provide substantial diachronic pecuniary knowledge externalities, the cost of external knowledge – a necessary and complementary input for the generation of new technological knowledge – falls to such levels that the supply of knowledge exhibits a downward shift from S_1 to S_2. It thus identifies, even with a knowledge demand schedule that reflects – with the downward shift from D_1 to D_2 – the negative effects of the transient appropriability of knowledge, the equilibrium point B where there is no knowledge undersupply, and the actual price of knowledge u_2 is lower than the standard price of knowledge u_1. When and if the institutional set-up of the system and the size of its knowledge stock are able to support the generation of new technological knowledge with large pecuniary knowledge externalities, the amount of technological knowledge that the system is able to generate is as large as if knowledge were a standard good, and its costs are actually lower.

In terms of quantity, there is no market failure and no knowledge undersupply when and if the quality of the knowledge governance and knowledge connectivity of the system are so high that the levels of the cost of external knowledge v and hence the cost of knowledge u are reduced to the minimum levels of u_2. In the range of conditions between the two extremes u_1 and u_2 some knowledge market failure with consequent undersupply takes place. Although firms can access external knowledge at costs that are lower than those of internal research activities, the equilibrium amount of knowledge generated by the system is below the equilibrium levels for standard goods. In these cases, the downward shift of the supply curve is not able to compensate for the downward shift in the demand curve.

In terms of value, on the other hand, the case for selective undersupply takes place. It stems from the portion of derived demand of knowledge that is no longer viable. High-quality, large-scale research projects can no longer be afforded. A selective, as opposed to generic, undersupply takes place. The downward shift in the supply of knowledge engenders only positive effects, and the downward shift in the demand of knowledge yields a selective undersupply.

There is a time element that has not been included in the analysis so far. The timing of the leakage and access to external knowledge may differ. The leaking into the public domain of one's own knowledge can occur faster than the appropriation of the knowledge of others. If this is the case, it could well be that a selection effect occurs in the short run that could have been prevented if access to outside knowledge had occurred faster. The Arrovian postulate would apply. On the contrary, however, it seems appropriate to consider the case with timing of the leakage that is much larger than the absorption lag. In this case, innovators can retain their competitive advantage by building on the knowledge generated by third parties that is rapidly absorbed. The Arrovian postulate would not apply.

The effects of knowledge indivisibility and non-exhaustibility augment the cases considered so far with major dynamic implications. For given levels of knowledge governance, it is clear that the larger the stock of public knowledge, the lower the cost of external knowledge – hence the lower the cost of knowledge as an output (u). With time, the stock of public knowledge keeps increasing, and consequently both the cost of external knowledge and the cost of knowledge as an output decline. This leads to an increase in the flow of knowledge generated at each point in time. The inter-temporal dynamics of knowledge costs is clearly characterized by a negative slope. As a consequence, the stock of public knowledge increases at faster rates. The dynamics is clearly self-reinforcing. At each point in time, countries with a larger stock of public knowledge enjoy not only lower levels of knowledge costs than countries with a small knowledge stock, but also faster rates of generation of new knowledge and faster rates of accumulation of the stock of knowledge. For a given small initial difference, the gap is deemed to increase over time.

The structure of knowledge interactions and transactions among agents within the business sector and between the business sector and the public research system becomes the central issue. Good knowledge governance mechanisms are able to improve the knowledge connectivity of the system, and hence access conditions to existing knowledge. Countries with large knowledge stocks and good knowledge governance able to implement good knowledge connectivity protocols can enjoy not only a large supply of technological knowledge, but also low technological knowledge costs – and hence a competitive advantage. Countries endowed with a smaller stock of knowledge and less able to command the good knowledge governance practices that are needed to implement high-powered knowledge connectivity protocols suffer the negative effects of Arrovian market failure, the undersupply of knowledge and a clear competitive disadvantage compared with countries where the absorption costs of the stock of existing knowledge are lower. The gap between countries increases over time because of the effects of the accumulation of larger flows of knowledge in countries with a larger stock.

A reduction in the cost of knowledge below the benchmark levels that would take place were knowledge a standard economic good has major economic implications that are both positive and negative. On the positive side, a fall in the price of knowledge below equilibrium levels accounts for total factor productivity levels and supports the introduction of innovations in the Schumpeterian framework of the creative response to out-of-equilibrium conditions. The negative consequences stem from the excess selection and hence selective undersupply of large-scale and high-quality projects. These negative consequences may be most relevant if large-scale and high-quality research projects are likely to enable the introduction of radical innovations. The excess selection of research projects may lead to the selective undersupply of projects with the exclusion of the high-yield ones. The consequences for the rate of technological change are clear. The introduction of incremental innovations stemming from small-scale, low-quality projects would be enhanced and the introduction of radical innovations stemming from large-scale and high-quality projects would be undermined. Finally, the dynamics of the process display typical non-ergodic characters that are self-reinforcing and fuel an increase in asymmetries. Yet the process is clearly far from deterministic: small events along the process can change its pace and direction. As such, this dynamics is non-ergodic but typically path dependent, as opposed to past dependent.

8.   Digital knowledge generation and the appropriability trade-off

New information and communication technologies (ICT) have been a radical innovation. As a general-purpose technology their introduction has enabled an array of technological and organizational changes in a wide variety of activities (Bresnahan and Trajtenberg, 1995; David and Wright, 2003; Brynjolfsson and Saunders, 2010; Bauer and Latzer, 2016).

Their impact on knowledge generation is one of the most important. ICT has induced significant innovations in the knowledge generation process, increasing its efficiency and profoundly changing its organization and structure. These changes, in turn, have had major effects on the role of knowledge spillover and the cost of new knowledge. New understanding of the actual role of appropriability on knowledge cost and revenue brought about by the organizational innovations associated with the introduction of ICT enables us to reconsider the Arrovian market failure hypothesis, to reframe the appropriability trade-off and to suggest an augmented role for telecommunications policy.

8.1   ICT AND THE DIGITAL GENERATION OF KNOWLEDGE

The changes brought about by the introduction and diffusion of ICT in the organization of the generation of technological and scientific knowledge are most likely to affect the knowledge appropriability trade-off, with important consequences in terms of firms' strategy and economic policy.

Different economic literatures have contributed to exploration of the effects of ICT on the knowledge generation process: the knowledge management literature, the economics of innovation and the economics of knowledge. The knowledge management literature has explored in depth the effects of ICT on the organization and structure of the knowledge generation process. It seems possible to identify two stages in this exploration. The first has focused on the internal organization of the research process. The second has identified and appreciated the new role of external knowledge made possible by the systematic use of ICT. The economics of innovation and knowledge have analysed in depth the consequences for economic analysis of the results of the previous stages (Antonelli, 2009). Let us consider them in turn.

In the first stage the knowledge management literature focused on the reorganization of research activities within corporations enabled by the introduction and intra-firm diffusion of an array of dedicated ICT applications. Multinational corporations lead in the adoption of ICT to improve the coordination and integration of their distribution activities (Antonelli, 1985, 1986).

Zuboff (1988) and Davenport and Prusak (1998) synthesize the main achievements of this stage of analysis. ICT is regarded as a process innovation that enables us to overcome the limits of the internal dissemination of information and data. According to Hendriks (1999), ICT lowers temporal and spatial barriers between knowledge workers and helps improve their motivation to share information. ICT improves the knowledge generation process, increasing the internal interfaces of the different activities of research laboratories and between them and the engineering, commercial, and financial functions of the firm. The improved quality of internal interactions favours the better use of internal information that was dispersed and better alignment of research strategies with corporate strategies. The diffusion of ICT applications trickles down with their rapid adoption by smaller firms. According to Hempell and Zwick (2008), ICT increases the ability of workers to cooperate and take decentralized decisions within an integrated context.

Dodgson et al. (2006) show how ICT enabled the introduction of an array of ICT-based innovations such as data mining, simulation, prototyping and visual representation. The increased efficiency of internal R&D activities coupled with the use of ICT applications widens the scope of the knowledge generation process and reduces the idiosyncratic advantages associated with the size of firms (Esposito and Mastroianni, 1998, 2001). The use of ICT to perform R&D overcomes the classic limits that favoured R&D activities conducted by large corporations and allows small firms to improve their internal R&D activities. The evidence provided by Morikawa (2004) confirms that Japanese small and medium-sized enterprises (SMEs) using ICT in innovative activities were better able to carry out R&D and introduce technological innovations than firms that had not adopted and implemented ICT in R&D.

The general consensus confirms that the adoption of ICT enables the introduction of major organizational innovations in the performance of internal research activities that enable firms to mobilize and integrate different sources of knowledge. These include the valorization of tacit knowledge and the interaction of different activities within the firm, with increased efficiency of internal R&D and the ultimate reduction of knowledge costs (Debackere and Van Looy, 2003; D'Adderio, 2004).

The second stage of the literature is the result of a major shift in the focus of analysis of the effects of ICT: from the internal organization of R&D activities to the appreciation and use of the large stock of external knowledge available in the system. ICT made it possible to improve drastically the economic value of the large stock of knowledge available in the system and to reduce its costs of absorption (Antonelli et al., 2000).

Cerchione et al. (2015) document the wide range of specific computer applications that enable us to widen the search in the stock of external knowledge available in the system. The use of new ICT-based techniques enables us to overcome the classic separation of scientific and technological knowledge. Earlier, the rich output of the scientific literature could be accessed and used only to a limited extent by competent and highly qualified experts. Only large corporations could take advantage of their skills. Much scientific literature could be not used to implement technological knowledge and consequently feed the introduction of innovations. The introduction of ICT-based innovation reduces such barriers and favours interaction between science and technology. Small firms especially benefit from the lowering of barriers to effective access to the stock of scientific knowledge to implement their own internal generation of new knowledge (Higon, 2011).

The systematic literature review by Pittaway et al. (2004) provides strong evidence of the effects of ICT-based procedures on access to the stock of external knowledge:

> identification of key words; construction of search strings; initial search and identification of further key words; choosing the citation databases; review of the selected citation databases using the search strings; review of the citations identified based on inclusion and exclusion criteria; review of the citation abstracts and separation into different lists; encoding abstracts according to their content; reviewing significant articles; the addition of further articles, based on professional recommendation and references from reviewed articles. (as quoted in Cerchione et al., 2015)

ICT applications enable the use of the huge amount of external knowledge available in the system through access to much more information and data. ICT allows a drastic reduction in resources that are necessary to implement the search, gathering, storing, screening, access, absorption and finally use of the knowledge spilling into the atmosphere.

ICT enables us to reduce the costs of distance in absorbing technological knowledge (Koellinger, 2008). There is much evidence documenting the negative role of distance in geographic, product and cognitive space in the absorption of external knowledge. Proximity aids access and use of external knowledge. Geographical proximity helps personal interaction. Cognitive proximity reduces the costs of decodification and screening processes (Audretsch and Feldman, 2004). Product proximity helps in the effective and timely imitation of both product and process innovations. The effects of distance reduces significantly the boundaries of the system in which the search for external knowledge could be performed (Boschma, 2005).

ICT-based innovations reduce drastically the role of distance both in geographic and cognitive space in a number of ways:

- Resources such as databases, discussion lists and notes improve knowledge distribution.
- Knowledge delivery is made more effective by innovations such as the Internet (World Wide Web), professional/social networks, intranets, e-mail and so on.
- Tacit knowledge can be mobilized through communication networks (video conferencing), and especially the creation of communities where digital infrastructure enables effective interaction by specialists in a particular knowledge domain (Subashini et al., 2012), for example the digitalization of heritage collections (Borowiecki and Navarrete, 2015).
- Most importantly, the sharing of protocols and procedures is facilitated by means of such applications as groupware (Soto-Acosta et al., 2014; Hafeez-Baig and Gururajan, 2012).
- Agents active in product markets that are unrelated to the innovation can access and extract a the knowledge relevant to their own innovation activities by means of digital decoding procedures based on digital content analysis.

ICT-based applications can reduce the role of knowledge gatekeepers and increase the number of agents who can interact directly in the system. Access to existing knowledge before the introduction of ICT-based applications was characterized by strong hierarchies that would give a pivotal role to gatekeepers able to centralize the search for and processing of knowledge. These systems would be characterized by networks where a central node interacts with a variety of isolated and disconnected agents unable to establish direct links with other agents. The introduction of ICT-based procedures for knowledge searching and screening has reduced significantly the role of such gatekeepers, favouring a reduction in the costs of access to external knowledge and increasing the scope of information flows (Whelan, 2007; Whelan et al., 2010).

ICT-based innovations in the knowledge generation process exert a powerful push towards the globalization of knowledge generation activities, both with respect to knowledge sourcing and to knowledge recombination. ICT allows expansion of the scope of the effective search for external knowledge, increasing not only the amount but also the variety of external knowledge that can be absorbed and used as input (Rosenkopf and Nerkar, 2001). The use of ICT has in fact enabled a dramatic increase in the geographic scope of knowledge search, selection and absorption activities carried out more and more in global markets, broadening the variety of possible knowledge suppliers and the opportunity to implement knowledge interactions nested with other transactions. The effects of ICT on agents' search capabilities and their consequences in terms of greater choice not only benefit the global broadening of knowledge outsourcing; they also benefit the increasing global offshoring with the selective localization of their knowledge-intensive activities in knowledge-intensive regions, including the recombinant generation of knowledge in a variety of specialized firms based in remote sites (Abramovsky and Griffith, 2006; Rasel, forthcoming).

Loebbecke and Crowston identify knowledge portals as a major organizational innovation introduced to synthesize widely dispersed knowledge and to interconnect individuals in order to aid the identification of and access to knowledge from each organization. The authors define knowledge portals (KPs) as:

> a type of portal that purposely supports and stimulates knowledge transfer, knowledge storage and retrieval, knowledge creation, knowledge integration, and knowledge application (i.e., the processes of knowledge management) by providing access to relevant knowledge artifacts. Repository-oriented components and functionalities of a KP include a knowledge organization system, repository access, search, and applications and services. In addition to the repository-oriented functionality of KPs, such a portal must also offer network-oriented components and functionalities. Some types of knowledge are most readily transferred through direct interaction between a knowledge seeker and another knowledgeable individual. To that end, a KP also provides functionalities to identify and connect users based on their expertise, such as collaboration and communication tools. (Loebbecke and Crowston, 2012: 3)

Knowledge portals can be seen as the evolution of internal mechanisms of knowledge management introduced by corporations to improve the quality of internal knowledge flows to, in turn, improve the quality of inter-organizational knowledge flows so as to improve the access to and use of the stock of quasi-public knowledge.

ICT-based applications enhance the opportunity to take advantage of and valorize the user–producer knowledge interactions that parallel vertical market transactions. Digital applications enable us to track the performance of capital goods and intermediary inputs at work in downstream production activities. Augmented storage capacity enables the accumulation of records and data about the strengths and weaknesses of the inputs at work. Augmented processing capabilities enable systematic processing of the information gathered, stimulating the generation of knowledge based on empowered interaction between the two parties (von Hippel, 2001).

The use of ICT has major effects on the generation not only of technological knowledge but also of scientific knowledge (Heimeriks and Vasileiadou, 2008). The digital generation of scientific knowledge is characterized by higher levels of interaction within the scientific community and between the scientific community and the business sector. The integration of data mining and data management technologies for scholarly enquiries becomes common practice, with major effects in terms of increased team organization, augmented levels of co-authorship, distributed interactions and cooperation between scholars in remote locations (Cobo and Naval, 2013). There is a strong consensus that the consequences are positive in terms of more efficient generation of scientific knowledge stemming from higher levels of division of labour and specialization (Hamermesh and Oster, 2002; Larson et al., 2014).

The digital generation of scientific knowledge, however, does not only affect knowledge costs; it also affects the organization and the architecture of scientific institutions. Agrawal and Goldfarb (2008) explore the consequences of the adoption of Bitnet in terms of increased cooperation between US universities, showing the asymmetric effects on the structure of academic research that favoured medium-ranked universities that could increase their interactions with top-ranked ones. According to Kim et al. (2009), elite universities are losing their competitive edge because of the enhanced opportunities for knowledge sharing and interaction among scholars based in peripheral universities. The creation of informal research cooperation mechanisms is favoured by the use of ICT with the implementation of computer-mediated communication procedures that empower distributed scientific work so that 'invisible' (virtual) colleges are being formed bringing together scholars based in a variety of research institutions (Walsh and Bayma, 1996). As Boppart and Staub (2016) note, centrifugal effects at institutional level take place together with centripetal effects on the visibility of academic stars. The easier access to the stock of scientific knowledge favours the concentration of citations and references to key authors, increasing the typical power law of the Matthew effect.

Van Schewick (2016: 309) highlights the powerful effects of the architecture of Internet networks on the organization of the innovation process.

The architecture of the Internet influences 'which actors can innovate, what incentives they have to do so and who controls whether an application can be developed, deployed and used'. The introduction of ICT has increased significantly the knowledge connectivity of the system, increasing the size and composition of the stock of quasi-public knowledge that can be accessed at low absorption costs.

The reduction in the levels of absorption costs of external knowledge has in turn major implications for the organization of knowledge generation activities. Appreciation of the recombinant character of knowledge generation and introduction of open innovation organizational methods can be regarded as a direct consequence of the new role of the stock of external knowledge made possible by the introduction of ICT.

According to Weitzman (1996), new knowledge is generated by means of the recombinants of existing knowledge items. As Brian Arthur puts it (2009: 2): 'I realized that new technologies were not "inventions" that came from nowhere. All the examples I was looking at were created – constructed, put together, assembled – from previously existing technologies. Technologies in other words consisted of other technologies, they arose as combinations of other technologies.' The greater variety of external knowledge that can be accessed at low absorption costs by means of ICT-based dedicated applications enables us to expand significantly the combinations of the recombinant process, and hence opportunities for the effective generation of new knowledge (Harada, 2003).

Appreciation of the recombinant character of knowledge generation and identification of the strict complementarity between external and internal knowledge (Antonelli and Colombelli, 2015a) leads to the introduction of the open innovation business model. Open innovation can be regarded as a major organizational innovation in the knowledge generation process. In this model, external knowledge is regarded as a necessary and indispensable input in the generation of new knowledge. Knowledge is generated more and more by assembling an array of knowledge items that have been outsourced. Firms keep funding R&D activities, but perform intramuros only a fraction of the total amount of research. The firm acts as a knowledge integrator that combines diverse knowledge items. Access to the stock of external knowledge is no longer regarded as an additional input, but as a necessary complementary input (Gehringer, 2011). Not only the amount of knowledge generated and its costs depend on the external knowledge that can be accessed, but also the type of innovations that can be generated. Strategic selection of external knowledge inputs becomes necessary (Chesbrough, 2003; Chesbrough et al., 2006, Dodgson et al., 2006; Enkel et al., 2009; Shearmur and Doloreux, 2013).

The use of digital technologies affects the generation of scientific and technological knowledge at three complementary levels: i) it reduces the cost of accessing the stock of quasi-public knowledge; ii) it makes knowledge interactions more effective; and iii) it favours the modularization of knowledge. Digital technologies enable the identification of modules of technological and scientific knowledge that can be better accessed and recombined.

The interaction of the protocols of software generation and the procedures applied in knowledge generation characterizes the evolution towards the digital generation of knowledge. The generation of new software consists in the recombination of existing software modules that are retrieved and applied as inputs. Free and open source practices have shown the advantages of the collective generation of new software packages based upon the cumulative contribution of myriad independent experts able to contribute to the enrichment and exploitation of an ever-increasing stock of public knowledge. The methodologies elaborated to implement the recombinant generation of new software packages are themselves the result of applying the procedures and protocols of the generation of new scientific and technological knowledge. Their evolution, however, has in turn reinforced the use of recombinatory procedures based upon the systematic use of existing modules of knowledge – properly framed – to generate new scientific and technological knowledge (David and Rullani, 2008).

Knowledge interactions supported by ICT enable us to share and access the strong tacit components of all knowledge items. Even the most codified knowledge items, such as scientific publications, include irreducible tacit components that can be shared only by means of personal interaction (Cowan et al., 2000). The digital generation of technological knowledge magnifies the role of the systematic interaction between knowledge holders and agents at large, not only within and among firms in the business sector but also between the members and the institutions of the scientific community and the business sector, as the key mechanism for increasing knowledge output.

ICT-based innovations change the organization of the knowledge generation process at the firm level through three different and yet complementary processes: i) the digital generation of technological knowledge is characterized by lower levels of vertical integration of research activities. The large intramuros research laboratories are squeezed and progressively integrated by the purchase of research inputs supplied by ii) knowledge-intensive business services (KIBS) that progressively become specialized suppliers able to substitute intramuros corporate research laboratories; and iii) the implementation of inter-firm coordination based on ICT platforms that help the organized cooperation of a variety of actors endowed with complementary capabilities and competences (Antonelli and Patrucco, 2016).

Once again digital technologies provide the essential infrastructure that supports the search for available information on existing knowledge and its active inclusion as an input in the knowledge generation process, based upon the systematic sharing and integration of modules of existing knowledge. The interactive use of large databases is key to making the management of knowledge outsourcing and its eventual integration possible and effective. Digital technologies – for example broadband-based procedures such as the Internet of things (IoT), big data and cloud computing – play a crucial role in making knowledge outsourcing and integration possible. This is because they allow the effective organization of research platforms guided by corporations for dedicated tasks, and myriad academic institutions and knowledge intensive business service suppliers contributing specialized inputs (Consoli and Patrucco, 2008, 2011).

Corporations keep funding research activities, but rely more and more on services from both the public research infrastructure and firms specializing in knowledge generation and application (KIBS) to conduct research on a contractual basis. The borders between private and public research institutions are becoming increasingly blurred as the latter are more and more involved in the global market for knowledge, with active roles as specialist suppliers of knowledge services outsourced by corporations.

This process does not only favour the division of labour, the specialization of research units and the selection of the best research capabilities; it also makes the interaction of knowledge holders, dispersed in the system, and the repeated use of existing knowledge items more and more effective. ICT enables us to better take advantage of: i) the indivisibility of knowledge, and hence the intrinsic complementarity of its components; ii) its substantial non-exhaustibility, and hence cumulability; and iii) its irreducible tacit content so as to make the digital generation of knowledge much more effective than the traditional corporate model.

The digital generation of knowledge seems a major organizational and institutional innovation that enables us to extract and better valorize the opportunities and positive aspects of the limited appropriability and exhaustibility of knowledge.

These advances in the exploration of new business models for the generation of new knowledge parallel the advances in the economics of innovation about the economic characteristics of the knowledge generation function. In the knowledge generation function, in fact, external knowledge enters as a necessary input, strictly complementary to internal R&D activities. The recombinant character of the knowledge generation function and the strict complementarity of external and internal knowledge stress the crucial role of external knowledge. Without external knowledge, the generation of new knowledge is actually impossible. Internal knowledge, in fact, can substitute for external knowledge only to a limited extent. If external knowledge is not available, the generation of new knowledge cannot actually take place (Antonelli and Colombelli, 2015a).

Access to external knowledge with low absorption costs, made possible by the introduction of ICT, has three distinct and powerful effects: i) it enables firms to generate new technological knowledge by making intensive use of external knowledge; ii) it reduces drastically the costs of new knowledge as an output (Antonelli and Colombelli, 2015b); iii) it is associated with significant increase in the performance and productivity of firms able to rely systematically on external knowledge (Tambe et al., 2012).

8.2 THE DIGITAL GENERATION OF KNOWLEDGE AND THE APPROPRIABILITY TRADE-OFF: CAN KNOWLEDGE SPILLOVERS COMPENSATE FOR MARKET FAILURE?

The notion of derived demand of knowledge implemented by Antonelli (2017) as an extension and enrichment of the CDM model enables us to articulate and operationalize analysis of the knowledge appropriability trade-off and provides an effective framework to assess the effects of ICT.

The analytical framework includes, in a single system, four equations: i) a knowledge generation function; ii) a technology production function; iii) a knowledge derived demand equation; and iv) a knowledge cost equation. In the knowledge generation function, knowledge is the output of an intentional and dedicated activity based on two strictly complementary inputs: internal research and learning activities and external knowledge. The cost of external knowledge is influenced by the size and access conditions of the stock of external quasi-public knowledge that stems from the limited appropriability of proprietary knowledge generated by all agents in the system.

In the technology production function the output is the result of traditional inputs, including technological knowledge supplied by the upstream knowledge generation function. The price of goods produced using technological knowledge will be lower the lower is the appropriability. With low levels of appropriability, in fact, imitators can easily enter the market place, shifting the supply curve to the right and hence engendering the fall in the price of the innovated products. Innovative incumbents may actually experience a fall in price of the innovated products below their unit costs that include knowledge costs. Imitators bear much lower knowledge costs as they can take advantage of limited appropriability.

Price levels in downstream product markets have a direct and evident effect on the position of the derived demand of knowledge. The derived demand of any input is nothing but the value of its marginal product. The position of the derived demand for knowledge consequently measures the negative effects of the limited appropriability of knowledge. The lower the appropriability of knowledge, the lower is the position of the derived demand for knowledge.

Finally, the knowledge cost equation defines the position and slope of the knowledge supply schedule. The lower the appropriability of knowledge and the larger the flow of knowledge spillover, the lower is the cost of external knowledge as an input in the knowledge generation function. Consequently, the lower the appropriability, the lower the position of the knowledge supply. The lower the position of the knowledge supply, the greater the positive effects of knowledge spillover.

Let us now explore the effects of the introduction of ICT and the spreading of the digital generation of knowledge on the framework elaborated so far to assess the knowledge appropriability trade-off. According to the literature review elaborated in section 8.1, it seems possible to claim that:

- ICT has little effect on the negative externalities of knowledge appropriability. Imitation of innovations by competent rivals engaged in head-to-head competition is poorly affected by ICT. Knowledge appropriability is already very low because of proximity in product and cognitive space. The introduction of ICT is not likely to yield further downward shifts in the derived demand for knowledge.
- ICT instead drastically reduces the cost of external, tacit and distant knowledge, and favour its use in the knowledge generation process. The introduction of ICT is most likely to favour the downward shift in the knowledge supply schedule. Because of the lower costs of external knowledge as an input in the knowledge generation, knowledge as the output has in turn lower costs.

On these bases it seems possible to argue that the Arrovian market failure does not hold in the specific conditions that take place after the introduction of ICT in knowledge generation when spillover helps reduce knowledge costs below the levels of knowledge were it a standard good, and favours a significant downward shift in the knowledge costs and supply curve.

Firms experience negative externality stemming from limited knowledge appropriability and consisting in a reduction of the expected revenue of their innovation activities that can be compensated for by the positive externalities stemming from limited knowledge appropriability, and consisting in the knowledge cost-reducing effects of knowledge spillovers. If the positive externalities augmented by the effects of the introduction of ICT-based innovations are able to compensate for the negative externalities, the marketplace is actually able to produce and use the same amount of knowledge that would be generated if knowledge were a perfect economic good in competitive markets. In these circumstances lack of incentives, market failure and the underproduction of knowledge would not actually occur; moreover, the lower cost of knowledge would have strong positive effects on the supply of knowledge and on total factor productivity levels. After the introduction of ICT in the digital generation of knowledge, the marketplace enriched by effective transactions-cum-knowledge interactions might actually generate a larger amount of knowledge at lower costs.

The introduction of ICT, with its powerful effects in terms of increased knowledge connectivity of the system and reduction of absorption cost, favours the reduction in the cost of external knowledge. The introduction of ICT in the knowledge generation process magnifies the positive side of the appropriability coin.

The reduction of absorption costs brought about by the introduction of ICT directly affects the cost of external and tacit knowledge, which in turn reduces the cost of knowledge and hence engenders a downward shift in the knowledge supply curve. If the fall in knowledge costs will be large, and consequently the shift in the supply of knowledge also large, the equilibrium demand for knowledge in the system will be actually larger than expected in the Arrovian framework, with positive effects both in terms of the equilibrium quantity and price of knowledge.

Figure 8.1 compares the effects of knowledge appropriability before and after the introduction of ICT on the derived demand of knowledge and its supply. The derived demand of knowledge as a standard good D_S lies above the derived demand of knowledge with its Arrovian properties D_A. The derived demand of knowledge with its Arrovian properties, in fact, reflects the low price of the good – which has been produced using knowledge as an input: a price that is well below the level it would have been were knowledge a standard good. Figure 8.1 shows three knowledge supply curves:

- S_S represents the position of knowledge supply were it a standard good.
- S_{BICT} represents the position of knowledge supply with its Arrovian properties before the introduction of ICT.
- S_{AICT} represents the position of the knowledge supply curve after the introduction of ICT.

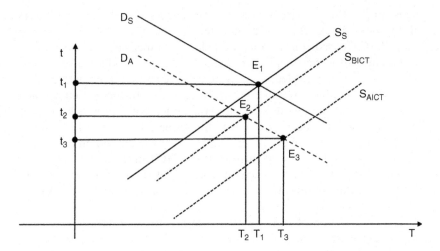

Note: The geometric exposition relies on the stylized facts presented and the hypothesis outlined in this chapter. Only dedicated empirical investigations can confirm whether or not it is consistent with the actual facts.

Figure 8.1   The digital generation and use of knowledge

We can now portray geometrically the effects of the introduction of ICT on the knowledge appropriability trade-off. The Arrovian properties of knowledge yield both positive and negative externalities. The position of the derived demand of knowledge is lower than it would have been. The positive externalities consist in the downward shift of the knowledge supply curve. The introduction of ICT empowers the positive externalities because of the reduction of knowledge absorption costs.

Figure 8.1 enables us to compare the two cases. Knowledge limited appropriability is the cause of the shift in derived demand of knowledge from D_S to D_A and the parallel shift in the knowledge supply curve from S_S to S_{BICT}. Equilibrium shifts from E_1 to E_2. The equilibrium quantity of knowledge T decreases from T_1 to T_2. The Arrovian hypothesis is confirmed: the market place is unable to allocate the appropriate amount of resources to the generation of knowledge, with the well-known consequences in terms of undersupply.

Note that the Arrovian hypothesis holds even when the positive effects of knowledge spillover are taken into account. The E_2 equilibrium solution is found at the intersection of the derived demand of knowledge after taking into account the negative effects of the reduction in price of the goods that have been produced using knowledge as an input and the supply curve (S_{BICT}) as determined by the positive effects of external knowledge.

After the introduction of ICT, however, the knowledge supply shifts to S_{AICT}. The new equilibrium is found in E_3. The equilibrium quantity of knowledge T increases from T_2 to T_3, where it is actually larger than it should have been in the benchmark condition that would have taken place if knowledge were a standard economic good.

The equilibrium quantity of knowledge that the market is able to allocate is much larger than the amount of knowledge that the market would have allocated were knowledge a standard good. The introduction of ICT makes the equilibrium supply of knowledge even larger and its costs actually lower. The Arrovian hypothesis of lack of incentive to generate knowledge, and hence its undersupply, does not hold.[1]

The knowledge market failure hypothesis could be tentatively questioned before the introduction of ICT, but it must be questioned after the introduction of ICT. Moreover, the market price of knowledge (t) is lower: it shifts from t_2 to t_3 because of the downward shift of the supply curve.[2] The low costs of knowledge, below competitive equilibrium levels, account for total factor productivity growth (Antonelli, 2013b).[3]

The appropriability trade-off can now be revisited. The value of knowledge that cannot be appropriated by the 'inventor' spills, but it does not disappear. The introduction of ICT enables other firms to use it to generate new technological knowledge in turn. After the introduction of ICT the generation of knowledge can now rely on external knowledge as an input that complements internal knowledge. The access and use of external knowledge is cheap(er) because the introduction of ICT favours knowledge interactions, and consequently access to the stock of quasi-public and quasi-tacit knowledge, and reduces its absorption costs.

It is clear that the actual effects of the introduction of ICT on knowledge interactions and the access and use of knowledge spillover on knowledge costs become the crucial issue. These effects are likely to be strongly affected by the properties of the system in which the process takes place. The structure and organization of the system play a major role in terms of knowledge connectivity. Some systems provide higher levels of interaction, communication and coordination in the use of knowledge than others. These in turn depend on:

- the variety and complementarity of knowledge(s) that are available in the system;
- the regional, industrial knowledge structure of the system;
- the quality and quantity of the communication channels among the system's units;
- the organization of knowledge interaction networks;

- the interactions that parallel and complement market transactions; and
- the strength of interactions between the academic and research community and the business system.

The quality of the telecommunications infrastructure, both in terms of physical infrastructure and of the regulatory environment that shapes its conditions of access and use, clearly plays a central role in this context.

The quality of the telecommunications infrastructure is the key factor in assessing the levels of knowledge connectivity of a system: the higher its knowledge connectivity, the larger its knowledge output. With high levels of connectivity, knowledge spillovers can be used again and again, and accessed at low costs. This is because of the quality of communication that improves the quality of knowledge interactions so as to support the generation of new knowledge at low costs due to the complementarity between external and internal knowledge.

The new framework enables us to appreciate the out-of-equilibrium conditions of knowledge generation and use and the levels of knowledge costs below equilibrium levels. It contrasts and yet complements the Arrovian framework, permitting us to formulate an improved framework of economic policy where telecommunication policy has much a wider and relevant role.

8.3   IMPLICATIONS

New information and communication technologies are pillars of the knowledge economy. Their introduction and diffusion enabled the mobilization and effective use of the large stock of quasi-public knowledge embedded in the economy of advanced countries. The systematic use of new ICT enabled increased knowledge connectivity of the system, drastically reducing knowledge absorption costs and hence the repeated use of knowledge as an input in the generation of new knowledge. New ICT enabled: industrialization of the recombinant generation of new knowledge favouring the division of knowledge labour; specialization and participation of an increasing variety of agents embodied by different and yet complementary knowledge items to its generation; and opportunities for more effective knowledge transactions and interactions in emerging knowledge markets and alongside user–producer interactions, with the eventual sharp increase in the efficiency of knowledge generation (Goldfarb et al., 2015).

Appreciation of ICT's positive role in the knowledge connectivity of an economic system enables us to reconsider the knowledge appropriability trade-off. The positive effects of the limited appropriability of knowledge in terms of knowledge spillovers, combined and augmented by ICT applications to the recombinant generation of knowledge, help reduce knowledge costs below equilibrium conditions. When and where such effects apply, the Arrovian framework and its implications for knowledge policy need to be reconsidered.

A new agenda for telecommunications policy – one that includes and highlights its economic role, aimed at increasing the knowledge connectivity of the system and the reduction of absorption of knowledge not entirely appropriated by inventors and spilling in the system – should be implemented. The larger the connectivity of the system, the stronger the positive effects of knowledge spillovers on knowledge costs are likely to be. The lower the actual knowledge costs, the larger the rates of increase of total factor productivity. The traditional framework for knowledge policy based upon the Arrovian analysis of knowledge market failure applies when and where knowledge spillovers cannot be used effectively to generate new technological knowledge at costs below equilibrium levels. The two agendas for knowledge policy can complement each other.

The remedy for the selective undersupply of knowledge can work only if public policies focus on both the supply and the demand for knowledge. Selective public procurement, both direct and indirect, able to provide reliable demand for radical innovations characterized by high levels of knowledge intensity and high-quality and large-scale research projects can compensate for the leftward shift in derived demand and complement the effects of supply policies on the position of the knowledge supply schedule.

These results seem important from many viewpoints. From an analytical viewpoint analysis of the derived demand for knowledge provides a novel approach to analysing the economic properties of knowledge as an intermediary economic good. It also highlights the risks that the price of knowledge – both the shadow prices within the corporation and the monetary prices in the markets for knowledge – falls well below the benchmark levels. The negative consequences in terms of excess selection of high-quality and large-scale projects and selective undersupply of knowledge – as opposed to the generic undersupply of the Arrovian approach – should be taken into account. From an empirical viewpoint this provides a field of investigation that can enrich and implement the CDM approach. From an economic policy perspective, it highlights the need to articulate and implement an integrated approach able to frame a set of public interventions that combine support to both the supply of knowledge and its derived demand.

NOTES

1. If we regard the demand curve as a pecking order, the reduction – from T_1 to T_2 – of the price of knowledge may exert negative consequences in terms of exclusion of high-quality research projects (Antonelli, 2017).
2. This price reduction is fully positive as it depends only on the shift of the supply curve.
3. The simultaneous solution of the model enables taking into account feedback of the reduction of the cost of knowledge on the supply of the goods that use it as an input, and hence a reduction of its costs with the consequent additional downward shift of the derived demand of knowledge. This secondary effect is not taken into account in Figure 8.1.

9. Knowledge governance, pecuniary knowledge externalities and total factor productivity growth

This chapter contributes to the endogenous technological change approach, arguing that innovation is an emerging property of the system in which the firm is embedded. It elaborates the view that innovation is the final result of the reaction to out-of-equilibrium conditions, both in factor and product markets, that can take place and become creative so as to lead to the generation of new technological knowledge and to the introduction of technological innovations only in localized circumstances that qualify the system in which the firm is embedded. The innovation process is affected by the costs and availability of internal and external knowledge. The latter, in turn, reflects the structural conditions of the system in terms of connectivity and knowledge governance. In so doing it contests the view that innovation is a homogeneous, inexorable process that depends only on the supply of knowledge and not on its cost or production process, as in the traditional growth theory.

The integration of the Schumpeterian and Marshallian legacies along the lines of the localized technological change approach provides a unifying methodology able to account for the origins of the levels and the dynamics of the residual. In this context, total factor productivity can be explained by joint appreciation of system characteristics, in terms of knowledge connectivity, and of the ability of individual firms to try to react to unexpected events by means of the introduction of technological innovations.

In the localized technological change approach, myopic firms are rooted in a limited portion of the technical, regional and knowledge space by substantial irreversibility. For that reason, they are exposed to unexpected events in their product and factor markets with which they cannot fully cope with traditional substitution. Nevertheless they can change intentionally their technology, provided a number of circumstances take place (Schumpeter, 1947a).

Firms caught in out-of-equilibrium conditions by unexpected changes in both factor and product markets, localized by the irreversibility of tangible and intangible inputs and by their idiosyncratic tacit competence accumulated by a learning process, try to generate new technological knowledge so as to introduce technological innovations. The generation of new technological knowledge may lead to the actual introduction of innovations that increase total factor productivity only if and when their economic system is characterized by high levels of knowledge governance. The latter enables the effective identification of, access to and use of external knowledge as key inputs in the recombinant generation of new technological knowledge at costs that are below equilibrium.

Innovation is made possible by the structural characteristics of the system that provide reacting firms with external knowledge at costs that, in specific locations, are below general equilibrium levels, and hence can account for localized total factor productivity: innovation is an emerging property of an economic system. If external knowledge cannot be accessed and used at costs that are below equilibrium levels, firms' reaction is adaptive rather than creative, and cannot lead to the introduction of productivity-enhancing innovations (Antonelli, 2008b, 2011).

In this approach the systemic conditions that qualify the access and use of external knowledge spilling from 'inventors' to generate new technological knowledge and support the introduction of innovations are crucial to understanding the actual introduction of productivity-enhancing innovations (Arthur et al., 1997; Lane, 2009).

This approach combines the Schumpeterian emphasis on the role of the reaction of firms in inducing attempts to introduce technological change with the Marshallian analysis of externalities. The combination of Schumpeterian reaction and Marshallian externalities provides an integrated framework in which out-of-equilibrium growth and development can be understood by partial equilibrium analysis. It thus enables us to combine a microeconomic analysis of short-term, instantaneous equilibrium with a long-term analysis of out-of-equilibrium growth and structural change at the system level (Marshall, 1920; Schumpeter, 1928; Metcalfe, 2007, 2009).

This approach makes it possible to appreciate the variety of localized contexts in which the generation of technological knowledge takes place. Moreover, it enables us to calculate when, where, why and how the pace of technological change is more or less rapid. The new growth theory, in contrast, is bound to postulate a homogeneous rate of introduction of technological change across space and time.

9.1   THE EFFECTS OF PECUNIARY KNOWLEDGE EXTERNALITIES ON TOTAL FACTOR PRODUCTIVITY

Technological knowledge is an economic good with particular characteristics such as limited appropriability, non-excludability and indivisibility, and hence complementarity, cumulativity and non-exhaustibility. For quite a long time the economics of knowledge has focused on the limits of knowledge as an economic good stemming from its limited appropriability, non-excludability and intrinsic information asymmetries. As a consequence the benefits stemming from its production and exchange in the market place are missing, together with incentives for the allocation of resources to generate it and opportunities for specialization. These characteristics would account for substantial market failure and major risks of undersupply. Because markets are unable to allocate the correct amount of resources to the generation of technological knowledge, public intervention is necessary (Nelson, 1959; Arrow, 1962, 1969).

This approach has been reconsidered when, instead of focusing on the negative aspects – in terms of missing incentives – of knowledge non-appropriability, attention has been directed to the positive effects of uncontrolled spillover of knowledge from 'inventors' to third parties. Technological knowledge generated by each firm affects, as an 'unpaid external' production factor, the production function of all other firms. Technological knowledge spilling in the atmosphere becomes an externality, and hence a resource for prospective recipients (Griliches, 1979, 1992; Adams, 1990; Link and Siegel, 2007).

The new growth theory has implemented analysis of the positive effects of knowledge non-appropriability, non-excludability, non-divisibility and non-exhaustibility, and elaborated models of endogenous growth based upon the role of knowledge externalities. In the first wave of new growth models the spilling of knowledge externalities is homogeneous and automatic, and enables the free utilization of the flows of knowledge generated in a system by third parties (Romer, 1986). Its accumulation through historic time takes place everywhere and at all times at no cost, benefiting lucky recipients who are just happy to be there (Romer, 1990). This literature implements analysis of a self-sustained process of economic growth based upon the benefits of knowledge characterized limited appropriability indivisibility that becomes available, like exogenous manna, at no cost to passive recipients who use it as an additional factor that increases their efficiency but does not alter their choices or their strategies (Romer, 1994; Lucas, 2008).

The powerful analytical framework elaborated by the first wave of the new growth theory has stimulated a wealth of empirical and analytical investigations into the economic characteristics of knowledge and their implications for economics at large, highlighting the uneven occurrence of productivity growth. Much evidence shows that the rates of technological change are far from being evenly distributed across historic times, industries and regional spaces, as suggested by the new growth theory. On the contrary, the introduction of technological change is concentrated in historic time within well-defined gales in defined portions of the industrial system and clusters in regional spaces that keep changing across time (Abramovitz and David, 1996; Mokyr, 1990, 2002; Metcalfe, 1995).

The growing empirical evidence provided by the economics of knowledge has progressively made clear that the use of knowledge spillovers is far from homogenous and free. It entails dedicated activities and well-identified resources. Knowledge does not fall from heaven to passive recipients; neither does it spill, freely, into the atmosphere. The prospective users of technological spillovers need to act intentionally in order to take advantage of them (Mansfield et al., 1981; Cohen and Levinthal, 1989, 1990).

Identification of the key role of tacit knowledge and the consequent understanding of the central role of user–producer interactions in users' access to the knowledge generated by third parties make clear that both knowledge cumulability and complementarity require the active participation of prospective users to access external knowledge and to use it in the generation of new technological knowledge (David, 1993).

New understanding of the mechanisms underlying the generation of technological knowledge substantiates the new approach. The generation of new technological knowledge by each firm consists in the recombination of existing modules of knowledge, and impinges upon high levels of complementarity with the knowledge generating activities in place in other firms and cumulability with the stock of existing knowledge. Technological knowledge is at the same time an output and an input of the recombinant generation of new technological knowledge, and external knowledge is an essential – indispensable – input. Eventually knowledge enters the production function of all goods; as such, it is twice an input: in the generation of new technological knowledge and in the generation of all the other goods. The firm is primarily a knowledge integrator able to bundle different sources of knowledge in order to generate new knowledge (Weitzman, 1996, 1998; Saviotti, 2007).

At each point in time, the system is endowed with a given amount of technological knowledge characterized by high levels of heterogeneity and diversity both with respect to epistemic content and location. Moreover, it is possessed by the myriad of agents that generated it and are generating it. As such, the stock of existing technological knowledge is not only heterogeneous but also dispersed and fragmented: much technological knowledge is external to each agent (Metcalfe, 1997, 2002).

External knowledge is strictly necessary to generate new technological knowledge, and its use entails dedicated interactions between the recipients and the possessors. More specifically, external knowledge that can be accessed either via market transactions or spilling from its possessors can be used by third parties only after dedicated interactions have been implemented and structured. Even knowledge spilling from the original possessor, because of limited appropriability, cannot be used freely by third parties. Appreciation of the notion of knowledge governance costs is crucial.

Dedicated interactions are necessary for its use to become possible not only when transactions in knowledge markets are involved, but also primarily and necessarily when spillovers are concerned. This is because it is dispersed in a myriad of highly idiosyncratic local contexts of application with high levels of irreducible tacit content. Moreover, it is codified in a variety of non-trivial codes and possessed by a myriad of heterogeneous agents with their own idiosyncrasies and routines. This implies that existing external technological knowledge can be used in the recombinant generation of new technological knowledge only after dedicated resources have been invested to identify, retrieve and extract it from its original context, and to learn from it and adapt it to a specific context of application. Most importantly, it becomes clear that the use of external knowledge requires, occasionally, transactions – but always and mainly dedicated intentional interactions with the actual possessors (Cassiman and Veugelers, 2006).

The access conditions of external knowledge depend upon the quality of knowledge governance of an economic system. Knowledge governance consists in the set of rules, procedures, modes and protocols that organize the use of knowledge in an economic system. It includes a variety of institutional factors that qualify the architecture of relations, ranging from the extremes of pure transactions to pure interactions, including hierarchical coordination within firms and, most importantly, transactions-cum-interactions. The quality of knowledge governance mechanisms at work – at each point in time within each economic system – can be seen as the spontaneous result of a systemic process of polycentric governance (Ostrom, 2010; Antonelli and Ferraris, 2011).

A variety of localized paths to organizing and managing at the system level the use of existing technological knowledge as an input in the recombinant generation of new technological knowledge, and the consequent introduction of total factor productivity enhancing technological change, can emerge and consolidate, according to the institutional setting of each system and its path-dependent characteristics (Link and Metcalfe, 2008).

The notion of pecuniary knowledge externalities applies far better than the traditional notion of pure externalities. External knowledge is not free and yet is strictly necessary. Active search, screening, identification and interpretation of existing knowledge are necessary in order to use knowledge again and again as an intermediary input in the production of new knowledge. At the same time, it now seems clear that external knowledge is an indispensable and non-disposable production factor, considering that its costs do affect the choice context of users. Pecuniary externalities matter when the costs of production factors differ from equilibrium levels: recipients are active and act intentionally, taking into account external effects so as to achieve more efficient production mixes. When pure externalities apply, external conditions affect the efficiency of the production process but do not enter the production set and the production choices: recipients are passive (Scitovsky, 1954; Antonelli, 2008a).

Pecuniary knowledge externalities are found where and when the knowledge governance costs incurred in accessing and using external knowledge are lower than its marginal product. The costs of accessing external knowledge reflect the localized conditions of using the existing knowledge that spills because of limited appropriability and can be used again because of non-exhaustibility.[1] Knowledge governance costs are determined by the quality of the knowledge interactions that make it possible to actually use the stocks of knowledge possessed by each agent as well as the flows of new knowledge generated by other agents. They include the costs of searching, screening, assessing, decodifying, extracting from its original context, learning and finally understanding the knowledge that cannot be fully appropriated by those who generated it.

Even in the extreme case that appropriability levels are nil and the possessors of technological knowledge can retain no control at all of the stream of rents associated with its use, so that the market price of technological knowledge is zero and all technological knowledge spills into the atmosphere, access to it and its use as external knowledge in the recombinant generation of new technological knowledge takes place at positive levels of knowledge governance costs. When appropriability levels are higher and the possessor of technological knowledge enters the market for knowledge, interaction activities are necessary to successfully perform the actual transaction and to assist prospective customers in the actual use of knowledge that has been purchased. In both cases external knowledge can be used, but only at a cost. The cost of external knowledge can be lower than equilibrium levels when its governance costs are especially low. Hence pecuniary knowledge externalities are influenced by the structure of the system, the distribution of agents within it that affect and qualify the activities that are necessary to engender the collective pursuit of generating new technological knowledge. In specific and qualified circumstances – highly localized in regional space, historic time and knowledge space – the levels of knowledge governance costs may be such that the cost of external knowledge is lower than equilibrium levels (Antonelli, 2007, 2008b).

The localized context of action emerges as a fundamental aspect of the innovation process. An understanding of the key role of the localized pools of existing technological knowledge that make possible the actual use of external knowledge in the generation of new technological knowledge opens up new prospects of enquiry regarding the effects that the costs of external knowledge have on the equilibrium growth of firms, industries and regions and the causes of pecuniary knowledge externalities (Porter, 2000; Antonelli and Barbiellini Amidei, 2011; Antonelli, 2011).

The new relevance of the role of external knowledge and its governance costs draw attention to the role of knowledge not only in the knowledge generation function but also in the cost equation. This contrasts a long-standing tradition focusing on just the production function. Ever since the Arrovian notion of learning, efforts to explain the determinants of total factor productivity have concentrated on analysing the contribution of technology to the production function. The new growth theory has framed a model where increasing returns at the system level are compatible with standard equilibrium based upon the hypothesis of knowledge cumulability and non-appropriability, and related free and spontaneous spillovers among firms.

9.2   A SIMPLE MODEL

This section articulates an alternative approach that builds upon the explicit identification of a knowledge generation function with internal and external knowledge as indispensable inputs and the related cost equation so as to accommodate the role of knowledge governance costs and the possible role of pecuniary knowledge externalities. We nest the knowledge generation function in a production function that includes technological knowledge as an input. In so doing we will show how pecuniary knowledge externalities can explain both total factor productivity levels and rates of change.

In the localized technological change approach the generation of new technological knowledge is activated when firms try to cope with unexpected events that affect their product and factor markets in order to introduce technological innovations as a form of reaction. The irreversibility of substantial portions of their tangible and intangible inputs limits their possibility of coping with such changes by means of traditional substitution processes. The reaction will be 'creative' if, when and where the generation of new technological knowledge and the eventual introduction of new technologies are supported by the actual availability of 'cheap' external knowledge to be used as an essential and indispensable production factor (Antonelli, 2008b).

In the knowledge generation function, internal knowledge obtained by means of research and development (R&D) activities and the valorization of learning processes is an essential input. Next to it, however, external knowledge is also indispensable, for nobody can command all the knowledge available at any point in time. External knowledge has been generated in previous periods and/or is currently used by other firms. In the recombinant generation of new technological knowledge, internal and external knowledge are complementary inputs that have to be combined in order to produce new technological knowledge (Nelson, 1982; Weitzman, 1996, 1998).

In our case, the generation function and the cost equation of technological knowledge of each firm can be written as follows:

$$T = (IK^a \, EK^b) \text{ with } a + b = 1 \qquad (9.1)$$

$$C = pIK + uEK \qquad (9.2)$$

where T represents new technological knowledge generated with constant returns to scale by means of internal knowledge (IK) and external knowledge (EK). Here p and u represent their respective unit costs. The unit cost of internal knowledge consists in the market price of the resources – primarily skilled labour – that are necessary to perform R&D and to valorize and maintain the internal stock of tacit knowledge and competence accumulated by means of learning processes. The unit governance costs of external knowledge include the costs of knowledge communication as well as knowledge networking, and consist in the resources needed to screen, identify, understand, purchase, learn and use knowledge generated, possessed and used by other agents in the system.

Pecuniary knowledge externalities are found where and when the governance costs of external knowledge (u) are below general equilibrium levels (u*). The latter would hold if and when knowledge were a standard economic good such that its equilibrium cost is found where its marginal and average costs meet its marginal product. According to the localized equilibrium condition:

$$a/b \, IK/EK = u/p \qquad (9.3)$$

If the governance cost of external knowledge (u*) is found where its marginal cost equals its marginal product, the optimal left-hand side ratio between internal and external knowledge would be equal to IK/EK*. When the actual cost of external knowledge is u < u*, then the right-hand side of equation (9.3) would diminish; and, in order to attain an optimum allocation, the left-hand side of the equation also has to be lower. This implies a relatively higher application of external knowledge. In other words, in the context of the opportunity cost described, pecuniary knowledge externalities apply, and the firm maximizing in a localized context will be using a mix characterized by more external than internal knowledge – that is, IK/EK < IK/EK*. Moreover, and most importantly, the amount of knowledge generated (T) will be greater than the equilibrium level (T*). The firm will produce more and cheaper technological knowledge than in a system where external knowledge has higher – equilibrium – costs.

Following Griliches (1979), technological knowledge enters directly the standard Cobb–Douglas production function of all the other goods with constant returns to scale of each firm. Hence:

$$Y = A \ (I^g \ T^d) \text{ with } g + d = 1 \tag{9.4}$$

$$C = cI + sT \tag{9.5}$$

where, for the sake of simplicity, I is a bundle of tangible inputs, c are their costs, T is technological knowledge, s its cost and A measures the total factor productivity level. According to the equilibrium condition:

$$g/d \ I/T = s/c \tag{9.6}$$

firms that can benefit from positive pecuniary knowledge externalities in access to external knowledge – and hence take advantage of the upstream localized generation of larger amounts of 'cheaper' technological knowledge with costs below equilibrium level (s < s*) – will use a technique characterized by higher level of T. Most importantly, they will also produce an output Y that is larger and cheaper than in general equilibrium conditions.

Following Abramovitz (1956), we know that total factor productivity is measured by the ratio between the real historic levels of output Y and the theoretical ones calculated as the equilibrium use of production factors:

$$A = Y/I^* \ T^* \tag{9.7}$$

Where I* and T* are the general equilibrium quantities of production factors, and A measures total factor productivity.

The case for the increase of total factor productivity takes place when access to technological knowledge as an input in the generation of new technological knowledge is affected by localized out-of-equilibrium conditions and is cheaper than in general equilibrium conditions. Hence the output of all the other goods produced downstream in localized equilibrium conditions characterized by pecuniary knowledge externalities will be larger than in general equilibrium conditions.

The results can be summarized as follows: firms produce more than expected, and hence experience a 'unexplained' residual in the actual levels of output that is larger than expected $(Y > Y^*)$, if and when:

- The localized governance costs of external knowledge in the upstream knowledge generation function are lower than in general equilibrium $(u < u^*)$.
- The localized output in terms of technological knowledge is larger than in general equilibrium conditions – i.e. the actual levels of T (T') are larger than the general equilibrium levels (T^*) $(T' > T^*)$.
- The costs of the localized technological knowledge that enters the Cobb–Douglas production function for all the other goods are also lower $(s < s^*)$.

These elementary passages enable us to support the basic proposition that total factor productivity levels (and their increase) depend upon the levels (and the rates of increase) of the discrepancy between the general equilibrium costs of external knowledge and the actual localized ones. Hence we can put forward the basic proposition that total factor productivity levels stem from pecuniary knowledge externalities:

$$A = f\ (T'/T^*) \tag{9.8}$$

$$T'/T^* = g\ (u/u^*) \tag{9.9}$$

$$A = h\ (g(u/u^*)) \tag{9.10}$$

Total factor productivity levels can be explained by the excess amount of output and technological knowledge determined by the localized governance costs of external knowledge that are below general equilibrium levels because of positive pecuniary knowledge externalities.

In such conditions, qualified by pecuniary knowledge externalities, each firm operates in localized (and transient) equilibrium conditions, but the aggregate output of the system is larger than expected in general equilibrium conditions. The working of pecuniary knowledge externalities is compatible with short-term, Marshallian, instantaneous equilibrium conditions at the firm level, while at the aggregate level the system is far from equilibrium.

From a dynamic viewpoint, total factor productivity growth can take place through time, that is:

$$dA/dt > 0 \qquad (9.11)$$

if, where and when

$$d\,(u^* - u)/dt = 0 \text{ or} > 0 \qquad (9.12)$$

The crucial distinction introduced by Schumpeter (1947a) between passive adaptation and creative reaction plays a central role at this point in the analysis to grasp the dynamics of the system and its effects, according to its localized conditions. Firms facing changes in their product and factor markets try to react with the generation of new technological knowledge. Their reaction will be creative if pecuniary knowledge externalities qualify the access conditions to external knowledge. In this case firms will be able to generate new technological knowledge at costs that are below equilibrium levels. The generation of technological knowledge will take place in conditions that make possible the introduction of productivity-enhancing innovations. The introduction of innovations will affect further the out-of-equilibrium conditions of the system and induce new firms to try to react in turn. A sustained dynamics of out-of-equilibrium growth is put in place; and it will continue as long as the system is able to provide its members with access to external knowledge at costs that are below equilibrium levels.

As long as there are pecuniary knowledge externalities and the local costs for external knowledge remain below general equilibrium levels, the typical complex system dynamics stemming from the positive feedback generated by knowledge cumulability and knowledge complementarity, implemented by good knowledge governance mechanisms and the convergence of knowledge generation activities, are at work. This outcome meets the basic expectations of the Schumpeterian tradition: 'Surplus values may be impossible in perfect equilibrium, but can be ever present because that equilibrium is never allowed to establish itself' (Schumpeter, 1942: 28).[2]

When the knowledge governance mechanisms are no longer suited to organizing access to the stock of technological knowledge available in the system, pecuniary knowledge externalities decline, and with them the opportunities to sustain the introduction of technological innovations, the increase in total factor productivity and hence the scope for dynamic increasing returns.

When the generation of technological knowledge cannot benefit from the availability of pecuniary knowledge externalities, the reaction of firms will be 'adaptive' as opposed to 'creative'. In these conditions firms can just introduce technical change as distinct from technological change, and will yield equilibrium levels of output. Firms will be able to move in the existing map of isoquants and the existing map of techniques, and no increase in the levels of total factor productivity can be detected. The equilibrium conditions of the system are not perturbed.

The essential argument elaborated so far is that productivity growth is a complex process that takes place in a heterogeneous environment. Technological innovation, which is the key to productivity growth, occurs as a result of a reaction to unexpected events that take place with costs of innovation being lower at particular points in time and space than the equilibrium level of those costs. Technological innovation occurs as a result of taking external knowledge (through screening, identification, understanding, purchasing and using) and recombining it with the use of internal knowledge. It is actually introduced by firms that, caught in out-of-equilibrium conditions, try to react to unexpected changes in their product and/or factor markets and can take advantage of pecuniary knowledge externalities that make it possible to access external knowledge at a cost that is below equilibrium levels ($u > u^*$).

9.3   IMPLICATIONS

This chapter takes issue with the idea, at the heart of the first generations of the new growth theory, that innovation is a homogeneous, inexorable process that depends only on the supply of knowledge and not its cost or process of production. It suggests that a new generation of endogenous growth theory can be elaborated building upon the view that innovation takes place as a form of creative reaction supported and actually made possible by the actual availability of internal and external knowledge, as determined by the knowledge governance mechanisms that cope with the structural conditions of the system.

In our approach firms are induced to try to generate new technological knowledge, so as to introduce innovations, when unexpected changes in both product and factor markets push them out of equilibrium. The recombinant generation of new technological knowledge is activated. Its outcome is crucially affected by the localized conditions of availability of external technological knowledge that has been already generated and used by third parties and yet, because of knowledge limited appropriability, can be accessed by third parties as external knowledge and, because of indivisibility and non-exhaustibility, can be used again.

At each point in time the system is endowed with a heterogeneous stock of technological knowledge possessed by a myriad of agents and embodied in a great variety of applications and uses with varying levels of actual connectivity. The generation of technological knowledge consists in the recombination of the existing bits of the heterogeneous stock of technological knowledge. Because of its intrinsic diversity, fragmentation and dispersion, much necessary technological knowledge is external to each agent. External knowledge is an essential input in the recombinant generation of new technological knowledge. Knowledge governance mechanisms enable the recollection of existing technological knowledge and enable firms to use it again. The governance of localized technological knowledge helps strengthen the knowledge connectivity of the system.

When knowledge governance is effective and enables the identification and actual use of external knowledge, at costs that are below equilibrium levels, the output of the recombinant generation of technological knowledge and of the downstream production of other goods increases beyond equilibrium levels. The localized generation of technological knowledge can take place at costs that are below general equilibrium levels. In these circumstances firms are successful in their attempt to cope with unexpected changes in their product and factor markets by means of the introduction of productivity-enhancing innovations. Localized access to external knowledge at out-of-equilibrium costs is the key to sustaining the introduction of productivity-enhancing technological innovations, as it can account for the empirical evidence of the increase in general efficiency of the production level beyond the levels of output expected in general equilibrium conditions.

The search for external knowledge, however, is a contingent process that takes place only when firms are in out-of-equilibrium conditions. The introduction of new technologies perturbs the system, engenders new out-of-equilibrium conditions and pushes new firms to try to react by means of the generation of additional technological knowledge. If the system provides access to pecuniary knowledge externalities, the process can keep going, sustained by the open-ended loop of positive feedback. In contrast, the reaction of firms caught in out-of-equilibrium conditions that try to react by changing the characteristics of their production processes or of their products without the support of pecuniary knowledge externalities will be merely adaptive, enabling the firms' mobility in the existing map of isoquants, feeding substitution processes and the introduction of novelties in product markets that, nevertheless, cannot increase their total factor productivity. In these circumstances firms can only adapt to the changing conditions of their product and factor markets by means of technical change – as opposed to technological change – with no increase in the levels of total factor productivity: general equilibrium conditions are restored.

Here the conditions of the systemic conditions of regions, in terms of knowledge governance mechanisms at work, affect the cost equation of the generation of new technological knowledge of each firm. Pecuniary knowledge externalities are found when and where external knowledge can be identified, retrieved and used at low costs. Only when pecuniary knowledge externalities are found can firms introduce technological innovations that can actually improve the general efficiency of the production process. By the same token, high levels of total factor productivity signal the positive effects of pecuniary knowledge externalities, and an increase in the levels of total factor productivity signals an increase in the levels of pecuniary knowledge externalities.

The access conditions to external knowledge, at costs that are below equilibrium levels, are not given or exogenous at the system level. They vary across historic times, regions, industries and countries. The levels of knowledge connectivity and the quality of knowledge governance mechanisms are endogenous to the system and strongly characterized by path dependence, as they are the result of the stratification and accumulation of firms' actions at each point in time, and their effects on both the composition of the system's knowledge structure and the viability of the knowledge governance mechanisms.

Dynamic increasing returns can take place if and when firms' attempts to try to generate new technological knowledge and introduce technological innovations – to cope with unexpected events and made possible by pecuniary knowledge externalities – are able to sustain over time appropriate levels of knowledge connectivity at the system level in terms of composition of the knowledge structure and quality of knowledge governance mechanisms.

This approach confirms that externalities are the basic component of the toolbox of economics that enables us to grasp the role of interactions between individual decision making and the properties of the system in which agents are placed. Analysis of knowledge as an endogenous endowment that has an intrinsic system character paves the way to understanding innovation as an emergent system property.

NOTES

1. The model by Romer (1990) assumes that the stock of knowledge, available to all agents, increases freely and automatically at a rate λ and does not investigates the costs of its accumulation and its possible variance. The notion of pecuniary knowledge externalities is meant to provide the analytical framework to investigate the determinants of λ.
2. I owe this quote to one of the anonymous referees.

10. A new framework of innovation and knowledge policy

The Arrovian framework has provided the foundations for the economics and policy of knowledge practised for almost half a century. The failure of the markets for knowledge leads to the undersupply of knowledge. Public interventions are necessary to remedy market failure. This approach has been implemented with four basic tools:

- public subsidies for R&D expenditures incurred by private firms to reduce the costs and related risks of firms so as to favour a downward shift in the knowledge supply curve (Hall and Van Reenen, 2000; David et al., 2000; Hall and Mairesse, 2006);
- the public supply of knowledge by means of a public research infrastructure so as to provide free access to basic knowledge and, again, reduce the final costs of knowledge and augment the downward shift in the knowledge supply curve;
- the public procurement of knowledge-intensive goods so as to reduce the risks of limited appropriability and favour the upward shift in the derived demand for knowledge (Edquist et al., 2015);
- the establishment of intellectual property (IP) rights protection to increase knowledge appropriability and, again, reduce the risks of limited appropriability and favour the downward shift in the supply of knowledge (Antonelli, 2013).

This chapter integrates recent advances in the economics of knowledge concerning its properties – ranging from the limited (transient) appropriability of knowledge to its indivisibility and non-exhaustibility – in order to analyse the full range of effects by applying the new tools of the economics of knowledge, the knowledge generation function combined with the technology-production function. It has applied this analytical framework to understand the effects on the technological knowledge markets of both a reduction in the derived demand of knowledge as an input in the technology production function and a reduction in the cost of technological knowledge in the knowledge generation function. It has identified a reduction in the price of knowledge as a key issue. A reduction in the price of knowledge has two consequences: i) positive effects on the supply of lower-quality knowledge; ii) negative effects on the supply of high-quality knowledge.

The implications of the analysis carried out so far are very important. Too much attention has been paid to the presumed generic undersupply of knowledge stemming from knowledge market failure. Too much effort has also been made to compensate for the presumed generic undersupply, with public interventions aimed at increasing all kinds of research efforts with the provision of indiscriminate subsidies to firms performing any kind of R&D and, most importantly, the direct supply of scientific and technological knowledge with the creation of a large public research system, including the academic system, deprived of any strategy. This generic approach applies only when the positive effects of knowledge externalities on the costs of external knowledge cannot compensate for the negative effects of transient appropriability on its use as an input in the production of all other goods.

Public policy should focus on two key issues: i) the laws of accumulation of the stock of public knowledge; ii) the selective exclusion of high-quality, large-scale research projects. Let us consider them in turn.

A reduction in the cost of technological knowledge stems from effective accumulation of the stock of public knowledge. The accumulation of an effective stock of public knowledge is not obvious and automatic. Knowledge items can remain dispersed and fragmentary across the system, engendering large screening and absorption costs. The levels of knowledge connectivity of the system play a major role in enforcing the accumulation of a well-structured and effective stock of public knowledge. The higher the levels of diachronic and pecuniary knowledge externalities, the greater the chance of generating new knowledge items; and hence, with given research costs, the lower the unit costs of new technological knowledge and the larger the actual amount of knowledge generated.

In a system characterized by high levels of knowledge connectivity and high levels of knowledge governance, there is little risk of generic knowledge market failures and systematic undersupply of the quantity of knowledge, as predicted by the Arrovian approach. The institutional characteristics of the system that are able to support the creative reaction of firms play a crucial role in this context since they affect the user costs of the stock of public knowledge.

The reduction in exclusivity of intellectual property rights and, more specifically, the extension of the trademark regime to patents with the implementation of compulsory licensing with royalties can play a major role in increasing the effective accumulation of the stock of public knowledge and favouring actual access to the existing stock of knowledge without harming the role of patents as an indispensable factor in the dissemination of information on existing knowledge (Antonelli, 2007, 2013).

An economic system that is able more easily to increase and make repeated use of technological knowledge to generate new technological knowledge, as well as all the other goods with governance mechanisms such as open innovation systems – for example Free/Libre and Open Source Software (FLOSS) – is likely to increase the positive effects of knowledge complementarity on the costs of knowledge as an input.

For this reason, public interventions should be directed towards improving the dissemination of existing technological knowledge by favouring interactions between knowledge users and producers and the mobility of creative workers. Interactions between the public research system, with special attention paid to the academic system, and firms should be the object of dedicated interventions. By the same token, user–producer interactions among firms should also be enhanced. The mobility of skilled personnel, with a focus on inventors, among firms and between firms and the public research systems should be supported by dedicated policy interventions. Although knowledge externalities have a strong local character, international flows of technological knowledge can be strengthened with public actions that link the imports of knowledge-intensive products to enhanced user–producer interactions with a strong local content (Montobbio and Kataishi, 2015).

The reduction in the price knowledge as determined by a downward shift in the derived demand of knowledge is likely to have serious, negative consequences in terms of excess selection of research projects and exclusion of large-scale and high-quality research undertakings, and hence selective undersupply of high-quality knowledge. Selective public policies finalized and specifically designed to increase the demand for large-scale and high-quality research projects seem necessary. The major risk of market failure stems from a selective exclusion of high-quality and large-scale research projects engendered by a downward shift in the derived demand of knowledge.

According to the results of the analysis carried out in this chapter, the second goal of public policy should consist in finding a solution to the selective undersupply of high-quality research projects. This goal can be achieved by means of selective and targeted knowledge policies specifically designed to support the generation of high-quality, large-scale research projects that are most likely to yield the introduction of radical innovations. Competent public procurement and strategic supply of basic knowledge by the public research infrastructure may help reduce the selective undersupply of high-quality knowledge.

The analysis carried out in this chapter yields two results:

- The negative effects of the limited appropriability of knowledge may be compensated by its positive effects on the supply of knowledge.
- The depreciation of knowledge stemming from the downward shift in the derived demand is a cause of major concern in terms of selective undersupply.

Identification of the fall in price of knowledge because of its Arrovian properties and its twin effects – positive if they stem from the shift in supply of knowledge and negative if they stem from the shift in demand of knowledge – seems an important result not only from the viewpoint of the economics of knowledge but also for its implications for knowledge policies. The positive effects stemming from the downward shift in the supply of knowledge call for an active policy that helps increase further the downward shift in the supply of knowledge. The negative consequences of knowledge depreciation in terms of excess selection of research projects may be quite important. High-quality projects, likely to involve major undertakings with high yields but also high risk, need to be sorted out (Arrow and Lind, 1970). The case of selective undersupply – as opposed to generic undersupply – should be taken into account. Targeted public policies aimed at contrasting selective undersupply are necessary. Substantial efforts are needed to complement and integrate support for the generation of knowledge by means of the public provision of knowledge (David et al., 2000) and subsidies for private R&D, with interventions able to shift actual derived demand for knowledge D_3 closer and closer to the benchmark position D_1 – that is, the position of the derived demand for knowledge if it were a standard economic good and even beyond. See also the systematic literature reviews by Hall and Van Reenen (2000) and Ientile and Mairesse (2009).

Public policies aimed at supporting the supply of knowledge in the system via the direct production of new knowledge by the public research infrastructure and the provision of public subsidies to firms that undertake R&D activities are most likely to reinforce the mechanisms that lead to the downward shift in the supply of knowledge, with all its positive effects. As such, they must be implemented. It should be clear, however, that supply policies cannot limit the negative effects of the depreciation of knowledge. Supply policies can help increase small-scale, low-productivity projects that are more likely to favour the introduction of incremental innovation. Supply policies cannot prevent the adverse selection engendered by the downward shift in derived demand.

Public policy should focus the negative effects on the system of knowledge depreciation that stems from the downward shift in the derived demand of knowledge. This downward shift, with the consequent depreciation of knowledge, leads in fact to the excess and adverse selection of knowledge generating projects, reducing the opportunity to take advantage of types of knowledge that can yield a large marginal output. Specifically, the downward shift in demand of knowledge risks excluding large-scale and high-quality research projects that are more likely to make the introduction of radical innovations possible. The occurrence of under-supply does not apply to the full range of research projects, but specifically only to high-yield ones. In fact, it takes place not because of the effects of the economic properties of knowledge on its supply, but because of the downward shift in derived demand for knowledge. As such, knowledge depreciation stemming from the downward shift in demand engenders an adverse selection that must be contrasted by an effective and dedicated knowledge policy. The case for selective undersupply, as opposed to the Arrovian generic undersupply, applies. As Arocena and Sutz (2010) note, the risk of under-demand and consequent excess selection and selective undersupply of knowledge is especially strong in developing countries.

The shift in the demand curve can be contrasted by targeted public policies that take into account the specific market failure determined by selective undersupply. This amounts to reconsidering the foundations of the demand-pull hypothesis. The large body of literature on demand pull makes it possible to identify three distinct components:

1. the sheer size effect: the larger the demand for a good, the greater the incentives and efforts of firms to invest in R&D in order to generate new knowledge. This effect would take place even if knowledge could be fully appropriated;
2. the user–producer interactions: greater demand from competent users should be able to support the efforts of upstream producers. This in turn requires that procurement is qualified and competent (Antonelli and Gehringer, 2015a);
3. the price effect: demand that is able to pay fair prices – that is, prices that are close to the benchmark costs of the new products, including R&D, can support effectively R&D expenses as firms can cope with lower risks of (poor) appropriability.

Support for the demand for high-quality and large-scale research projects can be implemented by means of both direct and indirect public interventions. Direct interventions consist in the demand of knowledge-intensive products by public administrations, for example states purchasing a wide range of goods direct from the private sector, from weapons to health-related products. Direct interventions can affect not only the size of demand and the quality of user–producer interactions, but also (and primarily) the price of knowledge-intensive products, and hence contribute directly to shifting D_3 closer and closer to the benchmark D_1.

Analysis of public procurement has highlighted the positive effects of the prices paid by specialized and competent public customers on the derived demand for R&D projects that focus on high-quality and large-scale projects. The rightward shift in demand for knowledge can take place when a reliable public demand for knowledge-intensive goods is implemented (Edquist et al., 2015). Dedicated procurement in weapons typically seems able to provide suppliers with a reliable price that includes the full appropriation of the resources invested in the use of knowledge as an input of their technology production function. The closer the price of goods in downstream markets to the benchmark, the higher the levels of derived demand for knowledge – hence the closer is D_3 to D_1. It seems important to try to apply this positive experience to other types of goods (Eliasson, 2010; Mowery, 2012).

Appreciation of the price effect has important implications for the selection procedures of public procurement. Beauty contests seem more appropriate than rebate auctions. The implementation of beauty contests, however, implies competent customers.

Indirect interventions consist in stimulating demand for knowledge by supporting the demand of downstream customers for knowledge-intensive products. Their implementation can take place by means of subsidies to dedicated knowledge-intensive products as well as by strategic standards able to direct demand towards innovative products. The effects on the size of the derived demand and the intensity of user–producer interactions are likely to be strong, but the effects on the price of the knowledge are weaker.

Public subsidies can support the purchase of knowledge embodied in intangible knowledge-intensive services by downstream firms. Indirect interventions to increase demand for knowledge might include specific subsidies for the purchase of patents, the payment of royalties and the outsourcing of research activities to the public research system (Guerzoni and Raiteri, 2015).

As Table 10.1 shows, support for the demand of knowledge as an input in the technology production function by downstream firms has a wide range of possible interventions, ranging from direct public procurement to indirect subsidies for the purchase of knowledge embodied in services and of disembodied knowledge. The distinction between size, knowledge interaction and price effect is useful to focus an effective demand side knowledge policy. Its implementation is successful as far as it is able to engender the shift of D_3 closer and closer to the benchmark D_1, pushing both knowledge quantity and price towards benchmark levels so as to mitigate knowledge 'under-demand'.

Table 10.1   Demand-side public interventions

	Size effect	Knowledge user–producer interactions	Price effect
Direct	Advanced public procurement	Competent public procurement	Public procurement with 'fair' prices
Indirect	Subsidies for the demand for knowledge-intensive goods	Subsidies for the purchase of knowledge-intensive business services (KIBS)	Subsidies for the purchase of KIBS
	Strategic standards	Subsidies for the purchase of patents and research contracts	Subsidies for the purchase of patents and research contracts

Analysis of the consequences of the actual position of the derived demand curve of knowledge with its specific and actual properties, as compared to the derived demand of a standard good, confirms not only that it exerts major effects on the actual working of the markets for knowledge. It also, and primarily, confirms that it is a necessary component of the array of interventions that may make it possible to remedy Arrovian market failure.

The framework elaborated in this chapter enables us to focus the effects of knowledge spillovers, empowered by the introduction of ICT, on the reduction of knowledge absorption cost and of knowledge costs and regard it as a major goal of a new alternative knowledge policy. This new analytical framework provides the foundations of a new augmented agenda for a telecommunications policy aimed at increasing the knowledge connectivity of the system, and hence the effects of spillovers on the reduction of knowledge costs. Dedicated interventions should be implemented in order to increase the reduction of knowledge absorption costs and the costs of knowledge as an output stemming from the use of external knowledge – spilling from 'inventors' – as key complementary inputs in the generation of new knowledge.

The effects of knowledge spillovers on the reduction of knowledge costs are limited by the costs of the activities that are necessary to absorb knowledge that is not appropriated by inventors.

The quality and coverage of the digital infrastructure has direct and powerful effects on the levels of knowledge connectivity of the system that favour the effective use of knowledge spillovers and empowers knowledge interactions. The digital divide has strong negative effects as it limits the connectivity of the system. It excludes a part of the system from the low-cost access to the stock of external knowledge. It engenders the loss of the increasing returns stemming from network externalities. Network externalities exert, in fact, their powerful effects also in access to the stock of knowledge. Network productivity increases at a more than proportionate rate, as the inclusion of each additional agent in the digital network has the twin effect of increasing access to the general stock of knowledge and its actual size. The working of network externalities finds a new powerful dimension of application and understanding.

The layer methodology articulated by Martin Fransman (2002) to study the evolution of ICT systems contributes to the understanding of the evolution of the knowledge generation process. The quality of the digital infrastructure, in fact, enables us to add a new layer to the generation of technological knowledge: the systematic access and valorization of the stock of external knowledge available in the system as a source of knowledge items that can enter the knowledge generation process.

The quality of the telecommunications infrastructure and of communications regulation, as measured by capillarity and inclusivity, becomes a crucial factor to increasing the knowledge connectivity of a system, and hence its rate of generation of new knowledge and introduction of innovations. The inclusive coverage of the digital infrastructure is a basic tool for a research policy aimed at increasing the knowledge connectivity of the system, and consequently the size and variety of the stock of knowledge that firms can access and use to generate additional knowledge at low absorption costs (Fransman, 2006).

Economic systems endowed with high-quality telecommunications networks are likely to support faster generation of technological and scientific knowledge, and hence faster increase in total factor productivity. The architecture and regulation of the Internet play major roles in this context. Limitations to and deviations from end-to-end arguments may affect the use of the Internet as a radical innovation in accessing and using the stock of existing knowledge to generate new knowledge (Bauer, 2014).

Net neutrality is likely to play an important role in this context. The set of rules that defines the interactions between Internet service providers (ISPs), content providers and customers can affect in depth the working of the digital generation of knowledge and the expected fall in the costs of accessing and using the stock of quasi-public external knowledge. Following Greenstein et al. (2016), the enforcement of net neutrality seems important to prohibit both one-sided pricing practices – that is, payments from content providers to (ISPs) – and prioritization of traffic with or without compensation. In both cases in fact access to the stock of quasi-public knowledge upon which the digital generation of knowledge rests risks suffering the consequences of discrimination and segmentation, with the consequent increase in knowledge absorption costs.

Support for the introduction of mobile broadband and for the adoption of mobile phones that provide high-speed Internet services seems to provide major opportunities for the diffusion of a new generation of digital modes of knowledge generation based on the IoT, big data and cloud computing. These are most likely to further enhance access to the stock of quasi-public knowledge so as to further reduce the costs of external knowledge and consequently the costs of new knowledge at large, increasing the extent to which the positive effects of knowledge spillovers are expected to overcome the negative effects of the limited appropriability of knowledge. Mobile broadband seems most important to reduce the digital divide that limits the diffusion of the digital generation of knowledge, excluding rural areas and small firms from its beneficial applications (Briglauer et al., 2013; Kongaut and Bohlin, 2016).

A good telecommunications policy aimed at reducing the digital divide and protecting the openness and neutrality of the Internet becomes a key (but not exclusive) component of a new research agenda aimed at increasing knowledge connectivity. Knowledge connectivity can be increased, favouring the knowledge interactions that occur in the system. Knowledge interactions may be enhanced in several ways:

- Non-exclusive intellectual property rights. The remuneration of IP rights is necessary to increase incentives to the generation of knowledge. At the same time it becomes more and more evident that patents block sequential innovation and reduce the rate of technological change (Galasso and Schankerman, 2015). Non-exclusive IP rights built upon fair levels of royalties associated with the non-discriminatory use of proprietary knowledge can increase the use of existing knowledge to generate new knowledge (Antonelli, 2015).
- Support for the mobility of scientists and inventors within, among and between firms and public research institutions. Tacit knowledge is embedded in human beings. Their mobility is the most effective means to favour the repeated use of existing knowledge, and hence the effective use of knowledge spillovers to generate new technological knowledge (Moen, 2005; Song et al., 2003).
- Knowledge outsourcing. The increasing reliance of firms on knowledge outsourcing is worth public support as it is likely to favour the repeated use of existing knowledge as an input in the generation of new knowledge (Shearmur and Doloreux, 2013; Chesbrough, 2003; Chesbrough et al., 2006). The provision of subsidies to purchase knowledge rather than generate it might have positive effects in terms of increased division of knowledge labour and less duplication and repetition. These positive effects would be especially strong

when the subsidies focus on knowledge transactions between universities and industry. The specialization of public research institutions and KIBS in research funded and purchased by firms specializing in recombination to generate new knowledge can help increase the rates of accumulation of the stock of quasi-public knowledge (Arora et al., 2001).

● Knowledge alliances. The creation of alliances between and among firms and public research institutions dedicated to the generation of knowledge, rather than its exploitation, can augment system connectivity and hence favour the use of existing knowledge in a larger variety of applications (Link and Antonelli, 2016).

The quality of the telecommunications infrastructure and of the regulatory framework of a country/region becomes an important factor in assessing the division of labour in the globalizing digital generation of knowledge. The better the telecommunications infrastructure and regulation, the higher the chances of: i) attracting global offshoring through localization of knowledge-intensive activities; ii) favouring the global reach of knowledge outsourcing for domestic firms; iii) favouring the participation of domestic research centres to the global knowledge markets. Finally, the quality of a country's telecommunications infrastructure and regulation are key to securing the localization of headquarters and central R&D laboratories of global corporations.

PART III

Endogenous Knowledge and Technological Congruence

11. Technological congruence and the economic complexity of technological change

Technological congruence is an important factor in economic growth both at the firm and the aggregate level. Technological congruence is defined by the relationship between the relative size of outputs' elasticity and the relative abundance and price of production factors. The study of technological congruence is likely to provide a major analytical platform that enables us to appreciate the implications of heterogeneity and variety at the microeconomic level for understanding the determinants of both the direction and the rate of technological change and their effects on the dynamics of output and structural change at the system level.

Technological congruence is a fundamental tool for understanding the economic complexity of technological change as it enables us to appreciate the necessary interplay between the characteristics of the technology and the properties of the system both in assessing the effects of technological change and its determinants. Analysis of technological congruence shows, in fact, that the economic effects of each technology depend crucially upon the characteristics of the system into which it is introduced. By the same token, the properties of the system, in terms of factor endowment, play a crucial role in understanding the direction of technological change (Antonelli, 2011).

Technological congruence has been little studied so far. Yet it is clear that output levels are strongly influenced by levels of technological congruence. Output will be larger when the production process technology enables us to use more intensively the production factors that are locally more abundant, and hence cheaper. The factor intensity of the production process, in fact, is determined not only by the relative costs of inputs but also by the relative size of the output elasticity of each production factor. The distribution of output elasticity among inputs and the relative size of the output elasticity of each input, in turn, are key features of the economic representation of a technology (Antonelli, 2003, 2012).

Technological congruence will be larger the larger is the relative output elasticity of the least expensive in local factor markets. For a given budget, the output of a firm will be larger the larger is the output elasticity of the production factor that is locally cheaper. At the system level it is clear that the output will be larger the larger the output elasticity of the production factors that are locally more abundant and hence cheaper.

The notion of technological congruence has received, so far, little attention. Analysis of its determinants and effects has been quite poor, with a scant appreciation of its relevance. Identification of its implications, however, is attracting growing attention (Zuleta, 2012). This substantial neglect can be considered a direct consequence of the widespread consensus on three strong economic assumptions: i) the stability and homogeneity of outputs elasticity; ii) the static and exogenous character of factor endowments; iii) the neutrality of technological change. Whereas major developments have been made to reconcile the last point, there is still a tendency to adopt the first two.

Recent developments in the economics of growth have drawn attention to the problem. The empirical evidence shows that output elasticity of inputs is far from stable at the aggregate level as it varies considerably across time and countries, as well as at the disaggregate level across firms, regions and industries (Krueger, 1999; Hall and Jones, 1999; Caselli and Coleman, 2006; Caselli and Feyer, 2004). The endowment of both tangible and especially intangible inputs can no longer be regarded as an exogenous and static character of economic systems. The relative abundance of many if not all production factors at each point in time can be considered the direct consequence of ongoing economic activities (Growiec, 2012). Technological change can no longer be regarded as an exogenous process as it is widely recognized that economic forces play a central role in determining its characteristics, including its direction, which is far from neutral (Acemoglu, 2003). The contributions that have now explored the role of economic factors in shaping the direction of technological changes have identified the effects of the relationship between levels of output elasticity of production factors and their costs on output levels, introducing the notion of 'factor-saving or factor-eliminating innovations' but not providing formal analyses (Sturgill, 2012; Zuleta, 2008).

With proper analytical foundations, the notion of technological congruence can acquire a much stronger role in economics. In the rest of the chapter section 11.2 provides an analytical demonstration of technological congruence and section 11.3 shows its effects on total factor productivity. Section 11.4 investigates the evolutionary complexity of the dynamics of technological congruence. Section 11.5 outlines its implications for both economic analysis and policy. The conclusions summarize the results of the analysis.

11.1   THE EXISTENCE OF TECHNOLOGICAL CONGRUENCE

The standard Cobb–Douglas production function seems a suitable and effective starting point. This specification, in fact, accommodates explicitly, with α and β the output elasticity of the production factors and enables us to analyse the effects of their changes. The standard Cobb–Douglas function takes the following format:

$$Y(t) = K^\alpha L^\beta \tag{11.1}$$

where K denotes the amount of capital and L the amount of labour. The cost equation is:

$$C = rK + wL \tag{11.2}$$

Firms select the traditional equilibrium mix of inputs according to the slope of the isocosts given by the ratio of labour costs (w) and capital rental costs (r) and the slope of isoquants. The equilibrium condition is:

$$w/r = (\beta/\alpha)(K/L) \tag{11.3}$$

Substitution of the equilibrium condition into the production function, assuming that $\alpha + \beta = 1$, leads to:

$$Y = (w/r)^\alpha (\alpha/\beta)^\alpha L \tag{11.4}$$

At this time we have not (yet) introduced the hypotheses that: i) the firm can change its technology so as to choose the output elasticity of the inputs; and ii) the sheer change of the output elasticity does affect the output. If this were the case it is obvious that the profit-maximizing firm should choose the α which maximizes output. This would amount to assuming that technological change is not neutral and that its direction is influenced by the profit opportunities stemming from relative factor cost. The positive effects of this choice, however, have yet to be demonstrated. This is what we are going to do here. To show the effect of α on the production function let us derive (11.4) with respect to α.

To do this, we exploit the derivation formula $D(f(\alpha)g(\alpha)) = f'(\alpha)g(\alpha) + f(\alpha)g'(\alpha)$, with $f'(\cdot)$ and $g'(\cdot)$ denoting the first derivative of the function, and we adopt the following substitutions: $f(\alpha) = L(w/r)\alpha$ and $g(\alpha) = [\alpha/(1-\alpha)]\alpha$, thus obtaining:

$$\frac{dY(L)}{d\alpha} = L\left(\frac{w}{r}\right)^{\alpha}\left(\ln\frac{w}{r}\right)\left(\frac{\alpha}{1-\alpha}\right)^{\alpha} + L\left(\frac{w}{r}\right)^{\alpha}\frac{d((\alpha/1-\alpha)^{\alpha})}{d\alpha} \tag{11.5}$$

To obtain $d[(\alpha/(1-\alpha))^{\alpha}]/d\alpha$, we apply the differentiation rule $D(f(\alpha)^{g(\alpha)}) = f(\alpha)^{g(\alpha)}[g'(\alpha)\ln f(\alpha) + g(\alpha)f'(\alpha)/f(\alpha)]$ where $f(\alpha) = \alpha\backslash(1-\alpha)$ and $g(\alpha) = \alpha$. We thus obtain:

$$\frac{d((\alpha/1-\alpha)^{\alpha})}{d\alpha} = \left(\frac{\alpha}{1-\alpha}\right)^{\alpha}\left(\ln\frac{\alpha}{1-\alpha} + \alpha\frac{1-\alpha}{\alpha}\frac{1-\alpha+\alpha}{(1-\alpha)^2}\right) \tag{11.6}$$

$$= \left(\frac{\alpha}{1-\alpha}\right)^{\alpha}\left(\ln\frac{\alpha}{1-\alpha} + \frac{1}{1-\alpha}\right)$$

By substituting (6) in (5), we obtain:

$$\frac{dY(L)}{d\alpha} = L\left(\frac{w}{r}\right)^{\alpha}\left(\ln\frac{w}{r}\right)\left(\frac{\alpha}{1-\alpha}\right)^{\alpha} + L\left(\frac{w}{r}\right)^{\alpha}\left(\frac{\alpha}{1-\alpha}\right)^{\alpha}\left(\ln\frac{\alpha}{1-\alpha} + \frac{1}{1-\alpha}\right) =$$

$$= L\left(\frac{w}{r}\right)^{\alpha}\left(\frac{\alpha}{1-\alpha}\right)^{\alpha}\left(\ln\frac{w}{r} + \ln\frac{\alpha}{1-\alpha} + \frac{1}{1-\alpha}\right)$$

$$= L\left(\frac{w}{r}\right)^{\alpha}\left(\frac{\alpha}{1-\alpha}\right)^{\alpha}\left(\ln\frac{w}{r}\frac{\alpha}{1-\alpha} + \frac{1}{1-\alpha}\right) \tag{11.7}$$

Since, by (6), $Y(L) = L (w/r \, \alpha/(1-\alpha))^{\alpha}$, (7) can be reformulated as.

$$\frac{dY(L)}{d\alpha} = Y\left(\frac{1}{1-\alpha} + \ln\frac{w}{r}\frac{\alpha}{1-\alpha}\right) \tag{11.8}$$

Using (3), identity (8) can be rewritten as:

$$\frac{dY(L)}{d\alpha} = Y\left(\frac{1}{1-\alpha} + \ln\frac{K}{L}\right) \tag{11.9}$$

Equation (11.9) confirms that output levels are influenced by the relative size of the output elasticity of the two production factors and by the levels of factor intensity that, according to equation (11.8), are determined by their relative costs. The direction of technological change – that is, changes in the mix of output elasticities of inputs – does affect output levels when the slope of the isocosts differs from 1. Specifically, the effect will be positive when directed technological change makes it possible to increase the output elasticity of the production factor that is relatively more abundant and hence cheaper. The effect will be negative when technological change is directed to increase the production factor that is relatively scarce and hence more expensive. There are no effects of directed technological change when r = w.

Let us now consider a slightly more general case, with three factors: capital (K), labour (L) and intermediate goods (X). Their elasticities to the output are respectively α, β and γ. The level of production Y is given by a Cobb–Douglas function with constant returns to scale:

$$Y = K^\alpha \ L^\beta \ X^\gamma \tag{11.10}$$

where $\alpha + \beta + \gamma = 1$.

The constant returns to scale assumption implies that:

$$d\alpha + d\beta + d\gamma = 0 \tag{11.11}$$

Let us assume the following relationships:[1]

$$\frac{d\beta}{d\alpha} = y_\beta; \tag{11.12}$$

$$\frac{d\gamma}{d\alpha} = y_\gamma \tag{11.13}$$

where either y_β or y_γ is negative.

Substituting (11.12) and (11.13) in (11.11), we obtain that, for any $d\alpha \neq 0$,

$$d\alpha + y_\beta \ d\alpha + y_\gamma \ d\alpha = 0 \Rightarrow d\alpha(1 + y_\beta + y_\gamma) = 0 \Rightarrow 1 + y_\beta + y_\gamma = 0 \tag{11.14}$$

Denoting with r, w and c the price of factors K, L and X and with p the output price, profits π are equal to:

$$\pi = pY - rK - wL - cX \tag{11.15}$$

from which $K = \dfrac{pY - \pi}{r} - \dfrac{w}{r}L - \dfrac{c}{r}X.$

From (11.10), we derive the marginal rate of technical substitution between K and L and X and L:

$$\frac{\partial Y/\partial L}{\partial Y/\partial K} = \frac{\beta K^\alpha L^{\beta-1} X^\gamma}{\alpha K^{\alpha-1} L^\beta X^\gamma} = \frac{\beta}{\alpha}\frac{K}{L} \quad \text{and} \quad \frac{\partial Y/\partial L}{\partial Y/\partial X} = \frac{\beta K^\alpha L^{\beta-1} X^\gamma}{\gamma K^\alpha L^\beta X^{\gamma-1}} = \frac{\beta}{\gamma}\frac{X}{L} \tag{11.16}$$

The equilibrium conditions for the factor pairs K–L and X–L are obtained by imposing (11.16) equal to the ratio of the prices of factors:

$$\frac{\partial Y/\partial L}{\partial Y/\partial K} = \frac{\beta}{\alpha}\frac{K}{L} = \frac{w}{r} \quad \text{and} \quad \frac{\partial Y/\partial L}{\partial Y/\partial X} = \frac{\beta}{\gamma}\frac{X}{L} = \frac{w}{c} \quad (11.17)$$

From (11.17), in equilibrium it must be:

$$K = \frac{w}{r}\frac{\alpha}{\beta}L \quad \text{and} \quad X = \frac{w}{c}\frac{\gamma}{\beta}L \quad (11.18)$$

By substituting (11.18) in (11.10), we obtain:

$$Y(L) = \left(\frac{w}{r}\frac{\alpha}{\beta}L\right)^{\alpha} L^{\beta}\left(\frac{w}{c}\frac{\gamma}{\beta}L\right)^{\gamma} = L\left(\frac{w}{r}\frac{\alpha}{\beta}\right)^{\alpha}\left(\frac{w}{c}\frac{\gamma}{\beta}\right)^{\gamma} \quad (11.19)$$

The following results will be useful to compute the effect of α on Y(L):

$$\frac{d(\alpha/\beta)}{d\alpha} = \frac{\beta z - y_{\beta}\alpha}{\beta^2} \quad (11.20)$$

$$\frac{d(\gamma/\beta)}{d\alpha} = \frac{\gamma_{\beta}\beta - y_{\beta}\gamma}{\beta^2} \quad (11.21)$$

The previous derivatives are obtained using the formula $D(f(\alpha)/g(\alpha)) = [f'(\alpha)g(\alpha) - f(\alpha)g'(\alpha)]/g^2(\alpha)$; for example, in (20), $f(\alpha) = \alpha$, $g(\alpha) = \beta(\alpha)$ and $d\beta(\alpha)/d\alpha = y_{\beta}$ from (12).

We can use (11.20) and (11.21) and the formula $D(f(\alpha)^{g(\alpha)}) = f(\alpha)^{g(\alpha)}[g'(\alpha)\ln f(\alpha) + g(\alpha)f'(\alpha)/f(\alpha)]$ to compute the expressions (11.22) and (11.23); for example, in (11.22), $f(\alpha) = (w\alpha/(r\beta))$ and $g(\alpha) = \alpha$:

$$\frac{d\left[L\left(\frac{w}{r}\frac{\alpha}{\beta}\right)^{\alpha}\right]}{d\alpha} = L\left(\frac{w}{r}\right)^{\alpha}\ln\left(\frac{w}{r}\right)\left(\frac{\alpha}{\beta}\right)^{\alpha} + L\left(\frac{w}{r}\right)^{\alpha}\left(\frac{\alpha}{\beta}\right)^{\alpha}\left[\ln\frac{\alpha}{\beta} + \alpha\frac{\frac{\beta - y_{\beta}\alpha}{\beta^2}}{\frac{\alpha}{\beta}}\right]$$

$$= L\left(\frac{w}{r}\frac{\alpha}{\beta}\right)^{\alpha}\left[\ln\frac{w}{r} + \ln\frac{\alpha}{\beta} + \frac{\beta - y_{\beta}\alpha}{\beta}\right] = L\left(\frac{w}{r}\frac{\alpha}{\beta}\right)^{\alpha}\left[\ln\frac{w}{r}\frac{\alpha}{\beta} + \frac{\beta - y_{\beta}\alpha}{\beta}\right] \quad (11.22)$$

$$\frac{d\left[\left(\frac{w}{c}\frac{\gamma}{\beta}\right)^{\gamma}\right]}{d\alpha} = \left(\frac{w}{c}\right)^{\gamma}y_{\gamma}\left(\ln\frac{w}{c}\right)\left(\frac{\gamma}{\beta}\right)^{\gamma} + \left(\frac{w}{c}\right)^{\gamma}\left(\frac{\gamma}{\beta}\right)^{\gamma}\left[y_{\gamma}\ln\frac{\gamma}{\beta} + \gamma\frac{\frac{y_{\gamma}\beta - y_{\beta}\gamma}{\beta^2}}{\frac{\gamma}{\beta}}\right]$$

$$= \left(\frac{w}{c}\frac{\gamma}{\beta}\right)^{\gamma}\left[y_{\gamma}\ln\left(\frac{w}{c}\frac{\gamma}{\beta}\right)+\frac{y_{\gamma}\beta-y_{\beta}\gamma}{\beta}\right] \tag{11.23}$$

We now differentiate (11.19) with respect to α. As $D(f(\alpha)g(\alpha)) = f'(\alpha)g(\alpha) + f(\alpha)g'(\alpha)$, by adopting $f(\alpha) = L(w\alpha/(r\beta))^{\beta}$ and $g(\alpha) = \{w\gamma/[c\beta(\alpha)]\}^{\gamma}$, and using the expression $f'(\alpha)$ and $g'(\alpha)$ obtained in (11.22) and (11.23), we can write:

$$\frac{dY(L)}{d\alpha} = L\left(\frac{w}{r}\frac{\alpha}{\beta}\right)^{\alpha}\left[\ln\frac{w}{r}\frac{\alpha}{\beta}+\frac{\beta-y_{\beta}\alpha}{\beta}\right]\left(\frac{w}{c}\frac{\gamma}{\beta}\right)^{\gamma}+L\left(\frac{w}{r}\frac{\alpha}{\beta}\right)^{\alpha}\left(\frac{w}{c}\frac{\gamma}{\beta}\right)^{\gamma}$$

$$\left[y_{\gamma}\ln\left(\frac{w}{c}\frac{\gamma}{\beta}\right)+\frac{y_{\gamma}\beta-y_{\beta}\gamma}{\beta}\right]$$

$$= L\left(\frac{w}{r}\frac{\alpha}{\beta}\right)^{\alpha}\left(\frac{w}{c}\frac{\gamma}{\beta}\right)^{\gamma}\left[\ln\left(\frac{w}{r}\frac{\alpha}{\beta}\right)+\frac{\beta-y_{\beta}\alpha}{\beta}+y_{\gamma}\ln\left(\frac{w}{c}\frac{\gamma}{\beta}\right)+\frac{y_{\gamma}\beta-y_{\beta}\gamma}{\beta}\right]$$

$$= L\left(\frac{w}{r}\frac{\alpha}{\beta}\right)^{\alpha}\left(\frac{w}{c}\frac{\gamma}{\beta}\right)^{\gamma}\left[\ln\left(\frac{w}{r}\frac{\alpha}{\beta}\right)+1-y_{\beta}\frac{\alpha}{\beta}+y_{\gamma}\ln\left(\frac{w}{c}\frac{\gamma}{\beta}\right)+y_{\gamma}-y_{\beta}\frac{\gamma}{\beta}\right]$$

$$= Y\left[\ln\left(\frac{w}{r}\frac{\alpha}{\beta}\right)+y_{\gamma}\ln\left(\frac{w}{c}\frac{\gamma}{\beta}\right)+1+y_{\gamma}-y_{\beta}\left(\frac{1-\beta}{\beta}\right)\right] \tag{11.24}$$

Using (11.14) and (11.17), the previous expression can alternatively be expressed as:

$$\frac{dY(L)}{d\alpha} = Y\left[\ln\left(\frac{K}{L}\right)+y_{\gamma}\ln\left(\frac{X}{L}\right)-\frac{y_{\beta}}{\beta}\right] \tag{11.25}$$

Equation (11.25) can be regarded as a generalization of equation (11.9) to n production factors. In equation (11.9) in fact, $y_{\gamma} = 0$ and $y_{\beta} = -1$. Equation (11.25) tells us that the output levels are clearly influenced by the relative size of the production factors. The latter in turn are influenced by their relative costs. Hence we can claim that the output levels are higher the larger the output elasticity of the cheaper input.

Specifically, we see that the effect that a change in α has on output is higher the lower is r with respect to w and the larger is α with respect to β. Moreover, it also depends on how the constant returns assumption affects the variations in elasticities: the effect that a change in α has on output is greater the stronger is the effect of an increase of α on the decrease of the elasticity of labour. Furthermore, the higher is the proportion of intermediate goods used with respect to labour, the stronger is the effect of an increase of α on the increase of the elasticity of intermediate goods.

Equation (11.25) proves the existence of technological congruence in a more general case of a Cobb–Douglas production function with three production factors. It seems clear that the unit of analysis plays a major role in assessing the relationship between inputs and outputs.

11.2   TECHNOLOGICAL CONGRUENCE AND TOTAL FACTOR PRODUCTIVITY GROWTH

Technological congruence has major effects on economic efficiency that can be measured with the appropriate methodology. Standard measures of total factor productivity growth assume that factor shares are constant (Solow, 1957). If factor shares change because of the introduction of new technologies that make possible a more intensive use of locally abundant factors, total factor productivity measures are influenced (Antonelli, 2003; Bailey et al., 2004). In order to appreciate the effects of technological congruence it becomes necessary to distinguish between a shift and a bias effect (Antonelli, 2006). The bias effect consists in the increase of total factor productivity that stems from the better matching between the distribution of output elasticity and the factor markets. The bias effect consists in the consequences of the changes in the slopes of the maps of isoquants. The shift effect consists in the sheer changes in the position of the map of isoquants. A new technology may have positive shift effects and negative bias ones. The actual effect depends on the algebraic relationship between the two effects (Antonelli and Quatraro, 2010; Zuleta, 2012).

Identification of bias effects can be implemented stretching the intuition of Solow (1957) beyond his own implementation. Solow's starting point assumes that the system is in equilibrium at each point in time and that no technological change takes place. The difference between the benchmark – (expected) output levels, calculated in equilibrium conditions with no changes to the technological conditions of the production process – and the actual output levels experienced in historic time will be considered as the result of the introduction of technological innovations.

This chapter follows closely this procedure, but with one major departure. We stretch the benchmark so as to assume that no change in the production function can take place, including all possible changes to the output elasticity of production factors. We replicate the growth accounting procedure assuming that α and β stay put at time t1. This assumption can be implemented keeping constant the levels of α and β but allowing all changes in K and L, as in Antonelli (2003 and 2006). This procedure has a clear limit in that it is not able to appreciate the effects of the introduction of directed technological change with the consequent changing slope of the isoquant, and hence the new equilibrium levels of factor intensity (Feder, 2015).

In order to overcome this limit we can keep constant the levels of α and β and yet sterilize the effects of the changing levels of the output elasticity of inputs on factor intensity.

In order to identify the effects of the changing output elasticity on the choice of equilibrium levels of K/L we proceed as follows. The empirical evidence provides the levels of K/L as well as the share of property in income at each point in time. According to the equilibrium conditions – see equation (11.4) – at time tn the actual historic levels of K/L are jointly determined by the new levels of relative factor costs, $(w/r)_{tn}$, and the new levels of relative output elasticity of production factors, $(\alpha/\beta)_{tn}$:

$$(K/L)_{tn} = (w/r)_{tn} \, (\alpha/\beta)_{tn} \tag{11.26}$$

because both $(K/L)_{tn}$ and $(\alpha/\beta)_{tn}$ are known, it is possible to calculate $(w/r)_{tn}$ as follows:

$$(w/r)_{tn} = (K/L)_{tn}/(\alpha/\beta)_{tn} \tag{11.27}$$

The substitution of $(\alpha/\beta)_{t1}$ in equation (11.26) enables us to identify the theoretical $(K/L)^*$ that should have been chosen in equilibrium conditions if no biased technological change had taken place:

$$(K/L)^* = (w/r)_{tn} \, (\alpha/\beta)_{t1} \tag{11.28}$$

The theoretical $(K/L)^*$ enables us to implement the standard growth accounting under the strict assumption that no kind of technological change has been taking place so as to identify a 'twice theoretical' output. The twice theoretical output differs from the theoretical output calculated by Solow as the former does not take into account the effects of introducing biased technological changes. The theoretical $(K/L)^*$ enables us to sterilize the effects of the introduction of directed technological changes on the equilibrium factor intensity so as to reflect only the effects of the changing relative costs of inputs.[2]

The difference between the twice theoretical equilibrium output calculated with this procedure and the historic output measures the full effects of technological change, including both shift and bias effects. It now becomes apparent that the difference between the theoretical equilibrium calculated with changing levels of output elasticity following the procedure first implemented by Solow and the historic output measures just shift the effects. Solow's procedure measures only a part of the total effects of technological change when it is non-neutral. The difference between the twice theoretical equilibrium level, calculated with the procedure elaborated in this chapter, and the theoretical output calculated following Solow's procedure provides a reliable account of the bias effects.

The following equations should help make the point clear. Solow measures the theoretical output per man-hour $(Y/L)^*$ – that is, equilibrium levels of output per man-hour with no technological change – and calculates the levels of total factor productivity, A_S (the ratio of the theoretical output per man-hour to the historic output per man-hour), $(Y/L)^H$, as follows:

$$(Y/L)^* = (K/L)_{tn}\alpha^{(t1)} \tag{11.29}$$

$$A_S = (Y/L)^H/(Y/L)^* \tag{11.30}$$

Equations (11.29) and (11.30) make clear that Solow's methodology allows change of both the output elasticity of capital and the capital intensity through time. In so doing this methodology allows us to count only the shift effects of the introduction of technological changes; it is not able to measure the bias effects stemming from the introduction of new, non-neutral technologies.

To fully sterilize the effects of the introduction of technological changes, whether neutral or not, it is possible to introduce the twice theoretical output per worker $(Y/L)^{**}$ measured as follows:

$$(Y/L)^{**} = ((K/L)^*)_{tn}\alpha^{(t1)} \tag{11.31}$$

where $(K/L)^*$ is defined by equation (11.28).

The levels of the new total factor productivity that account for the (logarithmic) sum of both shift and bias effects (A_T) are now measured as follows:

$$A_T = (Y/L)^H/(Y/L)^{**} \tag{11.32}$$

The logarithmic effects on total factor productivity of the introduction of directed technological changes, $\log(A_B)$, can be easily calculated as follows:

$$\log(A_B) = \log(A_T) - \log(A_S) \tag{11.33}$$

It is important to note that $\log(A_B)$ can assume both positive and negative values according to the levels of technological congruence. The introduction of radical capital-intensive technologies in a labour-abundant country may have positive shift effects but negative bias ones.

This new set of indicators can be used to identify the (bias) effects of the direction of technological change on total factor productivity growth as distinct from the (shift) effects of technological change. These tools enable us to grasp the endogenous dynamics of technological change.

11.3   THE EVOLUTIONARY COMPLEXITY OF TECHNOLOGICAL CONGRUENCE

The analysis of technological congruence shows that the match between the characteristics of each technology and the properties of the system into which it is being introduced plays a crucial role. The notion of technological congruence shows that the economic effects of each technology depend crucially upon the characteristics of the system into which it is introduced. By the same token, the properties of the system, in terms of factor endowment, play a crucial role in understanding the direction of technological change. Technological congruence is a crucial aspect of the economic complexity of technological change as it shows that there is a dynamic interplay between the characteristics of the technology and the properties of the system, both with respect to the effects of technological change and its determinants (Antonelli, 2011).

The dynamics of technological congruence has the intrinsic characteristics of an emergent system property where the dynamics is determined by the Schumpeterian reactions of agents to the effects of their own prior actions. The dynamics is typically path dependent – as opposed to past dependent – because it is at the same time non-ergodic and non-deterministic as its rate and direction are shaped not only by the initial conditions but also by the contingent events that take place along the process (Antonelli, 2015b).

The interactions between the effects of introducing directed technological change not only on total factor productivity growth but also on the prices of the (cheaper) inputs, and the feedback of its derived demand and supply curve, are the engine of the evolutionary complexity of the dynamics of technological congruence.

So far we have not considered the effects of directed technological change on the relative costs of production factors. At the firm level the introduction of directed technological change is not likely to affect the factor markets. The size of the changes in the derived demand of input after the introduction of new directed technologies cannot change the general conditions of factor markets.

At the system level, instead, the introduction of directed technological change affects the position and slope of both the derived demand and supply of inputs with clear effects on their price. Let us consider the range of possible outcomes:

1. With a given elastic (horizontal) factor supply, the shift in derived demand for the cheaper input determined by the introduction of directed technological change has no effects on its cost. Its introduction has positive effects.

2. When the position of the supply curve of the production factor is given, but exhibits a positive slope, changes in the position of its derived demand affect the prices of the input and (may) eliminate the expected positive effects of bias on output levels. There is actually room for the introduction of further directed technological changes according to the new levels of relative input costs. The system enters a loop with the eventual identification of the equilibrium levels of the relationship between output elasticities and factor prices.

3. Let us now consider the possibility that the rightward shift in demand for an input – determined by the introduction of directed technological change – attracts the entry of new firms with effects on the position (and slope) of the supply curve. The position of the supply curve of the input shifts towards the right. In this dynamic context the positive effects of technological congruence in terms of output and productivity are not limited by the increase in cost of the cheaper input. The relative size of the shifts in supply and demand curves may engender a self-sustained process of introduction of directed technological changes that will not identify equilibrium factor prices. The dynamics of the process is fully endogenous and unpredictable as it depends on the relationship between the extent of the shift in derived demand and the extent of the shift in the supply curve.

4. In an open economy the shift in the supply curve may be influenced by the international mobility of the input – the object of biased technological change – that can be activated by the rightward shift in derived demand. Labour or capital can move to the country where biased technological change has been taking place, increasing their demand. By the same token, additional exports of intermediary inputs can flow to the country where biased technological change has been introduced. In all cases the international mobility of production factors is likely to be attracted by the increased derived demand and affect the local supply curve with a downward shift. The price of the input is not necessarily going to increase after the introduction of the biased input. It may actually decrease further if the entry from abroad is significant (Rybczynski, 1955).

5. The introduction of new technologies in the upstream markets may be pulled by the shift in derived demand (Schmookler, 1966). The demand-pull hypothesis applies nicely to intermediary inputs, but can be stretched to take into account skilled labour. The introduction of skill-biased technological change in a skill-abundant region may have the effect of increasing wages sharply and reducing capital rental costs, changing the relative costs of production factors to the point of eliminating the expected positive effects on output levels. The supply of skills (and other intermediary inputs), however, may be in turn sensitive to the increased levels of demand. A demand-pull effect may take place with the eventual downward shift of the supply schedule of skilled labour. The expectations of an increase in demand for skilled labour may push towards a larger supply of skills. In this latter case the skill premium would not increase, as the amount of skilled labour available in the region would increase. The interaction between two classical mechanisms that account for the endogeneity of technological change – demand pull and induced technological change – is likely to feed a self-sustaining process. The introduction of induced technological change directed to increase the output elasticity of the cheaper input increases its derived demand, which in turn pulls the introduction of new technologies that increase the efficiency of the production process and reduce further the price of the input, feeding further rounds of introduction of induced technological change. The process is intrinsically dynamic, and highly path dependent, as it is exposed at each round to the changing outcomes of the innovation process and its effects on factor markets.

6. Let us now consider the effects of the accumulation of resources and the creation of stocks. This dynamics is relevant with respect to two inputs: wealth and knowledge. Yearly savings accumulate and add to and define the stock of wealth. With positive yearly savings the stock of capital keeps increasing over time (Picketty, 2014). The larger the rates of savings and growth of revenue, the larger will be the increase in the stock of knowledge. Advances in the economics of knowledge have made clear that cumulability and non-exhaustibility are intrinsic properties of knowledge. The stock of knowledge keeps increasing through time via the accumulation of new knowledge generated at each point in time (Antonelli and David, 2015). The accumulation of stocks of capital and knowledge affects their relative prices. We now have all the elements of a self-feeding loop dynamics between: i) the introduction of technological innovations; ii) the increase in total factor productivity; iii) the consequent growth of output and revenue; iv) the rates of accumulation of savings and knowledge; v) the

reduction in their prices; and vi) the introduction of new technological changes. Provided the shift in derived demand (determined by the introduction of biased technological change) is smaller than the shift in the supply curve (determined by the increasing size of the stocks), reduction of their relative prices takes place. Their price reduction stirs the creative reaction of firms to search for higher levels of technological congruence. When knowledge externalities are available, this search enables firms to introduce biased technological change directed towards the more intensive use of capital and knowledge. The system keeps evolving in a self-sustained dynamics with strong stochastic and path-dependent features that depend upon the comparative dynamics of the processes at work that is far from general equilibrium (Antonelli, 2015a).

The dynamics of technological congruence – and hence the incentives to introduce directed technological changes biased in favour of the inputs that are locally cheaper – share the intrinsic characteristics of an emergent system property. They also provide the foundations for a Schumpeterian model of endogenous growth where the interplay between demand pull and inducement mechanisms and the dynamics of accumulation of wealth and knowledge induces the introduction of directed technological change that accounts for the self-sustained increase in total factor productivity.

11.4 THE IMPLICATIONS OF TECHNOLOGICAL CONGRUENCE

The implications of technological congruence are far-reaching and spread in many important directions, opening new perspectives in many debates and fields of investigation. Their tentative list follows with a brief analytical sketch.

Technological Congruence and Technological Advance

The introduction of technological changes in different locations may have different effects according to the relative costs of production factors. A new technology may actually be more productive in one country and less productive, and consequently actually inferior to existing ones, in another country. Technological congruence impedes the objective ranking of technologies and questions the very notion of technological advance. A new technology can be considered superior or actually inferior to others only when the actual conditions of the local factor markets are taken into account (Abramovitz and David, 1996a; Antonelli, 2003). All this implies that technological congruence makes the notion of technological advance local and not global.

Technological Congruence and the Direction of Technological Change

Technological change is far from neutral. Much evidence confirms that technological change exhibits substantial directionality. Cliometric investigations confirm that technological change changes direction across time and across firms, industries and regions (Abramovitz and David, 1996a). The notion of technological congruence enables us to understand the incentives of firms and countries to try to direct the introduction of new technologies that make more intensive use of locally abundant factors. Here the notion of technological congruence enables us to make major progress in the debate about the determinant of so-called inducement mechanisms. There is a large and controversial literature on the direction of technological change (Ruttan, 1997, 2001; Acemoglu, 2003, 2010). The notion of technological congruence provides a new perspective to disentangle the key issues. Firms and countries have an incentive to direct the introduction of new technologies, not to substitute inputs that have become more expensive, as argued by John Hicks (1932), who revived the Marxian analysis of induced technological change, but to substitute inputs that are more expensive than others and to valorize the local availability of cheap production factors (David, 1975). The direction of technological change is successful when its bias enables us to valorize the relative abundance of inputs in local factor markets. The search for technological congruence keeps the introduction of technological changes within corridors defined by the intensity of local availability of cheap production factors.

Technological Congruence and the International Division of Labour

The international division of labour can no longer be regarded as the given result of an exogenous distribution of endowments. The specialization of countries in international markets can be considered the result of careful selection of appropriate technological corridors that enable them to valorize the relative abundance of some inputs in local factor markets. The specialization of countries is the direct consequence of their ability to introduce directed technological change with the right 'bias' – namely the larger output elasticity of the input that is cheaper in local factor markets. Hence the international specialization of both countries and firms is to a large extent endogenous. Countries and firms can shape their role in the international division of labour, favouring the emergence of an appropriate bias that intentionally shapes the direction of technological change that takes into account the existing characteristics of internal factor markets. For example, Portugal specialized in the production of Porto (port) and England in the production of cotton because labour and capital, respectively, were cheaper in their local factor markets (Habakkuk, 1962; Abramovitz and David, 1996a; Comin and Hobijn, 2004).

In the case of laggard countries, however, the availability on international markets of superior technologies in terms of shift effects, generated by advanced countries according to their own factor markets, may force the adoption of technologies with low levels of technological congruence. The algebraic sum of strong positive shift effect and the negative bias effect still yields a very positive total effect. In the case of laggard countries, technological congruence can be increased by adaptive adoptions able to yield good but still imperfect 'matching' between exogenous best practice technology and country factor endowments.[3] Following this line of analysis, it becomes evident that high levels of technological congruence can be implemented only by advanced countries with high levels of technological capabilities, while laggard countries are doomed to experience lower levels of technological congruence and hence total factor productivity (Cimoli and Porcile, 2009).

Technological Congruence, Firms' Strategies and the Emergence of Innovation Systems

The clear incentive of firms to try to target their activities so as to increase the output intensity of locally abundant inputs is likely to shape not only the individual strategies of each firm but also the emergence of local pools of collective knowledge. The local abundance of specific inputs, in fact, becomes a guiding factor that pushes all the firms co-localized to direct their generation of new technological knowledge towards complementary phases and components of a general production process that is more intensive in the same input locally abundant. The Ricardian specialization of Portugal in wine and England in cotton can be seen as the result of the collective specialization of Portuguese and English firms in the exploitation of dedicated and specific inputs that were locally abundant. The active search for complementarity helps the emergence of national and regional innovation systems centred on the exploitation of local endowments (Malerba, 2005). In this sense, differences in local industrial architectures might be viewed as a natural consequence of technological congruence shaping a particular sectoral system.

Technological Congruence and Location

As a corollary of the above considerations, technological congruence that might and – for efficiency reasons – should motivate exploitation of the relative abundance of a productive factor in a certain location might be viewed as a novel factor determining the local concentration of economic activities around industrial clusters. Indeed, technological congruence directly determines the direction and extent of external technological spillovers observable in a certain geographic location. The greater opportunity in terms of the availability of such external technological effects is perceived by the firms and motivates their location around the economic centre (Feldman, 1999; Antonelli and David, 2015).

Technological Congruence and the Diffusion of Innovations

Appreciation of the notion of technological congruence reinforces the supply school of analysis of the diffusion of innovations and reduces the appeal of the epidemic approach. Adoption takes place when and if the characteristics of the new technology are appropriate to the local context of action of potential adopters. Late adopters of new technologies should not be regarded as 'lazy', but – quite the opposite – as clever agents that are able to assess carefully the actual matching between the characteristics of the new technologies and their specific conditions. Late adopters may be rational agents that are able to wait until the characteristics of the new technologies change and become closer to the specific conditions. Actually, some countries and firms may decide that poor levels of technological congruence of a new technology do not warrant its adoption (David, 1969; Stoneman and Battisti, 2010).

Technological Congruence and Industrial Policies

Grasping the dynamics of technological congruence can help the design of economic policy directed at increasing the local supply of key production factors. Such intervention may become necessary when:

- a new superior technology introduced in country A with a large endowment of input X is actually most effective in country B where factor X is scarce because of major positive shift effects that compensate for the negative bias ones;
- the introduction and widespread diffusion of a new technology with a large output elasticity for a locally abundant input affects the derived demand for it and its market price.

In both cases, X can be identified as a key input. In such conditions there is a strong incentive to make the supply of the key input X locally stronger so as to accommodate the increasing demand and contrast its negative effects on market prices. Here market failures can deprive the system of the appropriate architecture, with strong negative effects: industrial policy has major responsibilities to implement the architecture of economic systems supporting the supply of intermediate products identified as key inputs.[4] The sectoral architecture of economic systems plays a central role in providing the rest of the system with a large and cheap supply of key inputs. Industrial policy should favour the emergence of 'good' sectoral architectures and target the creation and strengthening of the local supply of key intermediary factors. The same logic can help implement an effective training policy aimed at supporting the selective creation of dedicated skills and specific types of human capital (Mohnen and Röller, 2005; Gehringer, 2011). Moreover, in the spirit of interdependences between sectors, it could be efficient to support a technological upgrading of a sector – even with a relatively lower degree of technological congruence – if this is crucial to the activities of another sector(s) with already high technological congruence.

Technological Congruence and Innovation Policy

There is no single, homogeneous frontier of technological advance upon which all countries and firms are equally localized. The relative endowments of production factor shape and limit the portion of the frontier upon which each agent or country has a true incentive to try to make advances. Each agent should try to identify the direction of technological advance that better suits its specific factor endowments and focus its research capabilities accordingly. The variety of research paths on the frontier of technological advance is as intrinsically necessary as the variety of specializations in the international division of labour. Both are endogenous to the capability of firms, and countries at the system level, to identify how to increase technological congruence as much as possible. Innovation policies in the first place should identify sector-specific levels of technological congruence. Subsequently, they should target the introduction of dedicated technologies able to increase levels of technological congruence (Antonelli and Crespi, 2012). This should regard especially sectors considered as playing a crucial role in driving induced economic growth. Complementary to this, an intermediate goal of innovation policies requires building an efficient system of measures – targeting business aspects that are internal and external to the normal operating of the firm/industry – able to support the exploitation of technological congruence intrinsic in the system. In the global economy it is clear that high levels of technological capability are necessary to attain high levels of technological congruence.

Technological congruence is a powerful tool that helps us to grasp many aspects of the economics of growth accounting, international division of labour and structural change. It enables the appreciation of the role of the heterogeneity and variety of agents and factor markets in the innovation process. The economics of technological congruence is a fundamental tool to understanding the economic complexity of technological change with respect both to the effects and the determinants of the rate and direction of technological change (Antonelli, 2011).

Understanding the effects of technological congruence is most relevant to grasp the determinants of actual levels of efficiency and of the competitive advantage of firms and countries. At the same time, understanding the working of technological congruence helps in grasping the endogenous dynamics of the rate and direction of both technological and structural change.

Analysis of technological congruence can help implement new effective strategies at the firm level and – at the system level – the design of selective industrial and labour policies directed at increasing the local supply of key inputs. More precisely, within a broad design of industrial policies for technological lead, innovation policies should be directed at favouring the introduction of new technologies that are better able to match and valorize the local factor endowments.

NOTES

1. For simplicity's sake, the relationships (11.12) and (11.13) already include any cross-effect, such as the effect of a change of β on γ.
2. We are well aware that this procedure has its own limits, as it is not able to account for the consequences of changes in the output elasticity of production factors on their own derived demand, and hence on the market cost of production factors. We shall proceed assuming that the supply schedule of both capital and labour are flat.
3. As an anonymous referee notes, the abundance of natural resources in the eighteenth and early nineteenth century induced the United States to try to match with relatively high capital-intensive and natural resource-intensive technologies the exogenous best practice (labour-intensive) technologies imported from England.
4. I owe this point to an anonymous referee.

12. A Schumpeterian approach to endogenous specialization in international trade

Standard economics of international trade assumes that the specialization of trading countries is given and exogenous. Integration of the notions of creative response elaborated by Schumpeter (1947a) and of technological congruence (Antonelli, 2015) makes it possible to understand it as the result of an endogenous process.

This chapter contributes to the investigation of the economic determinants of the specialization of trading countries, elaborating a Schumpeterian version of the Heckscher–Ohlin (H–O) model of international trade. This analysis enables appreciation of the changing international specialization of trading partners as an aspect of endogenous structural and technological change stirred by the integration into the international markets of new trading partners (Meliciani, 2002; Urraca-Ruiz, 2013). The radical changes in the specialization of both advanced and industrializing countries that have been taking place since the last decades of the twentieth century can be regarded as the consequence of the radical technological and structural changes introduced to cope with the globalization of product and factor markets (Freeman, 1996; Perez, 2002).

12.1 GRAFTING THE SCHUMPETERIAN CREATIVE RESPONSE ON H–O

This section elaborates the grafting of innovation as an emergent system property approach based upon the Schumpeterian notion of creative response to analyse the dynamics of international trade. We assume as a starting point that unexpected events have brought the international economy to an out-of-equilibrium condition, and explore how endogenous and localized technological change can be integrated into the traditional H–O approach. For the sake of historic likelihood we shall assume that the pre-existing equilibrium in international markets has been shackled in the last decades of the twentieth century by the entry of new labour-abundant countries and the parallel liberalization of international capital markets. This analysis pays special attention to the effects on the capital-rich countries of the Organisation for Economic Co-operation and Development (OECD).

The well-known Heckscher–Ohlin (H–O) model provides the classic framework to analyse the effects of the entry of new labour-abundant countries in international product markets. The integration of these countries in international markets can be portrayed as an increase in the size of the production frontier of labour-intensive products. The consequence is straightforward as it consists in the change in slope of the isorevenue – which reflects the reduction in relative price of labour-intensive products and the increase in relative price of capital-intensive products – and a new international division of labour with the reduction in equilibrium output of labour intensive products manufactured in capital-abundant countries and higher levels of specialization of capital-abundant countries in capital-intensive products. The prices of the final goods decrease sharply, and the price of investment goods exhibits a minor increase.

Figure 12.1 represents the classical overlapping of the production possibility frontiers of two trading countries or groups of countries. On the vertical axis the intercept of the production possibility frontier of capital-abundant countries identifies the maximum amount of capital-intensive Y goods that can be produced, while the intercept on the horizontal axis identifies the maximum amount of labour-intensive X goods that labour-abundant countries can produce. The tangency with the isorevenue identifies the two equilibrium conditions for the two trading countries S and R. The entry of new labour-abundant countries in international product

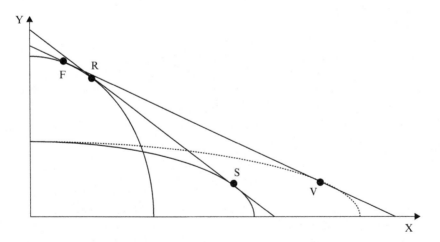

Figure 12.1   Globalization and specialization: the static version

markets affects the shape of the production possibility frontier of the group of labour-intensive countries, and consequently the isorevenue slope: the new equilibrium solutions F and V replace the old equilibrium solutions R and S, respectively, in the capital- and labour-abundant countries.

This graphical representation is the result of the following steps. Let us assume that the two overlapping frontiers of possible production are identified by four simple Cobb–Douglas production functions in two trading entities. The first two represent the two frontiers of possible production of the Z countries; the second couple identifies the frontiers of possible production of the T countries. They are characterized by their diverse endowment of capital and labour. Capital is abundant in Z countries and labour is abundant in T countries; Y represents capital goods and X final goods:

$$Y_Z = A_Z (K_Z)^a (L_Z)^b \tag{12.1}$$

$$X_Z = A_Z (K_z)^a (L_z)^b \tag{12.2}$$

$$Y_T = A_T (K_T)^c (L_T)^d \tag{12.3}$$

$$X_T = A_T (K_t)^c (L_t)^d \tag{12.4}$$

where Y_Z and X_Z are the output of Y and X goods in Z countries; K_Z and L_Z are capital and labour in countries Z engaged in the production of Y goods; K_z and L_z are capital and labour in countries Z engaged in the production of X goods. Y_T and X_T are the output of Y and X goods in T countries; K_T and L_T are capital and labour in countries T engaged in the production of Y goods; K_t and L_t are capital and labour in countries T engaged in the production of X goods; a,b , c, d measure the output elasticity of the production factors.

A_Z measures the levels of total factor productivity in Z countries in the production of capital goods Y and final goods X; A_T measures the levels of total factor productivity in T countries in the production of Y and X (for the sake of clarity we shall assume that in each country the two sectors have the same levels of total factor productivity).

The following cost functions apply:

$$C_Z = w_Z L_Z + r_Z K_Z \tag{12.5}$$

$$C_T = w_T L_T + r_T K_T \tag{12.6}$$

where w_Z measures the unit wage in Z countries and w_T measures the unit wage of T countries that interact in the globalized international product markets. By the same token, r_Z and r_T are the capital user costs in Z countries and T countries.

The standard, albeit often tacit, assumptions that a > b in Z countries and c < d in T countries enable the overlapping of the two possible production frontiers so as to yield gains from trade and international specialization. Following Maskus and Nishioka (2009) and Trefler (1993), we take into account differentiated efficiency levels and assume that $A_Z > A_z$, $A_T > A_t$ and $A_Z > A_t$.[1] Actually the larger are the difference between a and b, c and d, A_Z and A_T and the larger are the gains from trade.

Following the standard procedure for constructing the frontiers of possible production, we assume that:

$$X_Z = nY_Z \qquad (12.7)$$

$$X_T = mY_T \qquad (12.8)$$

Their slopes identify the two marginal rates of transformation, respectively MRT_Z and MRT_T. The isorevenue, describing the maximum production combination of goods X and Y, is defined as follows:

$$TR = Py\, Y + Px\, X \qquad (12.9)$$

The equilibrium conditions of the isorevenue slope are easily identified as follows:

$$Px/Py = MRT_Z = MRT_T \qquad (12.10)$$

The entry of new, large, low-wage, labour-abundant competitors increases L_T and the supply of X_T in global markets. This reduces the slope of the isorevenue, that is, conditions for the international division of labour and specialization of countries, and changes the relative conditions of the domestic factor markets in real terms.

In this context, in the H–O model firms based in capital-abundant countries face these relative changes in the new globalized factor (and product) markets only by means of textbook substitution, moving on the existing maps of isoquants towards higher levels of capital intensity. The shape, position and slope of the production possibility frontier cannot be changed by the intentional conduct of firms. Firms can cope with the new conditions of international factor and product markets only by moving on the existing frontier so as to reach the new equilibrium point identified by the tangency between MRT and the slope of the new isorevenue.[2]

When the Schumpeterian hypothesis of an endogenous and directed technological change induced by the mismatch between expected and actual factor markets conditions is taken into account, instead, firms can cope with the new conditions of international product and factor markets by means of the introduction of new technologies that change the slope, position and eventually the shape of the production possibility frontier.

12.2   THE S–H–O MODEL WITH TWO INPUTS

In the S–H–O approach firms – and, at the aggregate level, countries – can react to the effects of globalization by means of the introduction of biased technological innovations so as to change the position, slope and shape of the production possibility frontier. The S–H–O model rests on the integration of three basic issues:

- Firms caught in out-of-equilibrium conditions try to react.
- Their reaction can be creative when appropriate knowledge externalities are available in the system.
- The technological change will be biased towards the intensive use of production factors that became locally more abundant and relatively cheaper.

The analysis elaborated so far can be usefully framed with an approach based upon a Cobb–Douglas production function. In a standard two basic input production function, the S–H–O model allows the possible introduction of endogenous and biased technological change directed to increase total factor productivity and the output elasticity of the production factor that is locally more abundant and relatively cheaper.

Here, appreciation of the different time horizons of the consequences of globalization plays a crucial role. Factor cost equalization should be regarded as a secular process that displays its effects in the very long term. Its implementation requires radical changes in economic structure, the exit from labour-intensive industries and the growth of capital-intensive ones. This in turn requires major adjustments in labour and capital markets. The strength of trade unions causes further delays in the reduction of nominal wages. Only in the very long term, ceteris paribus, can factor cost equalization actually take place: wages in Z countries should fall and capital user costs rise. The changes in the relative prices of investment and final goods, instead, are instantaneous. The flows of imports from capital-intensive countries of labour-intensive goods have rapid effects on their relative market prices. In the short term, as a consequence, while factor costs change smoothly, the price of the final goods X falls drastically and the price of capital goods Y exhibits minor increases. As a consequence, in capital-abundant countries, real wages increase and real capital-user costs decline.

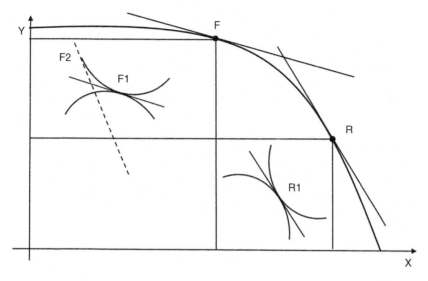

Note: Secular dynamics takes place in T countries.

Figure 12.2   Out-of-equilibrium in the Edgeworth box of Z countries

In the very long term the new isocost and the new isorevenue should be equal, as predicted by the factor costs equalization theorem. In the short term, however, this is not the case. Because of the discrepancy between the two conflicting time horizons, a typical out-of-equilibrium condition takes place. In the short term the real isocost is different from the isorevenue: the isocost is actually steeper than the isorevenue. Formally, this amounts to saying that the slope of the isocost in capital-abundant countries, already >1 before globalization, is even steeper after globalization:

$$(w_Z/P_X/r_Z/P_Y)_{t1} > (w_Z/P_X/r_Z/P_Y)_{t0} > 1 \qquad (12.11)$$

Figure 12.2 shows the changes within the Edgeworth box. After integration of international markets and the shift of the isorevenue from equilibrium point R to the new equilibrium R1, the factor costs equalization theorem assumes that the isocost of Z countries rotates together with a change in the size of the Edgeworth box. According to our hypothesis, because in Z countries (after globalization) real capital user costs will become relatively cheaper than real wages – and the slope of the real isocost will be steeper than before globalization – there is a major opportunity to grasp the benefits, in terms of increased total factor productivity, of an increase in technological congruence by means of the introduction of new capital-intensive technologies. The dotted isocost in Figure 12.2 shows that the actual isocost of Z countries in real terms shifts in the opposite direction. Isocost and isorevenue are no longer parallel. Z countries move away from equilibrium point R1, but are not able to reach the new equilibrium point F1: they actually move towards the out-of-equilibrium point F2.

The setting for the Schumpeterian creative reaction and the search for technological congruence is now ready. The disequilibrium condition with the actual increase in real wages and the decline of capital user costs leads to the introduction of a new, superior capital-intensive technology represented by a new production function in Z countries, with larger capital output elasticity and higher levels of total factor productivity. After the introduction of the biased capital-intensive technological change, the new production function in Z countries can be represented in formal terms as follows:[3]

$$Y_Z = A_{ZZ} (K_Z)^F (L_Z)^G \qquad (12.12)$$

where $A > a$, $B < b$ and $A_{ZZ} > A_Z$. The new total factor productivity, measured by A_{ZZ}, is larger than the former A_Z because of the introduction of biased technological change directed to the increase in output elasticity of capital, F, that has become cheaper because of globalization. The new production function reflects the introduction of capital-intensive technological change, and hence – given the changes in factor markets brought about by the out-of-equilibrium conditions engendered by globalization – higher levels of technological congruence and higher levels of total factor productivity.

In the S–H–O model, the endogenous introduction of biased technological change directed to increase the output elasticity of capital – the production factor that because of globalization has become relatively more abundant in local factor markets – changes the position, slope and shape of the production possibility frontier of the innovating countries and the international division of labour favouring an augmented (with respect to the H–O model) specialization of advanced countries in capital-intensive products (Montobbio and Rampa, 2005).

As Figure 12.3 shows, the production possibility frontier of the Z countries has changed position and shape because of the endogenous introduction of biased technological change directed to using more intensively the input that is locally and relatively most abundant – i.e. fixed capital.[4] The changes to the production possibility frontier do have direct effects on the international division of labour. The slope of the isorevenue is indeed affected by the changes in the production possibility frontier introduced in the Z countries. As a consequence, the equilibria are no longer found

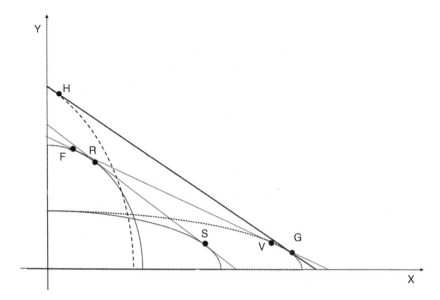

Figure 12.3   Globalization and specialization: the S–H–O version

respectively in F and V, but in H for the Z countries and in G for the T countries.

Figure 12.2 makes clear that the changes in the position and shape of the production possibility frontier of Z countries brought about by the introduction of productivity-enhancing and biased technological changes directed towards the more intensive use of the production factor that is locally most abundant change the slope of isorevenue. The new production possibility frontier of Z countries is in fact further away from the origin and taller.

The difference between the levels of total factor productivity and output elasticity of the inputs in the production functions of the goods Y and X in Z and T countries is not exogenous or random. It is, quite the opposite, the consequence of the effects of international trade on the rate and direction of endogenous technological change in trading partners. Each country has in fact an incentive to try to increase production efficiency by means of the exploitation of the technological opportunities that enable changing the output elasticity of the production factor that, after integration, happens to be locally and comparatively cheaper (Laursen, 1999).

The decline of factor shares experienced by advanced countries since 1990 is the consequence of endogenous directed technological change stirred by their increasing exposure to international trade and imports from labour-abundant countries (Bockerman and Maliranta, 2012).

The discrepancy between the time horizon in which the nominal price of goods changes in international markets and the nominal price of inputs changes in domestic markets has long-lasting consequences that make factor equalization impossible. The divergence between the changes in the nominal and real prices of both inputs and outputs, in fact, is at the origin of the search for technological congruence and the consequent introduction of biased technological change that is capital intensive in advanced countries. The latter in turn changes the equilibrium conditions in international markets, with the final consequence that the very foundations of factor equalization disappear.

Much evidence confirms the decline of the labour share experienced since 1990 by advanced countries. It confirms that technological change in the countries most exposed to increasing competition by labour abundant countries has been biased in favour of the introduction of capital-intensive technologies that could use resources that were locally more abundant (Zeira, 1998; Karabarbounis and Neiman, 2014).

12.3   THE S–H–O MODEL WITH KNOWLEDGE AS AN INPUT

When factor mobility is allowed for, the framework elaborated so far may change. The parallel globalization of product and financial markets in place since the last decades of the twentieth century undermined the opportunities for Z countries to cope with changes in the international division of labour by introducing new capital-intensive technologies. Major institutional changes affected the working of the system dynamics, deepening the out-of-equilibrium conditions for firms in Z economies. The globalization of financial markets played a central role here. The new international mobility of capital via both the flow of foreign direct investment of multinational companies and the international finance managed by international banks provided industrializing companies with a large supply of capital, undermining the profitability of a capital-intensive induced technological change of (formerly) capital-abundant countries (Perez, 2002, 2010).

The globalization of financial markets provided newcomers with readily available and cheap capital. The competitive advantage of Z economies could no longer be restored by means of capital-intensive technological changes and increased specialization in capital-intensive products. The introduction of radical technological changes became even more necessary. In countries where knowledge externalities were available, firms could cope with the entry into international product and capital markets of new, huge, labour-abundant and low-wage countries in the global economy. But this was only with major efforts to identify the input that was actually and specifically abundant in their local factor markets so as to direct their new technologies and increase production intensity.

The search for technological congruence led to identifying technological knowledge as the key abundant factor in Z economies exposed to the international mobility of goods and capital. The strong collective and systemic character of technological knowledge localizes it in the specific and highly idiosyncratic features of each economic system. Technological knowledge does not spill freely into the 'international' atmosphere, as suggested by extensions of the new growth theory to international economics; rather, it has a strong localized content based upon its tacit and sticky content that roots it in learning countries endowed with a strong knowledge base and advanced knowledge-governance mechanisms (Romer, 1994; Branstetter 2001; Montobbio and Kataishi, 2015).

Knowledge is abundant in Z countries because they are characterized by a complex web of networks that make knowledge user–producer interactions possible and effective (Breschi and Lissoni, 2001), and high-quality knowledge-governance mechanisms that favour the dissemination of knowledge spillovers and their actual use by third parties in the generation of new technological knowledge (Antonelli and Link, 2015). For these reasons Z countries could discover technological knowledge as a relatively abundant resource upon which a new competitive advantage could be built.

The relative abundance of technological knowledge in advanced countries activated and supported, at the same time, the mechanisms of knowledge congruence that led to the introduction of biased technological changes directed to the sharp increase in output elasticity of technological knowledge as an input and the complementary decline in output elasticity of low-skilled labour.

The technology production function elaborated by Griliches (1979, 1992) is a very effective tool for analysing the production process at a time characterized by the key role of knowledge as a production factor. The explicit integration of knowledge as a production factor into the production function enables us to grasp the effects of the central role of knowledge, characterized by high levels of skilled labour intensity, and its substitution to standard labour as key production factors.

We assume that in the out-of-equilibrium phase determined by twin globalization, in Z countries technological knowledge is more abundant and cheaper than in the T economies, where both capital and labour are relatively less scarce than technological knowledge. Hence the relative wages (w) and user costs of capital (r) are lower in T economies than in Z countries, while the relative cost (m) of the new input technological knowledge (TK) is lower in Z countries than in the T economies.

After the introduction of the new biased technological change, the Cobb–Douglas technology production function includes on the left-hand side capital goods (Y) that differ from the previous ones for their increasing intangible content. It also includes many knowledge-intensive business services (KIBS), on the right-hand side, along with standard capital (K) and labour (L), and the new production factor technological knowledge (TK), each with its respective output elasticity (C, B and E):

$$Y_Z = A_{ZZZ} (K_Z)^C (L_Z)^D (TK_Z)^E \qquad (12.13)$$

Comparison of the production functions (12.13) and (12.14) makes clear that $C = A$, $D < B$, $E > 0$. We assume in fact – with constant returns to scale, and hence $C + D + E = 1$ – that the new input technological knowledge (consisting primarily of intangible capital) displaces standard labour, but not fixed capital. Next, we assume that $A_{ZZZ} > A_{ZZ}$ (the levels of total factor productivity in the innovating countries Z) increase because of the higher levels of technological congruence made possible by the introduction of biased technological changes directed at increasing the output elasticity (E) of the input locally most abundant technological knowledge (TK).[5]

The introduction of TK, next to and together with the levels of total factor productivity A_{ZZZ}, stems from the Schumpeterian hypothesis that the amount of knowledge (TK) is a necessary but not sufficient condition for total factor productivity to increase. The amount of knowledge may engender knowledge externalities that may support the creative reaction of firms caught in out-of-equilibrium conditions.

Now the S–H–O model can take into account the effects of twin globalization and the discovery of technological knowledge as the most abundant production factors in Z countries so as to explain the introduction of induced technological change biased towards the increased output elasticity of the new input technological knowledge as an endogenous reaction that changes the shape of the production possibility frontier.

In order to cope with the twin globalization of the last decades of the twentieth century, Z countries introduced a wave of biased technological changes directed towards more intensive use of technological knowledge, while the rest of the international economy specialized in technologies with higher levels of capital output elasticity. In fact, because of technological congruence, Z countries found it convenient to increase as much as possible the intensity of the production factor that was locally relatively more abundant (Antonelli, 2008, 2015a).

The S–H–O framework elaborated so far is quite consistent with the results of Maskus and Nishioka (2009), who implement the H–O model with factor-specific productivities and factor-augmenting technological differences differentiated across countries. Their analysis suggests that factor-augmenting productivity gaps and factor abundance make the H–O framework compatible with the empirical evidence. They do not explain, however, how and why factor abundance guides the introduction of factor-augmenting productivity gaps. Previously, Nishioka (2005) had shown that the inclusion of knowledge as an input and output in the analysis of international trade flow helps increase the viability of the H–O model.

The S–H–O framework implemented so far seems to explain how such changes take place. The S–H–O approach shows that the introduction of biased technological changes directed at increasing the output elasticity of the locally cheaper input is the result of an out-of-equilibrium condition determined by changes in international product markets. The strength of the S–H–O model consists in the endogenous account of the specialization of the trading countries. From this viewpoint, the S–H–O framework differs from the Maskus–Nishioka approach as it stresses the process that underlies the endogenous definition of both the rate and direction of technological change.

After the endogenous introduction of the new directed technologies, the two economies will be far different than before. The specialization of Z countries in the generation, use and exploitation of technological knowledge will be even stronger than before, as the substitution process on the existing map of isoquants is enhanced and reinforced by the introduction of biased technologies that favour the more intensive use of technological knowledge. The introduction of endogenous and biased technological change alters the shape, position and slope of the production possibility frontier, and helps increase the specialization of innovating (knowledge-abundant) countries in the use of knowledge as both a key production factor and a key product (Abramovitz and David, 1996; Antonelli and Colombelli, 2011; Antonelli and Fassio, 2011).

In the S–H–O approach Z countries could face these relative changes in the new globalized factor markets by means of creative responses consisting in the introduction of new knowledge-intensive technologies that help them cope with the new conditions of both product and factor international markets.

Advanced countries discovered that the high quality of their knowledge-governance mechanisms, which made the exploitation of knowledge indivisibility and limited appropriability possible so as to favour its use and dissemination as a collective resource localized in their own economic systems, could become the base of a new knowledge-intensive comparative advantage (Guerrieri and Meliciani, 2005).

The effects on the flows of goods among trading partners are clear. Knowledge-abundant countries became the specialized providers of knowledge-intensive products to the rest of the world, exporting both knowledge-intensive tangible goods and intangible knowledge-intensive business services. Knowledge-abundant countries rely more and more on the rest of the world for imports of both capital- and labour-intensive products. The introduction of the new technological system based upon new information and communication technologies was the cause and consequence of the new specialization in the generation and exploitation of technological knowledge (Guerrieri et al., 2011).

The ultimate effect of the endogenous technological and structural change was the reshaping of countries' specialization in international product markets with the decline and exit from traditional low-tech manufacturing sectors and attempts to find new knowledge-intensive service industries that could support a new competitive advantage (Evangelista et al., 2013; Antonelli and Fassio, 2014).

The S–H–O framework accommodates the Leontief paradox. This is an apparent paradox that finds its explanation in the longstanding knowledge abundance of the US economy, and in a theoretical explanation centred on the endogenous direction of technological change biased towards the intensive use of locally abundant inputs.

12.4 IMPLICATIONS

This chapter has elaborated the S–H–O framework, a Schumpeterian version of the H–O model based upon the hypothesis that changes in international trade interact with endogenous and directed technological change biased towards the most intensive use of production factors that are locally most abundant in comparative terms. Changes in international markets and changes in technology do interact and feed each other, and shape the specialization of trading countries.

According to the Schumpeterian notion of innovation as the result of the creative reaction, firms caught in out-of-equilibrium conditions by the changing conditions of both factor and product markets try to react to the changing conditions of factor and product markets brought about by globalization by means of the introduction of biased technological changes, provided they can rely on substantial knowledge externalities.

Innovation as an emergent system property approach also integrates the recent advances of the new economics of knowledge that stress the strong systemic and localized character of technological knowledge and the analytical tradition of the induced technological change hypothesis.

The relative abundance of technological knowledge plays a twin role in this analysis. First, it makes it possible for firms to react creatively and introduce technological innovations: without a strong knowledge base their reaction could fail and be just adaptive. Second, because of the mechanisms of technological congruence, the very same strong knowledge base favours a new specialization in knowledge-intensive products. The two roles reinforce each other with positive feedback. The larger the knowledge abundance, the more creative the reaction of firms and countries in international markets can be; also, the stronger will be the direction of technological change towards the most intensive use of knowledge as the key production factor on which a new international specialization can be built.

The S–H–O approach integrates the H–O model with endogenous technological change, and shows that the levels of both total factor productivity and output elasticity of production factors are endogenous to the system. In the standard H–O model, the difference between trading countries in levels of output elasticity of inputs and total factor productivity is assumed to be exogenous, and factor cost equalization leads to the end of international trade and specialization. In S–H–O the technological specialization of each country, and specifically the mix of output elasticity of production factor, is not accidental: it reflects the search for technological congruence and the introduction of biased technological innovations directed at increasing the output elasticity of the inputs that are locally cheaper. While in the standard H–O approach trade takes place between countries because of their exogenous specialization, in S–H–O trade is the result of the intentional introduction of directed technological changes in countries that have differentiated factor markets. In the S–H–O approach international specialization, structural and technological change are but ingredients of a single ongoing, out-of-equilibrium process of transformation of economic systems.

The integration of the Schumpeterian approach into the H–O framework enables us to identify a window of opportunity determined by differences in the time horizon of changes in international isorevenue with respect to changes in the domestic isocost of countries exposed to international integration. If countries are able to take advantage of this window of opportunity to introduce directed technological changes, globalization is likely to have strong positive effects: the fall of nominal and real wages in advanced countries is no longer expected. If, however, countries are not able to take timely advantage of the window of opportunity, there is no possibility of combating the long-term decline of real wages (Samuelson, 2004).

Historically, this implies that knowledge-abundant countries could cope with the changed conditions of both product and factor markets brought about by globalization since the late twentieth century by means of the introduction of knowledge-intensive innovations and radical changes to their economic structure that enable them to complement the decline of the traditional manufacturing base with specialization in the new knowledge economy.

NOTES

1. Following Solow (1957), the term A measures the levels of total factor productivity, which measures the residual – that is, the amount of output that cannot be explained by the amount of input. A increases because of the introduction of innovations. Knowledge may account for the rate of technological change, but does not coincide with it. In a knowledge economy, based upon knowledge-intensive services, however, total factor productivity may be zero as no innovation is introduced.
2. Attempts have been made to elaborate a more inclusive version of the standard H–O model allowing for the mobility of inputs and, more specifically, for both labour and capital flow among countries. Even in this version of the H–O model, however, firms are not allowed to change their technologies: technological change is exogenous (Rybczynski, 1955).
3. The introduction of new biased technologies can also take place in the production of XZ. This, however, is not strictly necessary. Analysis of learning processes helps make this argument stronger. Z countries had the opportunity to accumulate more experience and competence based upon learning processes in Y goods than in X goods. Hence they have the opportunity to react to the new conditions of international product markets with the introduction of new superior and directed technologies that rely on the directed knowledge externalities available in their countries. The accumulation of tacit knowledge in capital-intensive products provides larger knowledge externalities in the generation of capital-intensive technologies than in the generation of labour-intensive technologies.
4. Note that the intercept on the X axis of the production possibility frontier of the Z countries in Figure 12.2 depends on the hypothesis that the introduction of innovations takes place only in the production of Y goods. The intercept can be larger if technological change takes place in Z countries also in the production of X goods. These alternative possibilities do not affect the outcome of the model that depends upon changes in the maximum output of Y goods in Z countries.
5. For the sake of clarity we identify the cost equation for the production of Y_Z goods in Z countries: $C_Z = r_Z K + w_Z L + m_Z TK$.

13. Schumpeterian growth: the creative response to knowledge exhaustibility

Recent advances in the economics of knowledge, innovation and techno-logical change and the reappraisal of the Schumpeterian framework of the creative response enable us to articulate a comprehensive model of Schumpeterian growth based on exhaustibility. The flow of knowledge generated at each point in time to fuel oligopolistic rivalry can be fully appropriated by 'inventors', albeit for a limited stretch of time. Eventually in fact, after a short period of appropriation, all the new knowledge becomes public and adds to the stock of public knowledge. At each point in time the system is in equilibrium as the marginal productivity of knowledge matches its costs. In the long term, however, an increase in the stock of public knowledge leads to a reduction in its cost as an input in the production of all other goods. This in turn engenders a mismatch in factor markets and stirs the creative reaction of firms, inducing the search for directed technological changes aimed at increasing the knowledge intensity of the technology production function. The motion of the system rests on the laws of accumulation of knowledge, its effects on the cost of knowledge and the factor markets and the induced search for technologi-cal congruence. As long as the accumulation of knowledge is sufficient to contrast the increased costs stemming from the shift in its derived demand, growth is sustainable.

This concluding chapter is structured as follows. The first section syn-thesizes briefly the main results of the analysis carried out in this book and recalls the Schumpeterian framework of the creative response, reviews recent advances in the economics of Schumpeterian rivalry, the revival of the directed technological change hypothesis and the new understanding of knowledge as the output of a dedicated and intentional generation process. This section stresses the role of knowledge externalities stem-ming from the exhaustibility, cumulability and transient appropriability of all knowledge. At each point in time new proprietary knowledge can be appropriated. Eventually, however, it spills and adds to the stock of public knowledge. The increasing stock of public knowledge yields pecu-niary externalities that feed the creative reaction of firms, the generation of additional knowledge and the introduction of further innovations. The notion of knowledge exhaustibility contrasts standard assumptions about the decomposability of knowledge in appropriable and non-appropriable components. The second section presents a simple model of endogenous economic growth based upon the interplay between knowledge externalities in knowledge generation and the increasing supply of technological knowledge, and the reduction of the relative user costs of technological knowledge in technology production with the consequent induced introduction of knowledge-intensive technological change. The conclusions summarize the main findings.

13.1   CONVERGENT ADVANCES IN THE ECONOMICS OF INNOVATION, TECHNOLOGICAL CHANGE AND KNOWLEDGE

The Schumpeterian framework of creative response has been somewhat neglected in the literature, but recent contributions have drawn attention to its merits (Antonelli, 2008, 2011, 2015). Schumpeter's 1947 contribution can be considered a major attempt to synthesize the different ingredients laid down in his earlier work. Firms are exposed to frequent mismatch between expected and actual conditions of product and factor markets. They can react by means of either adaptive or creative responses. Adaptive responses consist in price and quantity adjustments through technical changes within the given technology on the existing map of isoquants. Creative responses consist in the introduction of new technologies that change the existing map of isoquants. Adaptive responses take place when firms have no access to the necessary externalities. Creative responses are possible when firms can take advantage of externalities, and specifically knowledge externalities that make possible the generation of new technological knowledge and the eventual introduction of innovations.

This approach seems able to accommodate in a single and powerful framework of analysis different and yet complementary advances recently elaborated in three fields of investigation: i) the economics of innovation; ii) the economics of technological change; and iii) the economics of knowledge. Let us consider them briefly, in turn.

The Economics of Innovation

New evidence has revived the so-called neo-Schumpeterian literature confirming the crucial role of innovation as an indispensable competitive tool in product markets (Scherer, 1965, 1967, 1984; Geroski, 1994). Market competition is shaped by product rivalry. Price competition is integrated and augmented by the introduction of product and process innovations. The rate of introduction of innovations is larger in oligopolistic markets characterized by head-to-head competition. Schumpeterian competition in product markets feeds the flow of R&D activities (Aghion et al., 2014, 2015).

The Economics of Technological Change

New analyses have revived the so-called induced technological change approach (Ruttan, 2001). Technological change is intrinsically biased and far from neutral. It consists in the introduction of new technologies directed at increasing the output elasticity of inputs that are relatively cheaper in the factor markets (Acemoglu, 1998, 2015). The larger is the technological congruence, the larger the output (Antonelli, 2016). The direction of technological change depends on the conditions of factor markets. Firms active in labour/capital-abundant factor markets have clear incentives to introduce labour/capital-intensive technological change.

Introduction of the technology production function helps in appreciating the role of technological knowledge as a distinctive and indispensable input – besides capital and labour – in the production of all other goods (Griliches, 1979). The search for technological congruence is likely to favour the direction of technological change towards the introduction of more knowledge-intensive technologies in factor markets characterized by low costs of knowledge.

The Economics of Knowledge

Technological knowledge is the output of a specific activity. The Arrovian properties of knowledge – such as non-appropriability, non-exhaustibility and cumulability, and non-rivalry in use – characterize not only knowledge as an economic good, but also its generation (Arrow, 1962, 1969). The generation of technological knowledge consists in the recombination of existing knowledge items (Weitzman, 1996; Arthur, 2009). The stock of existing knowledge is a necessary and indispensable input in the generation of new knowledge as an output (Griliches, 1979). The generation of knowledge is a branching out process where new technologies are generated building upon the existing ones (Fleming and Sorenson, 2001). As a consequence, the recombinant knowledge generation is a process with clear non-ergodic characteristics: at each point in time the rate and direction of the process are influenced by the stock of existing knowledge (Antonelli, 2008).

The intrinsic non-excludability of knowledge limits its appropriability:

knowledge producers can retain control of their 'inventions' only for a stretch of time. Knowledge appropriability is limited because it is transient, not because it is partial.[1] Proprietary knowledge gradually, but inevitably, leaks out, spills and is eventually disseminated in the system. Because of knowledge cumulability and non-exhaustibility, the flows of knowledge spilling from 'inventors' add to the stock of knowledge. At the firm level, knowledge transient appropriability impedes its exclusive cumulativity intramuros (Griliches, 1979, 1992).

Knowledge non-exhaustibility and cumulativity display, instead, its powerful effects at the system level. The flow of new knowledge – with appropriate lags stemming from the duration of appropriation by inventors – adds to the stock of public knowledge and engenders diachronic knowledge externalities. Access and use of the stock of public knowledge is not free: the larger the stock, the lower its costs of absorption and use. Knowledge externalities are pecuniary, as they affect the costs of public knowledge as an input, and diachronic as their (powerful) effects are inter-temporal and take place through time.

The laws of accumulation of the stock of public knowledge play a crucial role in this context. The levels of knowledge connectivity of the system in which firms are embedded are most important. Systems with high levels of knowledge connectivity are able to integrate the different knowledge items that are generated at each point in time into an effective stock of knowledge. The effective rates of knowledge accumulation are larger: diachronic knowledge externalities are larger. At the same time, the stock of public knowledge can be accessed and used at low absorption costs: pecuniary knowledge externalities are larger. Systems with low levels of connectivity are not able to pull together the different knowledge items that remain dispersed in the system. The stock of knowledge is public but fragmented, and its rates of accumulation are smaller: diachronic knowledge externalities are lower. The costs of accessing and using it are much higher: pecuniary knowledge externalities are lower. In systems with high levels of knowledge connectivity, total knowledge externalities are high. In systems with low levels of knowledge connectivity, total knowledge externalities are low.

At each point in time the new vintages of knowledge generated by means of the flow of R&D activities add – with delays due to dissemination lags – to the public stock of knowledge that keeps increasing. Diachronic knowledge externalities are determined by two dynamic processes: i) the larger the stock of knowledge, the lower are its costs as an input in the knowledge generation process. The cost of knowledge as an input in knowledge generation keeps decreasing. At the same time: ii) the larger the stock of public knowledge, the larger the scope for recombination and knowledge output. Along with increasing stock of knowledge, efficiency of the knowledge generation process increases and the cost of the stock of knowledge decreases. Because of diachronic knowledge externalities, the generation of technological change takes place with costs that decrease along with the inter-temporal increase in the stock of knowledge. The sequential search for technological congruence pushes the direction of technological change to take into account the dynamic reduction in the price of technological knowledge and favours the eventual introduction of more knowledge-intensive technologies.

Let us now try to pull these converging threads together. The creative response framework is reinforced by integration so as to articulate a spiralling process. Mismatches between expected and actual market conditions take place both in the product and the factor markets. Schumpeterian rivalry engenders mismatches in the product market and sustains the flow of R&D expenditure. The consequent accumulation of stock of public knowledge causes the inter-temporal fall in the price of knowledge, which in turn engenders new emerging mismatches in factor markets. Both favour the creative reaction and increase the rates of generation of new technological knowledge in order to introduce innovations. The accelerated introduction of innovations acts as the chain effect to:

- reinforce mismatches between expected and actual product and factor market conditions;
- push the generation of new technological knowledge;
- increase the stock of existing technological knowledge;
- reduce further the price of knowledge; and
- reinforce the introduction of new, more knowledge-intensive technologies.

In the long term the reduction of knowledge costs stirs the creative reaction of firms and induces the introduction of biased technological changes directed at the introduction of knowledge-intensive technologies, which in turn leads to the accumulation of even larger stocks of public knowledge. The search for higher levels of technological congruence and the new direction of technological change aimed at increasing the match between declining costs of technological knowledge and its increasing output elasticity accounts for self-sustained Schumpeterian growth.

The knowledge-intensive direction of technological change can account for the shift of industrialized economies to knowledge economies characterized by the large output elasticity of knowledge as an input and the specialization of advanced countries in the generation and use of technological knowledge as both output and input. The growth path is interrupted when the shift of the derived demand for technological knowledge has a 'positive' impact on the cost of technological knowledge that is larger than the 'negative' effects of diachronic knowledge externalities stemming from the joint effects of knowledge non-exhaustibility, cumulativity and transient appropriability.

The endogenous growth model highlights the crucial role of the conditions of accumulation, access and use of technological knowledge that cannot be fully appropriated by its inventors. It enables us to appreciate the systemic conditions that shape the actual costs of knowledge. It shows that there is a constraint to the self-sustained process of growth that stems from the dynamic balance between the effects of increased derived demand of technological knowledge – determined by the knowledge-intensive direction of technological change – and the effects of knowledge non-exhaustibility and cumulativity. Identification of the constraint paves the way to specifying policy interventions finalized to keep the system in motion on the growth path and avoid falling into the trap of equilibrium.

13.2   THE MODEL

This section presents a simple model that shows the dynamics of the creative response. Let us assume that production is realized through a technology function characterized by the combined use of some amount F of physical factors (for example, capital and labour) and some level of technological knowledge T. Their elasticity to the output are, respectively, $1 - \delta$ and δ, so that the level of output produced is:

$$Y = F^{1-\delta} T^{\delta} \tag{13.1}$$

Denoting with z and u the price of factors F and T, the total cost equation is:

$$C = zF + uT \tag{13.2}$$

We assume that firms chose to keep total costs fixed and maximize the output. Formally, firms choose the values of F and T so as to solve the following problem:

$$\max_{F,T} Y = F^{1-\delta} T^{\delta} \tag{13.3}$$
$$\text{s.t. } zF + uT \leq \tilde{C}$$

where $\tilde{C}$ is the constant level of cost entailed by the production.

The marginal rate of technical substitution between F and T is:

$$\frac{\partial Y/\partial T}{\partial Y/\partial F} = \frac{\delta F}{(1-\delta)T} \tag{13.4}$$

Firms select the equilibrium mix of inputs by imposing the ratio between the input marginal costs equal to the slope of isoquants. The equilibrium conditions for the couple of factors $F - T$ is thus obtained by imposing (13.4) equal to the ratio of the marginal prices of factors:

$$\frac{\partial Y/\partial T}{\partial Y/\partial F} = \frac{\partial F}{(1-\delta)T} = \frac{u}{z} \tag{13.5}$$

From (13.5), in equilibrium it must be:

$$F^* = \frac{u(1-\delta)}{z\delta} T^* \tag{13.6}$$

The optimal mix of productive factors that would entail total costs equal to $\tilde{C}$ can be obtained as the solution of the following system:

$$\begin{cases} F^* = \dfrac{u(1-\delta)}{z\delta} T^* \\ \tilde{C} = zF^* + uT^* \end{cases} \tag{13.7}$$

The solution of (13.7) gives:

$$\begin{cases} T^* = \tilde{C}\,\dfrac{\delta}{u} \\ F^* = \tilde{C}\,\dfrac{1-\delta}{z} \end{cases} \tag{13.8}$$

Substituting (13.8) in (13.1), we can express the level of output that can be achieved at cost $\tilde{C}$:

$$Y^* = \tilde{C}\left(\frac{1-\delta}{z}\right)^{1-\delta}\left(\frac{\delta}{u}\right)^{\delta} \tag{13.9}$$

Building on the hypothesis that firms react to changes in the market price of inputs so as to improve their technological congruence, we assume that the output elasticity of inputs depends on their relative price: cumulated knowledge and physical factors. In particular, we assume that, because of the search for technological congruence, firms have a clear incentive to innovate and change their technology so that, when the ratio u/z falls, δ should increase. Hence:

$$\delta = \bar{\delta}e^{-u/z} + \underline{\delta} \qquad (13.10)$$

Equation (13.10) implies that $\delta \in (\underline{\delta}, \underline{\delta} + \bar{\delta}]$.

Let us now evaluate the effect of a variation of u on the level of production Y^*. We can write:

$$dY^*/du = \partial Y^*/\partial\delta \; \partial\delta/\partial u + \partial Y^*/\partial u \qquad (13.11)$$

To obtain $\partial Y^*/\partial\delta$, we apply to (13.7) the differentiation rule $D((f(x)g(x)) = f'(x)g(x) + f(x)g'(x)$, where $x = \delta$, $f(x) = \tilde{C}[((1-\delta)/z)^{1-\delta}]$ and $g(x) = (\delta/u)^\delta$.

In particular, to obtain $\partial[(\delta/u)^\delta]/\partial\delta$, we exploit the differentiation rule $D((h(x)^{l(x)}) = h(x)^{l(x)}[l'(x)\ln h(x) + l(x)h'(x)/h(x)]$ where $x = \delta$, $h(x) = \delta/u$ and $l(x) = \delta$. We proceed similarly to compute $\partial[((1-\delta)/z^{1-\delta}]]/\partial\delta$, where we use $h(x) = (1-\delta)/z$ and $l(x) = 1 - \delta$.

We thus obtain:

$$\frac{\partial Y^*}{\partial\delta} = \tilde{C}\left[\left(\frac{1-\delta}{z}\right)^{1-\delta}\left(-\ln\frac{1-\delta}{z} - 1\right)\left(\frac{\delta}{u}\right)^\delta + \left(\frac{1-\delta}{z}\right)^{1-\delta}\left(\frac{\delta}{u}\right)^\delta\left(\ln\frac{\delta}{u}\right)\right]$$

$$= \tilde{C}\left(\frac{1-\delta}{z}\right)^{1-\delta}\left(\frac{\delta}{u}\right)^\delta\left(\ln\frac{\delta z}{(1-\delta)u}\right) \qquad (13.12)$$

By substituting (13.9) and (13.6), equation (13.12) can be rewritten as:

$$\frac{\partial Y^*}{\partial\delta} = Y^*\left(\ln\frac{T^*}{F^*}\right) \qquad (13.13)$$

Moreover, by deriving (13.9), we obtain

$$\frac{\partial Y^*}{\partial u} = \tilde{C}\left(\frac{1-\delta}{z}\right)^{1-\delta}\left(\frac{\delta}{u}\right)^\delta\left(-\frac{\delta}{u}\right) = -Y^*\frac{\delta}{u} \qquad (13.14)$$

and, by taking derivative in (13.10), we have:

$$\frac{\partial\delta}{\partial u} = -\frac{\bar{\delta}}{z}e^{-u/z} \qquad (13.15)$$

Substituting (13.13), (13.14) and (13.15) into (13.11), we have:

$$\frac{\partial Y^*}{\partial u} = Y^*\left(-\frac{\overline{\delta}}{z}e^{-u/z}\ln\frac{T^*}{F^*} - \frac{\delta}{u}\right) \tag{13.16}$$

Given that, from (13.12), $\overline{\delta}e^{-u/z} = \delta - \underline{\delta}$, the previous equation becomes

$$\frac{\partial Y^*}{\partial u} = Y^*\left(-\frac{\delta - \underline{\delta}}{z}\ln\frac{T^*}{F^*} - \frac{\delta}{u}\right) \tag{13.17}$$

From the previous expression, we have that a sufficient condition for $dY^*/du < 0$ is $T^* > F^*$.

The demand for technological knowledge, from (13.8), is given by

$$T^* = \tilde{C}\frac{\delta}{u} \tag{13.18}$$

From expression (13.18), demand for technological knowledge is a decreasing function of u and increasing with δ. Note that when u decreases, Y increases even without technological change.

Let us assume that technological knowledge cumulates, so that the stock available at a given time t is equal to the sum of the technological knowledge that has been employed in all the previous periods. We denote with KN_t the stock of technological knowledge at time t, and with T_j the level of technology at time j:

$$KN_t = \sum_{j=0}^{t-1}T_j^* \tag{13.19}$$

Following Griliches (1979) and Weitzman (1996), we assume that the generation of technological knowledge is a recombinant and non-ergodic process where the stock of existing knowledge KN_t enters the knowledge generation function as an indispensable input alongside current R&D activities. The flows of additional knowledge add to the stock of existing knowledge that keeps increasing. As a consequence, assuming that the unit costs of access and use of the stock of knowledge decrease, the cost of the additional units of knowledge keeps decreasing.[2] Hence we can assume that u_t, the unit cost of technological knowledge as an output of the knowledge generation function at time t, is negatively correlated with the stock of technological knowledge KN_t at the same time t:

$$du_t/dKN_t < 0 \tag{13.20}$$

As $T^* > 0$ for any t, then $KN_t > KN_{t-1}$. By (13.20) this might imply a process where a reduction of u ($u_t < u_{t-1}$) is followed, by (13.10), by an increase of δ ($\delta_t > \delta_{t-1}$). If $T_t^* > F_t^*$, the reduction of u and increase of δ induces endogenously an increase in the level of production Y. The accumulation of technological knowledge shifts, by technological congruence, the production function towards more technologically intensive techniques; if the level of technological knowledge in use is higher than that of physical factors, the level of production increases given the same production costs.

Note that this process can take place only if the increase in the supply of knowledge is larger than the increase in its derived demand stemming from the biased technological change directed at increasing the output elasticity of knowledge in the production function.

Moreover, when some technological knowledge is first introduced, the level of cumulated knowledge KN tends to zero and the value of u is relatively high. Still, by (13.18), $T^* > 0$. This implies that a minimum amount of technological knowledge is indispensable to start any production process and, because of accumulation, its cost falls from the high levels found at the onset.

From the analysis above, as the elasticity of technological knowledge increases because of the search for higher levels of technological congruence and the consequent introduction of new biased technologies directed towards more knowledge-intensive technologies, the intensity of technological knowledge also increases.

Let us now extend the result to a macroeconomic level. On the demand side, as $u_{t+1} < u_t$ and $\delta_{t+1} > \delta_t$, it must be, from (13.18), $T^*(u_{t+1}, \delta_{t+1}) > T^*(u_t, \delta_t)$. It must be noted, moreover, that, over time, the derived demand of technological knowledge T shifts to the right, also because of the positive effects on Y of the decline of u.

On the supply side, the supply of technological knowledge at a given time t is assumed to be an increasing function of u and knowledge KN_t:

$$T_t^s(u; KN_t) = kKN_t + \varepsilon u \qquad (13.21)$$

with $k, \varepsilon > 0$.

In factor markets the equilibrium price of technological knowledge is found by balancing the demand for technological knowledge from (13.18) with its supply from (13.21):

$$\frac{Y\delta}{u} = kKN + \varepsilon u \qquad (13.22)$$

Figure 13.1 represents the variation in equilibrium price of technological knowledge when the demand for technological knowledge shifts to the

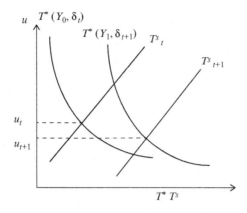

Figure 13.1   Equilibrium in the market for technological knowledge

right because of the increased levels of Y and δ together with the supply driven by the increase of δ from δ_t to δ_{t+1}.

The accumulation of technological knowledge over time induces, by (13.22), a decrease of u from u_0 to u_1. This reduction causes a right shift of the derived demand of technological knowledge. This shift will take place both with an adaptive and a creative reaction. In the latter case it will be stronger. Let us explore the matter in detail.

The derived demand for technological knowledge shifts to the right, because of the positive effects on Y of the decline of u, even if firms – because of the low quality of knowledge governance mechanisms at work in their economic system – are not able to implement a creative reaction and introduce biased technological changes aimed at increasing the output elasticity of technological knowledge δ. Their adaptive reaction will consist just in changes of production techniques on the existing map of isoquants. Yet the decline of u yields and increase of Y, and hence a positive (albeit smaller) shift in the derived demand for technological knowledge.

When, instead, the quality of the institutional mechanisms of knowledge governance is high, firms will be able to take advantage of the reduction of u with a creative reaction and the consequent introduction of biased technological innovations. In this case the right shift of the derived demand for technological knowledge is much larger because of the twin effects of the increase in δ and the larger increase of Y caused not only by the reduction of u but also by the increase in total factor productivity.

As represented in Figure 13.1, when the reaction is adaptive the demand for technological knowledge shifts slightly to the right because of the increase of Y. When, instead, a creative reaction takes place, and firms can introduce directed technological innovations, δ increases from δ_t to δ_{t+1}. This produces, by (13.16) together with the effects of the increasing levels of Y, a much larger increase in demand for technological knowledge, shifting the relative function to $T^*(\delta_{t+1})$. On the supply side, the working of cumulativity and non-exhaustibility explains the shift in knowledge schedule over time.

If $u_{t+1} < u_t$, the accumulation of technological knowledge sets in motion an endogenous decrease in the price of technological knowledge, leading to a process directed towards a more technology-based production mix (by means of an increase in T/F) and technological knowledge-intensive technology production function (by means of an increase in δ), resulting in the long run in increased total factor productivity and level of production Y.

When the supply of additional technological knowledge is not able to compensate for the increase in its derived demand, the price of technological knowledge increases and the dynamics of the system stops. The need to avoid these risks identifies the scope for a dedicated economic policy aimed at implementing the dynamics of knowledge-intensive technological change.

13.3   CONCLUSIONS

This chapter has accommodated within the Schumpeterian framework of creative response the recent advances in the economics of innovation, technological change and innovation. Their integration enables us to articulate a Schumpeterian model of growth characterized by out-of-equilibrium conditions determined by the endogenous accumulation of knowledge. The model analysed the effects of knowledge indivisibility, articulated in knowledge complementarity and cumulativity, and transient appropriability on the generation of technological knowledge – at each point in time and through time – on the creative reaction of firms; the search for technological congruence; the introduction of induced technological change; and the consequent growth of output and total factor productivity in the long term.

The notion of knowledge as an endogenous endowment based upon diachronic knowledge externalities plays a central role. Diachronic knowledge externalities stem from the accumulation of knowledge generated as proprietary, but appropriated by its 'inventors' only for a limited stretch of time. The current vintages of knowledge gradually but inevitably become part of the stock of public knowledge that can be accessed and used in the generation of new knowledge by every firm at decreasing cost, through time. The notion of diachronic knowledge externalities enables us to reconsider the effects of the Arrovian properties of knowledge as a special economic good. Analysis of the knowledge generation process, in fact, allows us to balance the negative effects of transient appropriability, in terms of missing incentives to generate new technological knowledge, with the positive effects of knowledge cumulativity and non-exhaustibility on the dynamics of the costs of knowledge. Standard economic goods are fully appropriable, but do suffer wear and tear. The intuition of Zvi Griliches that spillovers are the other – positive – side of the transient appropriability coin is augmented and empowered by appreciation of its inter-temporal aspects.

Appreciation of the limited exhaustibility and cumulability of knowledge with the consequent diachronic knowledge externalities enables us to overcome the limits of current endogenous growth models. They allow elaboration of an alternative solution to the problem of combining instantaneous competitive conditions in both product and factor markets with dynamic increasing returns (Romer, 1994). At each point in time firms fund and carry out R&D according to their marginal productivity as they can appropriate their returns. Firms cannot appropriate the extra returns of knowledge that stem from knowledge cumulativity and non-exhaustibility, another Arrovian property. The assumption of monopolistic competition or oligopolistic rivalry is no longer necessary to accommodate increasing returns (Romer, 1990). The inter-temporal accumulation of knowledge that spills, with appropriate lags, from inventors and adds to the stock of public knowledge accounts for the decrease in costs of knowledge as an input, and hence the reduction of knowledge as an output.

This chapter has applied the analytical framework of the creative response elaborated by Schumpeter (1947a) to understanding economic growth as a consequence of the reduction of the user cost of technological knowledge stemming from knowledge complementarity, non-exhaustibility and cumulability. The reduction in the cost of technological knowledge stemming from the effects of these intrinsic properties of knowledge in its recombinant generation process, where new items of technological knowledge are generated by means of the recombination of existing ones, has the consequence that the larger is the stock of public knowledge and the larger are pecuniary knowledge externalities, the greater the chance to generate new knowledge items and hence, with a given research cost, the lower the unit costs of new technological knowledge.

The reduction of the user cost of technological knowledge enhances the Schumpeterian – creative reaction – of firms that try to cope with both the changing conditions of product markets and market rivalry and the endogenous changes in the factor markets, specifically in the markets for technological knowledge. When the reaction, supported by a viable institutional set-up, is creative, firms are able to search for higher levels of technological congruence that lead to fostering the innovation process and skewing it towards the introduction of technological changes directed at increasing the output elasticity of technological knowledge as an input.

This Schumpeterian growth model highlights the crucial role of the laws of accumulation of the stock of public knowledge and of the conditions of access and use of technological knowledge that cannot be fully appropriated by its inventors. It enables us to appreciate the systemic conditions that shape the actual costs of knowledge. In this context it is clear that the levels of knowledge connectivity of a system are crucial to overcome the constraint to the self-sustained process of growth that stems from the dynamic balance between the effects of the increased derived demand of technological knowledge – determined by the knowledge-intensive direction of technological change – and the effects of knowledge cumulativity.

Identification of the constraint paves the way to specifying policy interventions finalized to keep the system in motion on the growth path and to avoid to falling into the trap of equilibrium. Effective knowledge governance enables systems to accumulate faster the flows of new knowledge into the stock of public knowledge and to reduce the costs of accessing and using it. Larger knowledge pecuniary and diachronic externalities favour the rates of reduction in the cost of knowledge, and hence balance the effects of the increasing levels of derived demand for knowledge.

The new knowledge-intensive technologies account not only for the growth of output and total factor productivity but also for the further accumulation of technological knowledge, which, in turn, feeds the reduction of its cost. This dynamics seems able to account for the shift of advanced economies away from the manufacturing industry typically characterized by strong capital intensity, to knowledge economies characterized by large output elasticity of knowledge and strong knowledge intensity. In an open economy framework of analysis this dynamics is reinforced by the competitive advantage stemming from the relative size of the knowledge stock that strengthens specialization in the generation and use of technological knowledge as both output and input.

NOTES

1. Following Arrow (1962), Romer (1990, 1994) portrays the appropriability of knowledge as partial. Knowledge is split into two parts: appropriable and non-appropriable. Following Schumpeter (1911/34), this chapter articulates the alternative hypothesis that the appropriability of knowledge is transient. Like Schumpeterian profits, all knowledge can be appropriated for a limited – transient – stretch of time. Eventually, all knowledge becomes public.
2. To make our argument clear, we explicate here the two postulates of our analysis: first,

that the unit costs of accessing and using the stock of knowledge decrease with its size. It seems plausible to assume that the amount of searching necessary to identify and absorb the relevant knowledge items declines with the size of the knowledge stock. Second, the quality of knowledge governance mechanisms does not decline along with the size of the stock of knowledge. We assume consequently that – with a given budget – knowledge output increases along with the stock of external knowledge.

References

Abramovitz, M. (1956), 'Resources and output trends in the US since 1870', *American Economic Review*, **46**, 5–23.

Abramovitz, M. and David, P.A. (1996a), 'Convergence and delayed catch-up: Productivity leadership and the waning of American exceptionalism', in R. Landau, T. Taylor and G. Wright (eds), *The Mosaic of Economic Growth*, Stanford, CA: Stanford University Press, pp. 21–62.

Abramovitz, M. and David, P.A. (1996b), 'Technological change and the rise of intangible investments: The US economy growth path in the twentieth century', in OECD (ed.), *Employment and Growth in the Knowledge-Based Economy*, Paris: OECD, pp. 35–60.

Abramovsky, L. and Griffith, R. (2006), 'Outsourcing and offshoring of business services: How important is ICT?', *Journal of the European Economic Association*, **4** (2–3), 594–601.

Acemoglu, D. (1998), 'Why do new technologies complement skills? Directed technical change and inequality', *Quarterly Journal of Economics*, **113**, 1055–89.

Acemoglu, D.K. (2002), 'Directed technical change', *Review of Economic Studies*, **69**, 781–809.

Acemoglu, D. (2003), 'Labor- and capital-augmenting technical change', *Journal of European Economic Association*, **1**, 1–37.

Acemoglu, D.K. (2010), 'When does labor scarcity encourage innovation?', *Journal of Political Economy*, **118**, 1037–78.

Acemoglu, D. (2015), 'Localized and biased technologies: Atkinson and Stiglitz's new view, induced innovations, and directed technological change', *Economic Journal*, **125** (3), 443–63.

Acemoglu, D. and Zilibotti, F. (2001), 'Productivity differences', *Quarterly Journal of Economics*, **116**, 563–606.

Adams, J.D. (1990), 'Fundamental stocks of knowledge and productivity growth', *Journal of Political Economy*, **98**, 673–702.

Adams, J.D. (2006), 'Learning internal research and spillovers', *Economics of Innovation and New Technology*, **15**, 5–36.

Adams, J.D. and Clemmons, R.J. (2013), 'How rapidly does science leak out? A study of the diffusion of fundamental ideas', *Journal of Human Capital*, **7**, 191–229.

Aghion, P. and Howitt, P.H. (1997), *Endogenous Growth*, Cambridge, MA: MIT Press.

Aghion, P. and Jaravel, X. (2015), 'Knowledge spillovers innovation and growth', *Economic Journal*, **125**, 533–45.

Aghion, P., Akcigit, U. and Howitt, P. (2014), 'What do we learn from Schumpeterian growth theory?', in P. Aghion and S. Durlauf (eds), *Handbook of Economic Growth*, Vol. 2, Amsterdam: Elsevier, pp. 515–63.

Aghion, P., Akcigit, U. and Howitt, P. (2015), 'Lessons from Schumpeterian growth theory', *American Economic Review*, **105**, 94–9.

Aghion, P., Bloom, N., Blundell, R. and Howitt, P. (2005), 'Competition and innovation: An inverted-U relationship', *Quarterly Journal of Economics*, **120** (2), 701–28.

Agrawal, A. and Goldfarb, A. (2008), 'Restructuring research: Communication costs and the democratization of university innovation', *American Economic Review*, **99** (4), 1578–90.

Albin, P.S. (1998), *Barriers and Bounds to Rationality: Essays on Economic Complexity and Dynamics in Interactive Systems*, Princeton: Princeton University Press.

Alchian, A. (1950), 'Uncertainty evolution and economic theory', *Journal of Political Economy*, **58** (3), 211–21.

Andersen, E.S. (2009), *Schumpeter's Evolutionary Economics: A Theoretical, Historical and Statistical Analysis of the Engine of Capitalism*, London: Anthem Press.

Anderson, P. and Tushman, M. (1990), 'Technological discontinuities and dominant designs: A cyclical model of technological change', *Administrative Science Quarterly*, **35** (4), 604–35.

Anderson, P.W., Arrow, K.J. and Pines, D. (eds) (1988), *The Economy as an Evolving Complex System*, Redwood, CA: Addison-Wesley.

Antonelli, C. (1985), 'The diffusion of an organizational innovation: International data telecommunications and multinational industrial firms', *International Journal of Industrial Organization*, **3** (1), 109–18.

Antonelli, C. (1986), 'The international diffusion of new information technologies', *Research Policy*, **15** (3), 139–147

Antonelli, C. (1989), 'A failure inducement model of research and development expenditure: Italian evidence from the early 1980', *Journal of Economic Behavior and Organization*, **12** (2), 159–80.

Antonelli, C. (1995), *The Economics of Localized Technological Change and Industrial Dynamics*, Boston: Kluwer Academic.

Antonelli, C. (2003), *The Economics of Innovation New Technologies and Structural Change*, London: Routledge.

Antonelli, C. (2006), 'Localized technological change and factor markets:

Constraints and inducements to innovation', *Structural Change and Economic Dynamics*, **17**, 224–47.

Antonelli, C. (2007a), 'The system dynamics of collective knowledge: From gradualism and saltationism to punctuated change', *Journal of Economic Behavior and Organization*, **62**, 215–36.

Antonelli, C. (2007b), 'Knowledge as an essential facility', *Journal of Evolutionary Economics*, **17** (4), 451–71.

Antonelli, C. (2008a), 'Pecuniary knowledge externalities: The convergence of directed technological change and the emergence of innovation systems,' *Industrial and Corporate Change*, **17**, 1049–70.

Antonelli, C. (2008b), *Localized Technological Change: Towards the Economics of Complexity*, London: Routledge.

Antonelli, C. (2009), 'The economics of innovation: From the classical legacies to the economics of complexity', *Economics of Innovation and New Technology*, **18**, 611–46.

Antonelli, C. (ed.) (2011), *Handbook on the Economic Complexity of Technological Change*, Cheltenham, UK and Northampton, MA, USA: Edward Elgar Publishing.

Antonelli, C. (2012), 'Technological congruence and productivity growth', in M. Andersson, B. Johansson, C. Karlsson and H. Lööf (eds), *Innovation and Growth: From R&D Strategies of Innovating Firms to Economy-Wide Technological Change*, Oxford: Oxford University Press, pp. 209–32.

Antonelli, C. (2013a), 'Compulsory licensing: The foundations of an institutional innovation', *WIPO Journal*, **4**, 157–74.

Antonelli, C. (2013b), 'Knowledge governance, pecuniary knowledge externalities and total factor productivity growth', *Economic Development Quarterly*, **27**, 62–70.

Antonelli, C. (2015a), 'Innovation as a creative response: A reappraisal of the Schumpeterian legacy', *History of Economic Ideas*, **23**, 99–118.

Antonelli, C. (2015b), 'A Schumpeterian growth model: Wealth and directed technological change', *Journal of Technology Transfer*, **41** (3), 395–406.

Antonelli, C. (2016), 'The economics of technological congruence and the economic complexity of technological change', *Structural Change and Economic Dynamics*, **38**, 15–24.

Antonelli, C. (2017), 'The derived demand for knowledge', *Economics of Innovation and New Technology*, **26** (1–2), 183–94.

Antonelli, C. (forthcoming), 'Endogenous innovation: The creative response', *Economics of Innovation and New Technology*.

Antonelli, C. and Barbiellini Amidei, F. (2011), *The Dynamics of Knowledge*

Externalities: Localized Technological Change in Italy, Cheltenham, UK and Northampton, MA, USA: Edward Elgar Publishing.

Antonelli, C. and Colombelli, A. (2011), 'Globalization and directed technological change at the firm level: The European evidence', in Libecap, G. (ed.), *Advances in the Study of Entrepreneurship, Innovation and Economic Growth*, Vol. 22, Cambridge: Emerald, pp. 1–20.

Antonelli, C. and Colombelli, A. (2015a), 'External and internal knowledge in the knowledge generation function', *Industry and Innovation*, **22** (4), 273–98.

Antonelli, C. and Colombelli, A. (2015b), 'The cost of knowledge', *International Journal of Production Economics*, **168**, 290–302.

Antonelli, C. and Colombelli, A. (forthcoming), 'The locus of knowledge externalities and the cost of knowledge', *Regional Studies*, DOI 10.1080/00343404.2017.1331294.

Antonelli, C. and Crespi, F. (2012), 'Matthew effects and R&D subsidies: Knowledge cumulability in high-tech and low-tech industries', *Giornale degli Economisti e Annali di Economia*, **71**, 5–31.

Antonelli, C. and David, P.A. (eds) (2015), *The Economics of Knowledge and the Knowledge Driven Economy*, London: Routledge.

Antonelli, C. and Fassio, C. (2011), 'Globalization and innovation in advanced economies', in Libecap, G. (ed.), *Advances in the Study of Entrepreneurship, Innovation and Economic Growth*, Vol. 22, Cambridge: Emerald, pp. 21–46.

Antonelli, C. and Fassio, C. (2014), 'The economics of the light economy: Globalization, skill biased technological change and slow growth', *Technological Forecasting and Social Change*, **87**, 89–107.

Antonelli, C. and Fassio, C. (2016), 'The role of external knowledge(s) in the introduction of product and process innovations', *R&D Management*, **46** (1), 979–91.

Antonelli, C. and Ferraris, G. (2011), 'Innovation as an emergent system property: An agent based model', *Journal of Artificial Societies and Social Simulation*, **14**, n.p.

Antonelli, C. and Ferraris, G. (2017), 'The creative response and the endogenous dynamics of pecuniary knowledge externalities: An agent based simulation model', *Journal of Economic Interaction and Coordination*, DOI 10.1007/s11403-017-0194-3 (forthcoming).

Antonelli, C. and Ferraris, G. (forthcoming), 'The Marshallian and Schumpeterian microfoundations of evolutionary complexity: An agent based simulation model', in U. Cantner and A. Pyka (eds), *Foundations of Economic Change: Behaviour, Interaction and Aggregate Outcomes*, Berlin: Springer.

Antonelli, C. and Gehringer, A. (2015a), 'The competent demand pull hypothesis: Which sectors play the role?', *Economia Politica*, **32** (1), 97–134.

Antonelli, C. and Gehringer, A. (2015b), 'The competent demand pull hypothesis', in F. Crespi and F. Quatraro (eds), *The Economics of Knowledge, Innovation and Systemic Technology Policy*, London: Routledge, pp. 48–69.

Antonelli, C. and Gehringer, A. (2015c), 'Knowledge externalities and demand pull: The European evidence', *Economic Systems*, **39** (4), 608–31.

Antonelli, C. and Gehringer, A. (2016), 'The cost of knowledge and productivity growth', in A.N. Link and C. Antonelli (eds), *Strategic Alliances: Leveraging Economic Growth and Development*, London: Routledge.

Antonelli, C. and Link, A. (eds) (2015), *Handbook of the Economics of Knowledge*, London: Routledge.

Antonelli, C. and Patrucco, P.P. (2016), 'Organizational innovations, ICTs and knowledge governance: The case of platforms', in J.M. Bauer and M. Latzer (eds), *Handbook on the Economics of the Internet*, Cheltenham, UK and Northampton, MA, USA: Edward Elgar Publishing, pp. 323–43.

Antonelli, C. and Quatraro, F. (2010), 'The effects of biased technological change on total factor productivity: Empirical evidence from a sample of OECD countries', *Journal of Technology Transfer*, **35**, 361–83.

Antonelli, C. and Scellato, G. (2011), 'Out-of-equilibrium profit and innovation', *Economics of Innovation and New Technology*, **20** (5), 405–21.

Antonelli, C. and Scellato, G. (2013), 'Complexity and innovation: Social interactions and firm level productivity growth', *Journal of Evolutionary Economics*, **23** (1), 77–96.

Antonelli, C., Crespi, F., Mongeau, C. and Scellato, G. (2016), 'Knowledge composition, Jacobs externalities and innovation performance in European regions', LEI&BRICK Working Paper 07/2016.

Antonelli, C., Crespi, F. and Scellato, G. (2012), 'Inside innovation persistence: New evidence from Italian micro-data', *Structural Change and Economic Dynamics*, **23** (4), 341–53.

Antonelli, C., Crespi, F. and Scellato, G. (2013), 'Internal and external factors in innovation persistence', *Economics of Innovation and New Technology*, **22** (3), 256–80.

Antonelli, C., Crespi, F. and Scellato, G. (2015), 'Productivity growth persistence: Firm strategies, size and system properties', *Small Business Economics*, **45** (1), 129–47.

Antonelli, C., Geuna, A. and Steinmueller, E. (2000), 'New information and communication technologies and the production distribution and use of knowledge', *International Journal of Technology Management*, **20** (1–2), 72–94.

Antonelli, C., Krafft, J. and Quatraro, F. (2010), 'Recombinant knowledge and growth: The case of ICTs', *Structural Change and Economic Dynamics*, **21**, 50–69.

Antonelli, C., Patrucco, P.P. and Quatraro, F. (2011), 'Productivity growth and pecuniary knowledge externalities: An empirical analysis of agglomeration economies in European regions', *Economic Geography*, **87** (1), 23–50.

Arocena, R. and Sutz, J. (2010), 'Weak knowledge demand in the south: Learning divides and innovation policies', *Science and Public Policy*, **37** (8), 571–82.

Arora, A. and Gambardella, A. (1990), 'Complementarity and external linkages: The strategies of the large firms in biotechnology', *Journal of Industrial Economics*, **38**, 361–79.

Arora, A. and Gambardella, A. (1994), 'Evaluating technological information and utilizing it: Scientific knowledge, technological capability and external linkages in biotechnology', *Journal of Economic Behavior and Organization*, **24**, 91–114.

Arora, A., Fosfuri, A. and Gambardella, A. (2001), *Markets for Technology*, Cambridge, MA: MIT Press.

Arrow, K.J. (1962), 'Economic welfare and the allocation of resources for invention', in Nelson, R.R. [NBER] (ed.), *The Rate and Direction of Inventive Activity: Economic and Social Factors*, Princeton: Princeton University Press, pp. 609–625.

Arrow, K.J. (1969), 'Classificatory notes on the production and transmission of technical knowledge', *American Economic Review*, **59**, 29–35.

Arrow, K.J. and Lind, R.C. (1970), 'Uncertainty and the evaluation of public investment decisions', *American Economic Review*, **60** (3), 364–78.

Arthur, B. (2014), 'Complexity economics and innovation complexity economics: A different framework for economic thought', Presentation to the 15th Schumpeter Society Conference, 'Foundations of Economic Change: Behavior, Interaction and Aggregate Outcomes', Jena, 27–30 July.

Arthur, B. (2015), *Complexity and the Economy*, Oxford: Oxford University Press.

Arthur, W.B. (2009), *The Nature of Technology: What It Is And How It Evolves*, New York: Free Press.

Arthur, W.B. (2010), 'Complexity, the Santa Fe approach and nonequilibrium economics', *History of Economic Ideas*, **18** (2), 149–66.

Arthur, W.B., Durlauf, S. and Lane, D. (eds) (1997), *The Economy as an Evolving Complex System II*, Reading, MA: Addison-Wesley.

Audretsch, D.B. (1995), *Innovation and Industry Evolution*, Cambridge, MA: MIT Press.

Audretsch, D.B. (2006), *Entrepreneurship Innovation and Economic Growth*, Cheltenham, UK and Northampton, MA, USA: Edward Elgar Publishing.

Audretsch, D.B. (2007), *The Entrepreneurial Society*, Oxford: Oxford University Press.

Audretsch, D.B. and Feldman, M.P. (2004), 'Knowledge spillovers and the geography of innovation', in J. Vernon Henderson and J.-F. Thisse (eds), *Handbook of Regional and Urban Economics*, Vol. 4, Amsterdam: Elsevier, pp. 2713–39.

Audretsch, D.B., Lehmann, E. and Hinger, J. (2015), 'From knowledge to innovation: The role of knowledge spillover entrepreneurship', in C. Antonelli and A. Link (eds), *The Routledge Handbook of the Economics of Knowledge*, London: Routledge, pp. 20–28.

Bailey, A., Irz, X. and Balcombe, K. (2004), 'Measuring productivity growth when technological change is biased: A new index and an application to UK agriculture', *Agricultural Economics*, **31**, 285–95.

Bandura, A. and Cervone, D. (1986), 'Differential engagement of self-reactive influences in cognitive motivation', *Organizational Behavior and Human Decision Processes*, **38**, 92–113.

Bauer, J.M. (2014), 'Platforms, systems competition, and innovation: Reassessing the foundations of communications policy', *Telecommunications Policy*, **38** (8–9), 662–73.

Bauer, J.M. and Latzer, M. (eds) (2016), *Handbook on the Economics of the Internet*, Cheltenham, UK and Northampton, MA, USA: Edward Elgar Publishing.

Bloom, N., Schankerman, M. and Van Reenen, J. (2013), 'Identifying technology spillovers and product market rivalry', *Econometrica*, **81**, 1347–93.

Blume, L.E. and Durlauf, S.N. (2006), *The Economy as an Evolving System, III*, Oxford: Oxford University Press.

Bockerman, P. and Maliranta, M. (2012), 'Globalization, creative destruction, and labour share change: Evidence on the determinants and mechanisms from longitudinal plant-level data', *Oxford Economic Papers*, **64**, 259–80.

Bonifati, G. (2010), '"More is different", exaptation and uncertainty: Three foundational concepts for a complexity theory of innovation', *Economics of Innovation and New Technology*, **19** (8), 743–60.

Boppart, T. and Staub, K.E. (2016), 'Online accessibility of scholarly literature and academic innovation', Mimeo.

Borowiecki, K.J. and Navarrete, T. (2015), 'Digitization of heritage collections as indicator of innovation', Discussion papers on business and economics, University of Southern Denmark, 14/2015.

Boschma, R. (2005), 'Proximity and innovation: A critical assessment', *Regional Studies*, **39** (1), 61–74.

Branstetter, L. (2001), 'Are knowledge spillovers international or intranational in scope? Microeconometric evidence from Japan and the United States', *Journal of International Economics*, **53** (1), 53–79.

Breschi, S. and Lissoni, F. (2001), 'Knowledge spillovers and local innovation systems: A critical survey', *Industrial and Corporate Change*, **10**, 975–1005.

Bresnahan, T.J. and Trajtenberg, M. (1995), 'General purpose technologies: "Engines of growth"?', *Journal of Econometrics*, **95**, 83–108.

Briglauer, W., Gugler, K. and Bohlin, E. (2013), 'Regulatory approaches and investment in new communications infrastructure', *Telecommunications Policy*, **37** (10), 815–18.

Brynjolfsson E. and Saunders, A. (2010), *Wired for Innovation: How Information Technology is Reshaping the Economy*, Cambridge, MA: MIT Press.

Caldari, K. (2105), 'Marshall and complexity: A necessary balance between process and order', *Cambridge Journal of Economics*, **39** (4), 1071–85.

Caselli, F. and Coleman II, W.J. (2006), 'The world technology frontier', *American Economic Review*, **96** (3), 499–522.

Caselli, F. and Feyer, J. (2007), 'The marginal product of capital', *Quarterly Journal of Economics*, **122**, 535–68.

Cassata F. and Marchionatti R. (2011), 'A transdisciplinary perspective on economic complexity: Marshall's problem revisited', *Journal of Economic Behavior and Organization*, **80** (1), 122–36.

Cassiman, B. and Veugelers, R. (2006), 'In search of complementarity in the innovation strategy: Internal R&D and external knowledge acquisition', *Management Science*, **52**, 68–82.

Cerchione, R., Esposito, E. and Spadaro, M.R. (2015), 'The spread of knowledge management in SMEs: A scenario in evolution', *Sustainability*, **7**, 10210–32.

Chesbrough, H. (2003), *Open Innovation: The New Imperative for Creating and Profiting from Technology*, Boston, MA: Harvard Business School Press.

Chesbrough, H., Vanhaverbeke, W. and West, J. (eds) (2006), *Open Innovation: Researching a New Paradigm*, Oxford: Oxford University Press.

Cimoli, M. and Porcile, G. (2009), 'Sources of learning paths and technological capabilities: An introductory roadmap of development processes', *Economics of Innovation and New Technology*, **18**, 675–94.

Clemence, R.V. (ed.) (1989), *Essays on Entrepreneurs, Innovations, Business Cycles, and the Evolution of Capitalism*, New Brunswick: Transaction.

Cobo, C. and Naval, C. (2013), 'Digital scholarship: Exploration of strategies and skills for knowledge creation and dissemination', Proceedings of the 1st International Conference on Internet Science, Brussels, 9–11 April.

Cohen, W.M. and Levinthal, D.A. (1989), 'Innovation and learning: The two faces of R&D', *Economic Journal*, **99**, 569–96.

Cohen, W.M. and Levinthal, D.A. (1990), 'Absorptive capacity: A new perspective on learning and innovation', *Administrative Science Quarterly*, **35**, 128–52.

Comin, D. and Hobijn, B. (2004), 'Cross-country technology adoption: Making the theories face the facts', *Journal of Monetary Economics*, **51**, 39–83.

Consoli, D. and Patrucco, P.P. (2008), 'Innovation platforms and the governance of knowledge: Evidence from Italy and the UK', *Economics of Innovation and New Technology*, **17** (7), 701–18.

Consoli, D. and Patrucco, P.P. (2011), 'Complexity and the coordination of technological knowledge: The case of innovation platforms', in Antonelli, C. (ed.), *Handbook on the Economic Complexity of Technological Change*, Cheltenham, UK and Northampton, MA, USA: Edward Elgar Publishing, pp. 201–20.

Cowan, R., David, P.A. and Foray, D. (2000), 'The explicit economics of knowledge codification and tacitness', *Industrial and Corporate Change*, **9**, 211–53.

Craft, N. (2010), 'Cliometrics and technological change: A survey', *European Journal of History of Economic Thought*, **17** (5), 1127–47.

Crépon, B., Duguet, E. and Mairesse, J. (1998), 'Research and development, innovation and productivity: An econometric analysis at the firm level', *Economics of Innovation and New Technology*, **7**, 115–58.

D'Adderio, L. (2004), *Inside the Virtual Product: How Organizations Create Knowledge through Software*, Cheltenham, UK and Northampton, MA, USA: Edward Elgar Publishing.

Dasgupta, P. and David, P.A. (1994), 'Toward a new economics of science', *Research Policy*, **23** (5), 487–521.

Dasgupta, P. and Stiglitz, J. (1980), 'Industrial structure and the nature of innovative activity', *Economic Journal*, **90** (358), 266–93.

Davenport, T.H. and Prusak, L. (1998), *Working Knowledge*, Boston, MA: Harvard Business School Press.

David, P.A. (1969), *A Contribution to the Theory of Diffusion*, Stanford, CA: Research Center in Economic Growth.

David, P.A. (1975), *Technical Choice Innovation and Economic Growth*, Cambridge: Cambridge University Press.

David P. (1993), 'Knowledge, property and the system dynamics of technological change', in L.S. Summers and S. Shah (eds), *Proceedings of the World Bank Annual Conference on Development Economics*, Washington, DC: International Bank for Reconstruction and Development, pp. 215–48.

David, P.A. (2005), 'Path dependence in economic processes: Implications for policy analysis in dynamical systems contexts', in K. Dopfer (ed.), *The Evolutionary Foundations of Economics*, Cambridge: Cambridge University Press, pp. 151–94.

David, P.A. (2007), 'Path dependence: A foundational concept for historical science', *Cliometrica*, **1** (1), 91–114.

David, P.A. and Rullani, F. (2008), 'Dynamics of innovation in an "open source" collaboration environment: Lurking laboring and launching FLOSS projects on SourceForge', *Industrial and Corporate Change*, **17**, 647–710.

David, P.A. and Wright, G. (2003), 'General purpose technologies and surges in productivity: Historical reflections on the future of the ICT revolution', in P.A. David and T. Mark (eds), *The Economic Future in Historical Perspective*, Oxford: Oxford University Press, pp. 135–66.

David, P.A., Hall, B.H. and Toole, A.A. (2000), 'Is public R&D a complement or substitute for private R&D? A review of the econometric evidence', *Research Policy*, **29**, 497–529.

Dawid, H. (2006), 'Agent-based models of innovation and technical change', in L. Tesfatsion and K.L. Judd (eds), *Handbook of Computational Economics, Vol. 2: Agent-Based Computational Economics*, Amsterdam: North-Holland, pp. 1235–72.

Debackere, K. and Van Looy, B. (2003), 'Managing integrated design capabilities in new product design and development', in B. Dankbaar (ed.), *Innovation Management in the Knowledge Economy*, London: Imperial College Press, pp. 213–34.

Depken, C.A. and Ward, M.R. (2009), 'Sited, sighted, and cited: The effect of JSTOR in economic research', SSRN Working Paper No. 1472063.

Dodgson, M., Gann, D. and Salter, A. (2006), 'The role of technology in the shift towards open innovation: The case of Procter & Gamble', *R&D Management*, **36** (3), 333–46.

Dosi, G., Marsili, O., Orsenigo, L. and Salvatore, R. (1995), 'Learning, market selection and the evolution of industrial structures', *Small Business Economics*, **7** (6), 411–36.

Edquist, C., Vonortas, N.S., Zabala-Iturriagagoitia, J.M. and Edler, J.

(eds) (2015), *Public Procurement for Innovation*, Cheltenham, UK and Northampton, MA, USA: Edward Elgar Publishing.

Eliasson, G. (2010), *Advanced Public Procurement as Industrial Policy: The Aircraft Industry as a Technical University*, Berlin: Springer.

Enkel, E., Gassmann, O. and Chesbrough, H. (2009), 'Open R&D and open innovation: Exploring the phenomenon', *R&D Management*, **39** (4), 311–16.

Esposito, E. and Mastroianni, M. (1998), 'Technological evolution of personal computers and market implications', *Technological Forecasting and Social Change*, **59**, 235–54.

Esposito, E. and Mastroianni, M. (2001), 'Information technology and personal computers: The relational life cycle', *Technovation*, **22**, 41–50.

Evangelista, R., Lucchese, M. and Meliciani, V. (2013), 'Business services innovation and sectoral growth', *Structural Change and Economic Dynamics*, **25**, 119–32.

Feder, C. (2015), 'A measure of total factor productivity with biased technological changes', WP Dipartimento di Economia e Statistica Cognetti de Martiis.

Feldman, M.A. (1999), 'The new economics of innovation, spillovers and agglomeration: A review of empirical studies', *Economics of Innovation and New Technology*, **8**, 5–25.

Fisher, F.M. and Temin, P. (1973), 'Returns to scale in research and development: What does the Schumpeterian hypothesis imply?', *Journal of Political Economy*, **81** (1), 56–70.

Fleming, L. and Sorenson, O. (2001), 'Technology as a complex adaptive system: Evidence from patent data', *Research Policy*, **30**, 1019–39.

Fontana, M. (2010), 'The Santa Fe perspective on economics', *History of Economic Ideas*, **18** (2), 167–96.

Foster J. and Metcalfe, J.S. (2012), 'Economic emergence: An evolutionary economic perspective', *Journal of Economic Behavior and Organization*, **82** (2), 420–32.

Fransman, M. (2002), 'Mapping the evolving telecoms industry: The uses and shortcomings of the layer model', *Telecommunications Policy*, **26** (9–10), 473–83.

Fransman, M. (2010), *The New ICT Ecosystem Implications for Policy and Regulation*, Cambridge: Cambridge University Press.

Fransman, M. (ed.) (2006), *Global Broadband Battles: Why the U.S. and Europe Lag While Asia Leads*, Stanford: Stanford University Press.

Freeman, C. (ed.) (1996), *The Long Wave in the World Economy*, Cheltenham, UK and Northampton, MA, USA: Edward Elgar Publishing.

Freeman, C., Clark, J. and Soete, L. (1982), *Unemployment and Technical*

Innovation: A Study of Long Waves in Economic Development, London: Frances Pinter.

Friedman, M. (1953), *Essays in Positive Economics*, Chicago: University of Chicago Press.

Galasso, A. and Schankerman, M. (2015), 'Patents and cumulative innovation: Causal evidence from the courts', *Quarterly Journal of Economics*, **130**, 317–69.

Gehringer, A. (2011), 'Pecuniary knowledge externalities and innovation: Intersectoral linkages and their effects beyond technological spillovers', *Economics of Innovation and New Technology*, **20**, 495–515.

Geroski, P. (1994), *Market Structure Corporate Performance and Innovative Activity*, Oxford: Clarendon.

Goldfarb, A., Greenstein, S.M. and Tucker, C. (eds) (2015), *Economic Analysis of the Digital Economy*, Chicago: University of Chicago Press.

Greenstein, S., Peitz, M. and Valletti, T. (2016), 'Net neutrality: A fast lane to understanding the trade-offs', *Journal of Economic Perspectives*, **30**, 127–50.

Griliches, Z. (1979), 'Issues in assessing the contribution of research and development to productivity growth', *Bell Journal of Econometrics*, **10** (1), 92–116.

Griliches, Z. (1984/98), 'Patent statistics as economic indicators: A survey', in Z. Griliches (ed.), *R&D and Productivity: The Econometric Evidence*, Chicago: University of Chicago Press.

Griliches, Z. (1986), 'Productivity, R&D, and basic research at the firm level in the 1970s', *American Economic Review*, **77** (1), 141–54.

Griliches, Z. (1992), 'The search for R&D spillovers', *Scandinavian Journal of Economics*, **94**, (Supplement), 29–47.

Griliches, Z. (1995), 'R&D and productivity: Econometric results and measurement issues', in P. Stoneman (ed.), *Handbook of the Economics of Innovation and New Technology*, Oxford: Blackwell, pp. 52–89.

Griliches Z. (ed.) (1998), *R&D and Productivity: The Econometric Evidence*, Chicago: University of Chicago Press.

Growiec, J. (2012), 'The world technology frontier: What can we learn from the US States?', *Oxford Bulletin of Economics and Statistics*, **74**, 777–807.

Guerrieri, P. and Meliciani, V. (2005), 'Technology and international competitiveness: The interdependence between manufacturing and producer services', *Structural Change and Economic Dynamics*, **16**, 489–502.

Guerrieri, P., Luciani, M. and Meliciani, V. (2011), 'The determinants of investment in information and communication technologies', *Economics of Innovation and New Technology*, **20**, 387–403.

Guerzoni, M. and Raiteri, E. (2015), 'Demand-side vs. supply-side technology policies: Hidden treatment and new empirical evidence on the policy mix', *Research Policy*, **44** (3), 726–47.

Habakkuk, H.J. (1962), *American and British Technology in the Nineteenth Century*, Cambridge: Cambridge University Press.

Hafeez-Baig, A. and Gururajan, R. (2012), 'Does information and communication technology (ICT) facilitate knowledge management activities in the 21st Century?', *Journal of Software*, **7** (11), 2437–42.

Hall, B.H. and Mairesse, J. (2006), 'Empirical studies of innovation in the knowledge driven economy', *Economics of Innovation and New Technology*, **15** (4–5), 289–99.

Hall, B.H. and Van Reenen, J. (2000), 'How effective are fiscal incentives for R&D? A review of the evidence', *Research Policy*, **29** (4–5), 449–69.

Hall, B.H., Mairesse, J. and Mohnen, P. (2010), 'Measuring the returns to R&D', in B.H. Hall and N. Rosenberg (eds), *Handbook of the Economics of Innovation*, Vol. 2, Amsterdam: Elsevier, pp. 1033–82.

Hall, R.E. and Jones, C.I. (1999), 'Why do some countries produce so much more output per worker than others?', *Quarterly Journal of Economics*, **114**, 83–116.

Hamermesh, D.S. and Oster, S.M. (2002), 'Tools or toys? The impact of high technology on scholarly productivity', *Economic Enquiry*, **40** (4), 539–55.

Harada, T. (2003), 'Three steps in knowledge communication: The emergence of knowledge transformers', *Research Policy*, **32**, 1737–51.

Harper, D.A. and Lewis, P. (2012), 'New perspectives on emergence in economics', *Journal of Economic Behavior and Organization*, **82** (2–3), 329–37.

Heimeriks, G. and Vasileiadou, E. (2008), 'Changes or transition? Analysing the use of ICTs in the sciences', *Social Science Information*, **47** (1), 5–29.

Hempell, T. and Zwick, T. (2008), 'New technology, work organization, and innovation', *Economics of Innovation and New Technology*, **17** (4), 331–54.

Hendriks, P.H.J. (1999), 'Why share knowledge? The influence of ICT on the motivation for knowledge sharing', *Knowledge and Process Management*, **6** (2), 91–100.

Hendriks, P.H.J. (2001), 'Many rivers to cross: From ICT to knowledge management systems', *Journal of Information Technology*, **16**, 57–72.

Hicks, J.R. (1932), *The Theory of Wages*, London: Macmillan.

Higon, D.A. (2011), 'The impact of ICT on innovation activities: Evidence from UK SMEs', *International Small Business Journal*, **30** (6), 684–99.

Hildago, C.A. and Hausmann, R. (2009), 'The building blocks of economic complexity', *Proceedings of the National Academy of Science*, **106** (26), 10570–75.

Ientile, D. and Mairesse, J. (2009), 'A policy to boost R&D: Does the R&D tax credit work?', *EIB Papers*, **14**, 144–68.

Iwai, K. (1984), 'Schumpeterian dynamics: An evolutionary model of innovation and imitation', *Journal of Economic Behavior and Organization*, **5** (2), 159–90.

Iwai, K. (2000), 'A contribution to the evolutionary theory of innovation, imitation and growth', *Journal of Economic Behavior and Organization*, **43** (2) 167–98.

Jaffe, A. (1986), 'Technological opportunity and spillovers of R&D: Evidence from firms' patents, profits, and market value', *American Economic Review*, **76**, 984–1001.

Jerzmanowski, M. (2007), 'Total factor productivity differences: Appropriate technology vs. efficiency', *European Economic Review*, **51**, 2080–110.

Kahneman, D. and Tversky, A. (1979), 'Prospect theory: An analysis of decision under risk', *Econometrica*, **47** (2), 263–92.

Kaldor, N. (1981), 'The role of increasing returns technical progress and cumulative causation', *Economie Appliquée*, **34** (3), 593–617.

Kamien, M. and Schwartz, N. (1982), *Market Structure and Innovation*, Cambridge: Cambridge University Press.

Karabarbounis, L. and Neiman, B. (2014), 'The global decline of the labor share', *Quarterly Journal of Economics*, **129**, 61–103.

Kim, E.H., Morse, A. and Zingales, L. (2009), 'Are elite universities losing their competitive edge?', *Journal of Financial Economics*, **93** (3), 353–81.

Koellinger, P. (2008), 'The relationship between technology, innovation, and firm performance: Empirical evidence from e-business in Europe', *Research Policy*, **37**, 1317–28.

Kongaut, C. and Bohlin, E. (2016), 'Investigating mobile broadband adoption and usage: A case of smartphones in Sweden', *Telematics and Informatics*, **33** (3), 742–52.

Krueger, A. (1999), 'Measuring labor's share', *American Economic Review*, **89**, 45–51.

Krugman, P. (1994), 'Complex landscapes in economic geography', *American Economic Review*, **84** (2), 412–17.

Krugman, P. (1995), *Development Geography and Economic Theory*, Cambridge, MA: MIT Press.

Lane, D.A. and Maxfield, R. (1997), 'Foresight complexity and strategy', in W.B. Arthur, S.N. Durlauf and D.A. Lane (eds), *The Economy as an Evolving Complex System, II*, Reading, MA: Addison-Wesley, pp. 169–98.

Lane, D.A. and Maxfield, R.R. (2005), 'Ontological uncertainty and innovation', *Journal of Evolutionary Economics*, **15** (1), 3–50.

Lane, D.A., Pumain, D., van der Leeuw, S. and West, G. (eds) (2009), *Complexity Perspectives in Innovation and Social Change*, Berlin: Springer.

Langlois R.N. (2007), *The Dynamics of Industrial Capitalism: Schumpeter, Chandler, and the New Economy*, London: Routledge.

Larson, R.R. et al. (2014), 'Integrating data mining and data management technologies for scholarly inquiry', IEEE International Conference on Big Data.

Laursen, K. (1999), 'The impact of technological opportunity on the dynamics of trade', *Structural Change and Economic Dynamics*, **10** (3–4), 341–57.

Lee, R. and Wu, T. (2009), 'Subsidizing creativity through network design: Zero-pricing and net neutrality', *Journal of Economics Perspectives*, **23**, 61–76.

Levinthal, D.A. (1997), 'Adaptation on rugged landscapes', *Management Science*, **43** (7), 934–50.

Link, A.N. and Antonelli, C. (2016), 'Strategic alliances: An introductory framework', in A. Link and C. Antonelli (eds), *Strategic Alliances: Leveraging Economic Growth and Development*, London: Routledge.

Link, A. and Metcalfe, J.S. (2008), 'Technology infrastructure: Introduction to the special issue', *Economics of Innovation and New Technology*, **17**, 611–14.

Link, A. and Siegel, D. (2007), *Innovation, Entrepreneurship, and Technological Change*, Oxford: Oxford University Press.

Loebbecke, C. and Crowston, K. (2012), 'Knowledge portals: Components, functionalities, and deployment challenges', 33rd International Conference on Information Systems, Orlando.

Lööf, H. and Johansson, B. (2014), 'R&D strategy, metropolitan externalities and productivity: Evidence from Sweden', *Industry and Innovation*, **21**, 141–54.

Loomes, G. and Sugden, S. (1982), 'Regret theory: An alternative theory of rational choice under uncertainty', *Economic Journal*, **92** (368), 805–24.

Louçã F. (2010), 'Bounded heresies: Early intuitions of complexity in economics', *History of Economic Ideas*, **18** (2), 77–114.

Lucas, R.E. (2008), 'Ideas and growth', *Economica*, 76, 1–19.

Mairesse, J. and Jaumandreu, J. (2005), 'Panel data estimates of the production function and the revenue function: What difference does it make?', *Scandinavian Journal of Economics*, **107** (4), 651–72.

Malerba, F. (2005), 'Sectoral systems of innovation: A framework for linking innovation to the knowledge base structure and dynamics of sectors', *Economics of Innovation and New Technology*, **14**, 63–82.

Malerba, F. and Orsenigo, L. (1995), 'Schumpeterian patterns of innovation', *Cambridge Journal of Economics*, **19** (1), 47–65.

Malerba, F. and Orsenigo, L. (1996), 'Schumpeterian patterns of innovation are technology-specific', *Research Policy*, **25** (3), 451–78.

Malerba, F., Nelson, R.R., Orsenigo, L. and Winter S.G. (1999), '"History-friendly" models of industry evolution: The computer industry', *Industrial and Corporate Change*, **8** (1), 3–40.

Malerba, F., Nelson, R.R., Orsenigo, L. and Winter S.G. (2001), 'History-friendly models: An overview of the case of the computer industry', *Journal of Artificial Societies and Social Simulation*, **4** (3), n.p.

Mansfield, E. (1985), 'How rapidly does new industrial technology leak out?', *Journal of Industrial Economics*, **34**, 217–23.

Mansfield, E., Schwartz, M. and Wagner, S. (1981), 'Imitation costs and patents: An empirical study', *Economic Journal*, **91**, 907–18.

Marshall, A. (1920 [1890]), *Principles of Economics*, 8th edition, London: Macmillan.

Martin, R. and Boschma, R. (eds) (2010), *The Handbook of Evolutionary Economic Geography*, Cheltenham, UK and Northampton, MA, USA: Edward Elgar Publishing.

Martin, R. and Sunley, P. (2012), 'Forms of emergence and the evolution of economic landscapes', *Journal of Economic Behavior and Organization*, **82** (2–3), 338–51.

Maskus, K.E. and Nishioka, S. (2009), 'Development-related biases in factor productivities and the HOV model of trade', *Canadian Journal of Economics*, **42**, 519–53.

Meliciani, V. (2002), 'The impact of technological specialization on national performance in a balance-of-payments-constrained growth model', *Structural Change and Economic Dynamics*, **13**, 101–18.

Metcalfe, J.S. (1995), 'Technology systems and technology policy in historical perspective', *Cambridge Journal of Economics*, **19**, 25–47.

Metcalfe, J.S. (1997), *Evolutionary Economics and Creative Destruction*, London: Routledge.

Metcalfe, J.S. (2002), 'Knowledge of growth and the growth of knowledge', *Journal of Evolutionary Economics*, **12**, 3–16.

Metcalfe, J.S. (2007), 'Alfred Marshall's Mecca: Reconciling the theories of value and development', *Economic Record*, **83**, S1–22.

Metcalfe, J.S. (2009), 'Replicator dynamics', in H. Hanusch and A. Pyka (eds), *Elgar Companion to Neo-Schumpeterian Economics*, Cheltenham, UK and Northampton, MA, USA: Edward Elgar Publishing, pp. 44–52.

Metcalfe, J.S. (2010), 'Complexity and emergence in economics: The road from Smith to Hayek (via Marshall and Schumpeter)', *History of Economic Ideas*, **18** (2), 45–76.

Metcalfe, J.S. (2014), 'Capitalism and evolution', *Journal of Evolutionary Economics*, **24** (1), 11–34.

Metcalfe, J.S. and Boden, M. (1992), 'Evolutionary epistemology and the nature of technology strategy', in R. Coombs, P.P. Saviotti and V. Walsh (eds), *Technological Change and Company Strategies*, London: Academic Press, pp. 65–93.

Miller, J.H. and Page, S.E. (2007), *Complex Adaptive Systems*, Princeton: Princeton University Press.

Moen, J. (2005), 'Is mobility of technical personnel a source of R&D spillover?', *Journal of Labor Economics*, **23**, 81–114.

Mohnen P. and Röller, L. (2005), 'Complementarities in innovation policy', *European Economic Review*, **49**, 1431–50.

Mokyr, J. (1990), *The Lever of Riches: Technological Creativity and Economic Progress*, Oxford: Oxford University Press.

Mokyr, J. (2002), *The Gifts of Athena: Historical Origins of the Knowledge Economy*, Princeton: Princeton University Press.

Montobbio, F. and Kataishi, R. (2015), 'The international dissemination of technological knowledge', in C. Antonelli and A. Link (eds), *Handbook of the Economics of Knowledge*, London: Routledge, pp. 165–88.

Montobbio, F. and Rampa, F. (2005), 'The impact of technology and structural change on export performance in nine developing countries', *World Development*, **33** (4), 527–47.

Morikawa, M. (2004), 'Information technology and the performance of Japanese SMEs', *Small Business Economics*, **23** (3), 171–7.

Mowery D.C. (2012), 'Defense-related R&D as a model for "Grand Challenges" technology policies', *Research Policy*, **41** (10), 1703–15.

Nelson, R.R. (1959), 'The simple economics of basic scientific research', *Journal of Political Economy*, **67**, 297–306.

Nelson, R.R. (ed.) (1962), *The Rate and Direction of Inventive Activity: Economic and Social Factors*, Princeton: Princeton University Press, pp. 609–25.

Nelson, R.R. (1982), 'The role of knowledge in R&D efficiency', *Quarterly Journal of Economics*, **97** (3), 453–70.

Nelson, R.R. (ed.) (1993), *National Systems of Innovation: A Comparative Study*, Oxford: Oxford University Press.

Nelson, R.R. and Winter, S.G. (1973), 'Toward an evolutionary theory of economic capabilities', *American Economic Review*, **63** (2), 440–49.

Nelson, R.R. and Winter, S.G. (1982), *An Evolutionary Theory of Economic Change*, Cambridge, MA: Belknap Press of Harvard University Press.

Nesta, L. and Saviotti, P.P. (2005), 'Coherence of the knowledge base and the firm's innovative performance: Evidence from the U.S. pharmaceutical industry', *Journal of Industrial Economics*, **53** (1), 123–42.

Nesta L. and Saviotti, P.P. (2006), 'Firm knowledge and market value in biotechnology', *Industrial and Corporate Change*, **15** (4), 625–52.

Nishioka, S. (2005), 'An explanation of OECD trade with knowledge capital and the HOV model', Working Paper No. 05-06, Department of Economics, University of Arizona.

North, D.C. (2010), *Understanding the Process of Economic Change*, Princeton: Princeton University Press.

Ostrom, E. (2010), 'Beyond markets and states: Polycentric governance of complex economic systems', *American Economic Review*, **100** (3), 641–72.

Page, S. (2011), *Diversity and Complexity*, Princeton: Princeton University Press.

Pakes, A. and Griliches, Z. (1984), 'Patents and R&D at the firm level: A first look', in Z. Griliches (ed.), *R&D Patents and Productivity*, Chicago: University of Chicago Press, pp. 55–72.

Penrose, E.T. (1952), 'Biological analogies in the theory of the firm', *American Economic Review*, **42** (5), 804–19.

Penrose, E.T. (1953), 'Rejoinder to Armen A. Alchian', *American Economic Review*, **43** (4), 603–9.

Perez, C. (2002), *Technological Revolutions and Financial Capital: The Dynamics of Bubbles and Golden Ages*, Cheltenham, UK and Northampton, MA, USA: Edward Elgar Publishing.

Perez, C. (2010), 'Technological revolutions and techno-economic paradigms', *Cambridge Journal of Economics*, **34**, 185–202.

Phillips F. (2004), 'Trading down: The intellectual poverty of the new free trade agreements', *Technological Forecasting and Social Change*, **71**, 865–76.

Picketty, T. (2014), *Capital in the Twenty-First Century*, Cambridge, MA: Harvard University Press.

Pittaway, L., Robertson, M., Munir, K., Denyer, D. and Neely, A. (2004), 'Networking and innovation: a systematic review of the evidence', *International Journal of Management Reviews*, **5–6** (3–4), 137–68.

Porter, M.E. (2000), 'Location, competition, and economic development: Local clusters in a global economy', *Economic Development Quarterly*, **14**, 15–34.

Rasel, F. (forthcoming), 'ICT and global sourcing: Evidence for German manufacturing and service firms', *Economics of Innovation and New Technology*.

Ravix, J.-L. (2012), 'Alfred Marshall and the Marshallian theory of the firm', in M. Dietrich and J. Krafft (eds), *Handbook on the Economics and Theory of the Firm*, Cheltenham, UK and Northampton, MA, USA: Edward Elgar Publishing, pp. 49–54.

Rizzello, S. and Turvani, M. (2002), 'Subjective diversity and social learning: A cognitive perspective for understanding institutional behavior', *Constitutional Political Economy*, **13** (2), 197–210.

Robert, V. and Yoguel, G. (2013), 'El Enfoque de la Complejidad y la Economía Evolucionista de la Innovación', Paper presented at the ECLA workshop analytical tools and policy implications for innovation, ICT and growth, Santiago del Chile.

Romer, P.M. (1986), 'Increasing returns and long-run economic growth', *Journal of Political Economy*, **94**, 1002–37.

Romer, P.M. (1990), 'Endogenous technological change', *Journal of Political Economy*, **98**, S71–102.

Romer, P.M. (1994a), 'The origins of endogenous growth', *Journal of Economic Perspectives*, **8**, 3–22.

Romer, P.M. (1994b), 'New goods old theory, and the welfare costs of trade restrictions', *Journal of Development Economics*, **43**, 5–38.

Romer, P.M. (2015), 'Mathiness in the theory of economic growth', *American Economic Review*, **105** (5), 89–93.

Rosenberg, N. (1974), 'Science innovation and economic growth', *Economic Journal*, **84** (333), 90–108. Reprinted in N. Rosenberg (1976), *Perspectives on Technology*, Cambridge University Press: Cambridge, pp. 260–79.

Rosenkopf, L. and Nerkar, A. (2001), 'Beyond local search: Boundary-spanning, exploration, and impact in the optical disk industry', *Strategic Management Journal*, **22**, 287–306.

Rosser, J.B. (ed.) (2009), *Handbook of Research on Complexity*, Cheltenham, UK and Northampton, MA, USA: Edward Elgar Publishing.

Ruttan, V.W. (1997), 'Induced innovation evolutionary theory and path dependence: Sources of technical change', *Economic Journal*, **107**, 1520–29.

Ruttan, V.W. (2001), *Technology Growth and Development: An Induced Innovation Perspective*, Oxford: Oxford University Press.

Rybczynski, T.M. (1955), 'Factor endowment and relative commodity prices', *Economica*, **22**, 336–41.

Safarzyńska, K. and van den Bergh, J.C.J.M. (2010), 'Evolutionary models in economics: A survey of methods and building blocks', *Journal of Evolutionary Economics*, **20** (3), 329–73.

Samuelson, P.A. (2004), 'Where Ricardo and Mill rebut and confirm arguments of mainstream economists supporting globalization', *Journal of Economic Perspectives*, **18**, 135–46.

Saviotti, P.P. (2007), 'On the dynamics of generation and utilisation of knowledge: The local character of knowledge', *Structural Change and Economic Dynamics*, **18**, 387–408.

Saviotti, P. and Pyka, A. (2013), 'The co-evolution of innovation, demand and growth', *Economics of Innovation and New Technology*, **22** (5), 461–82.

Scherer, F.M. (1982), 'Interindustry technology flows in the United States', *Research Policy*, **11**, 227–45.

Scherer, F.M. (1965), 'Firm size, market structure, opportunity, and the output of patented inventions', *American Economic Review*, **55**, 1097–125.

Scherer, F.M. (1967), 'Market structure and the employment of scientists and engineers', *American Economic Review*, **57**, 524–31.

Scherer, F.M. (1982), 'Demand-pull and technological invention: Schmookler revisited', *Journal of Industrial Economics*, **30** (3), 225–37.

Scherer, F.M. (1984), *Innovation and Growth: Schumpeterian Perspectives*, Cambridge, MA: MIT Press.

Schmookler, J. (1966), *Invention and Economic Growth*, Cambridge, MA: Harvard University Press.

Schumpeter, J.A. (1911–34), *The Theory of Economic Development*, Cambridge, MA: Harvard University Press.

Schumpeter J.A. (1928), 'The instability of capitalism', *Economic Journal*, **38** (151), 361–86.

Schumpeter J.A. (1939), *Business Cycles: A Theoretical, Historical and Statistical Analysis of the Capitalist Process*, New York: McGraw-Hill; abridged version with introduction by Rendigs Fels, available at http://classiques.uqac.ca/classiques/Schumpeter_joseph/business_cycles/business_cycles.html (last accessed April 2017).

Schumpeter J.A. (1941), 'Alfred Marshall's Principles: A semi-centennial appraisal', *American Economic Review*, **31** (2), 236–48.

Schumpeter, J.A. (1942), *Capitalism, Socialism and Democracy*, New York: Harper & Brothers.

Schumpeter, J.A. (1947a), 'The creative response in economic history', *Journal of Economic History*, **7** (2), 149–59.

Schumpeter, J.A. (1947b), 'Theoretical problems of economic growth', *Journal of Economic History*, **7** (Suppl.), 1–9.

Scitovsky, T. (1954), 'Two concepts of external economies', *Journal of Political Economy*, **62** (2), 143–51.

Shearmur, R. and Doloreux, D. (2013), 'Innovation and knowledge-intensive business service. The contribution of knowledge-intensive business service to innovation in manufacturing establishments', *Economics of Innovation and New Technology*, **22** (8), 751–74.

Simon, H.A. (1947), *Administrative Behavior: A Study of Decision-Making Processes in Administrative Organization*, London: Macmillan.

Simon, H.A. (1969), *The Sciences of Artificial*, Cambridge, MA: MIT Press.

Simon, H.A. (1979), 'Rational decision making in business organizations', *American Economic Review*, **69** (4), 493–513.

Simon, H.A. (1982), *Metaphors of Bounded Rationality: Behavioral Economics and Business Organization*, Cambridge, MA: MIT Press.

Solow, R.M. (1957), 'Technical change and the aggregate production function', *Review of Economics and Statistics*, **39** (3), 312–20.

Song, J., Almeida, P. and Wu, G. (2003), 'Learning-by-hiring: When is mobility more likely to facilitate knowledge transfer?', *Management Science*, **49** (4), 351–65.

Sorenson, O., Rivkin, J.W. and Fleming, L. (2006), 'Complexity, networks and knowledge flow', *Research Policy*, **35** (7), 994–1017.

Soto-Acosta, P.A., Colomo-Palacios, R.B. and Popa, S.A. (2014), 'Web knowledge sharing and its effect on innovation: An empirical investigation in SMEs', *Knowledge Management Research and Practice*, **12**, 103–13.

Stoneman, P. and Battisti, G. (2010), 'The diffusion of new technology', in B.H. Hall and N. Rosenberg (eds), *Handbook of the Economics of Innovation*, Amsterdam: Elsevier.

Sturgill, B. (2012), 'The relationship between factor shares and economic development', *Journal of Macroeconomics*, **34**, 1044–62.

Subashini, R., Rita, S. and Vivek, M. (2012), 'The role of ICTs in knowledge management (KM) for organizational effectiveness', in P.V. Krishna, M.R. Babu and E. Ariwa (eds), *Global Trends in Information Systems and Software Applications: 4th International Conference, ObCom 2011, Vellore, TN, India, December 9–11, 2011. Proceedings, Part II*, Berlin: Springer, pp. 542–9.

Tambe, P., Hitt, L. and Brynjolfsson, E. (2012), 'The extroverted firm: How external information practices affect innovation and productivity', *Management Science*, **58** (5), 843–59.

Tassey, G. (2005), 'The disaggregated knowledge production function: A new model of university and corporate research', *Research Policy*, **34** (3), 287–303.

Trefler, D. (1993), 'International factor price differences: Leontief was right!', *Journal of Political Economy*, **101**, 961–87.

Urraca-Ruiz, A. (2013), 'The "technological" dimension of structural change under market integration', *Structural Change and Economic Dynamics*, **27**, 1–18.

Utterback, J.M. (1994), *Mastering the Dynamics of Innovation*, Boston, MA: Harvard Business School Press.

Utterback, J.M. and Abernathy, W.J. (1975), 'A dynamic model of product and process innovation', *Omega*, **36**, 639–56.

van Schewick, B. (2016), 'Internet architecture and innovation in applications', in J.M. Bauer and M. Latzer (eds), *Handbook on the Economics of the Internet*, Cheltenham, UK and Northampton, MA, USA: Edward Elgar Publishing, pp. 288–322.

Veblen T. (1898), 'Why is economics not an evolutionary science?', *Quarterly Journal of Economics*, **2** (4), 373–97.

von Hippel, E. (2001), 'User toolkits for innovation', *Journal of Product Innovation Management*, **18**, 247–57.

Walsh, J. and Bayma, T. (1996), 'The virtual college: Computer-mediated communication and scientific work', *Information Society*, **12**, 343–63.

Weitzman, M.L. (1996), 'Hybridizing growth theory', *American Economic Review*, **86** (2), 207–12.

Weitzman, M.L. (1998), 'Recombinant growth', *Quarterly Journal of Economics*, **113**, 331–60.

Whelan, E. (2007), 'Exploring knowledge exchange in electronic networks of practice', *Journal of Information Technology*, **22**, 5–13.

Whelan, E., Teigland, R., Donnellan, B. and Golden, W. (2010), 'How internet technologies impact information flows in R&D: Reconsidering the technological gatekeeper', *R&D Management*, **40** (4), 400–413.

Windrum, P. and Birchenhall, C. (2005), 'Structural change in the presence of network externalities: A co-evolutionary model of technological successions', *Journal of Evolutionary Economics*, **15**, 123–48.

Winter, S.G., Kaniovski, Y.M. and and Dosi, G. (2000), 'Modeling industrial dynamics with innovative entrants', *Structural Change and Economic Dynamics*, **11** (3), 255–93.

Wolff, E. (2012), 'Spillover, linkages, and productivity growth in the US economy, 1958–2007', in M. Andersson, C. Karlsson, B. Johansson and H. Lööf (eds), *Innovation and Growth: From R&D Strategies of Innovating Firms to Economy-Wide Technological Change*, Oxford: Oxford University Press, pp. 233–66.

Young, A.A. (1928), 'Increasing returns and economic progress', *Economic Journal*, **38** (152), 527–42.

Zeira, J. (1998), 'Workers, machines and economic growth', *Quarterly Journal of Economics*, **113**, 1091–113.

Zuboff, S. (1988), *In the Age of the Smart Machine: The Future of Work and Power*, New York: Basic Books.

Zuleta, H. (2008), 'Factor saving innovations and factor income shares', *Review of Economic Dynamics*, **11**, 836–51.

Zuleta, H. (2012), 'Variable factor shares measurement and growth accounting', *Economics Letters*, **114**, 91–93.

Index

Abernathy, W.J. 68
Abramovitz, M. 89, 130, 135, 167, 168, 169, 183
Abramovsky, L. 114
Acemoglu, D.K. 154, 167, 189
Adams, J.D. 84, 93, 104, 129
Aghion, P. 16, 41, 45, 49, 83, 98, 99, 189
Agrawal, A. 115
Akcigit, U. 97
Albin, P.S. 48
Alchian, A. 6, 48
Andersen, E. 22
Anderson, P. 47
Anderson, P.W. 21, 35, 37, 67
Antonelli, C. 6, 13, 26, 28, 35, 36, 37, 38, 40, 41, 42, 44, 45, 46, 48, 49, 50, 52, 63, 64, 65, 66, 69, 71, 74, 77, 82, 83, 84, 86, 87, 89, 92, 99, 111, 112, 116, 118, 119, 123, 126, 128, 131, 132, 133, 134, 141, 143, 145, 149, 150, 153, 160, 161, 163, 165, 166, 167, 170, 171, 172, 181, 182, 183, 184, 188, 189
Arocena, R. 145
Arora, A. 86, 89, 150
Arrovian
    analysis 5, 96
    analysis of knowledge 125
    approach 142
    framework 95–6, 121, 124, 125, 141
        and extreme Arrovian conditions 96
    good 103
    good in equilibrium 102
    hypotheses 122–3
    hypothesis of 'failure of the market' 96
    market failure 96, 110, 120, 147
    methodology 90
    postulate 81–2, 107–8

properties 105
properties of knowledge 81, 83, 101, 102, 121, 122, 198
remedy 106
see also derived demand for knowledge
Arrow, K.J. 15, 81, 87, 88, 90, 95, 96, 98, 129, 144, 189, 200
Arthur, B. 21, 43, 116
Arthur, W.B. 35, 37, 51, 52, 67, 128, 189
Audretsch, D.B. 40, 41, 65, 113

Bailey, A. 160
Bandura, A. 40
Barbiellini Amidei, F. 133
Battisti, G. 169
Bauer, J.M. 110, 148
Bayma, T. 115
Birchenhall, C. 12
Bitnet, adoption of 115
Bloom, N. 16, 82, 83
Blume, L.E. 62
Bockerman, P. 179
Boden, M. 47
Bohlin, E. 149
Bonifati, G. 51
Boppart, T. 115
Borowiecki, K.J. 113
Boschma, R. 46, 113
Branstetter, L. 181
Breschi, S. 181
Bresnahan, T.J. 110
Briglauer, W. 149
Brynjolfsson, E. 110
Business Cycles 19, 30, 32, 33, 67; *see also* Schumpeter, J.

Caldari, K. 35
Capitalism, Socialism and Democracy 3, 20, 33, 67; *see also* Schumpeter, J.